14-50

Beyond the Courtroom

Programs in Community Justice and Conflict Resolution

Benedict S. Alper
Lawrence T. Nichols
Boston College

LexingtonBooks
D.C. Heath and Company
Lexington, Massachusetts

Library of Congress Cataloging in Publication Data

Alper, Benedict Solomon, 1905-
  Beyond the courtroom.

  Bibliography: p.
  Includes index.
  1. Criminal justice, Administration of—United States. I. Nichols,
Lawrence T., joint author. II. Title.
KF9223.A937   345.73'05   78-20376
ISBN 0-669-02724-3

Copyright © 1981 by D.C. Heath and Company

Published simultaneously in Canada

Printed in the United States of America

International Standard Book Number: 0-669-02724-3

Library of Congress Catalog Card Number: 78-20376

*To the countless citizens
dedicated to achieving justice
in their communities*

Contents

Contents   ix

Foreword

Our system of justice is adversarial. Lawyers argue the rightness of their case within a corpus of law as interpreted by a judge or jury. The laws change. Those served by the law change. Free legal service is now available in some form or other to the poor and to juveniles. Before long, children may be represented in custody disputes.

Yet something is wrong, drastically wrong, in the courts of our country. Justice in teeming urban centers all too often is characterized by haste, ill-prepared and harassed defense attorneys, interminable waiting, frightened victims, most of whom can ill afford time lost from work, and defendants who see the entire system as having little real relevance to their lives. Their cynical view is that more money can buy a better brand of justice, which means, to them, "a better shake." Sentences mean little; fines often go unpaid; a term on probation usually means, given present high probation case loads, neither sufficient oversight nor adequate help.

The crime that sets the cumbersome machine of criminal justice in motion is seen by the typical urban defendant in terms of its components—lawyers, judges, occasionally the law itself—components that operate in the setting of crowded, noisy courtrooms. At best, a defendant's view of the crime seems a technical one, a crime that could be wiped out "if only I had money to pay for a better lawyer."

Where is there consideration for the human dimension of the crime? How much consideration is paid to victims and their hurts? Why is a broader sense of true justice not imparted? Where is the sense that people are involved and that a community fabric, however frail, has been further torn by a criminal act? Where is the sense that both victim and victimizer are members of the human family, of a community? For the most part, these aspects are absent, woefully absent, so that justice, if perceived at all, is seen as a thing apart from the lives of those whom it touches.

Although the law and the techniques of its administration have improved in many significant respects, from my vantage point it seems that the law and its attendant machinery have drifted further and further from the essentials, from touching in human terms the lives of defendant and complainant alike. The processes of criminal justice should be viewed not as a distant, objective entity but as an extension of people, of a community, of society.

Some of the "new" forms of justice that this book describes (the roots of which, curiously, go back several millennia) are beginning to give depth and breadth to our Anglo-Saxon common-law traditions of justice. Mediation, arbitration, citizen disposition panels, restitution, victim-assistance, and alternative-sentencing modes appear as hopeful signs, in differing forms but all resting on the same basic assumptions. Victims meet victimizers in the presence of neutral moderators or mediators, themselves community residents, volunteers who attempt to reach beneath the surface "right-wrong" aspects of the conflict in an effort to discover a mutual acknowledgment of the problem and to craft a solution that is meaningful in human terms to each of the disputing parties. To ensure that justice does not become tribal, decisions reached by such proceedings are thereafter reviewed and approved by lawyers and judges.

I have seen remarkable results from mediated disputes and from citizen-levied sentences in criminal areas. Young offenders have been sentenced to guard frightened welfare recipients when they cash their checks; offenders have been sentenced to coach basketball, to work in hospitals, and to tutor in day-care centers. Work crews made up of offenders, while receiving CETA wages, have cleaned up parks and assisted in school maintenance. A portion of CETA wages is returned weekly by the offender to his victim. I have seen such programs work wonders with offenders who were labeled chronic or incorrigible and for whom the most expensive services of treatment had previously been provided—and had failed. Responsibility is fixed on the defendant, and the defendant is enlisted to redress his or her criminal act in specific, human terms.

What is really different about this? First, the defendant is made responsible in both legal and human terms. Next, the defendant is treated as part of his community, which he has a right (even an obligation) to be involved in. Last, the defendant, having wrested something from a victim and, by extension, from the community, is treated as a person of worth who has something of worth to return to that community or victim, or both. It is both a process of citizen involvement and an outcome, through sentence or mediated settlement, cast in specific and human terms.

Thousands of citizens in the last decade have become active participants in areas heretofore walled off by professionals. Community schools, community health centers, and citizen mental-health boards are pertinent examples. The field of justice seems the final bastion.

Community modes of justice do not rest on a foundation of innocent-guilty, right-wrong, win-lose, victor-vanquished. The foundation here is one of healing, of reconciliation, of defendant with complainant as well as with the community. That this book addresses this new movement and sets out examples of various programs to be found today in all parts of our country, as well as abroad, is extremely encouraging to all those who seek to improve the administration of criminal justice.

Commissioner John A. Calhoun
Administration for Children, Youth and Families
Department of Health and Human Services
Washington, D.C.

Acknowledgments

So many friends and colleagues have helped in gathering and preparing the materials presented here that it is impossible to acknowledge them all. Grateful acknowledgment is made to Nancy Dube and to the generosity of the G. Howland Shaw Foundation in covering some research and typing costs. To our student-colleagues—Peter Cordella for his work on arbitration, Diane Daley for diversion, Keith Merron for mediation, Rory Fields for historical research, and Angela Miragliotta for victim compensation—as well as to the students in our classes on whom we have tried out some of what here appears, gratitude for their hours of plodding research, their critical advice, and their encouragement. To Madeleine Chrone of the Pretrial Services Resource Center in Washington, D.C., Daniel McGillis of the Harvard Law School; Alan Harland of the Criminal Justice Research Center; Joseph Stulberg, formerly of the Rochester 4-A Program; Anne Schneider and Peter Schneider of the Institute of Policy Analysis; Neil Houston, director of the Crime and Justice Foundation, Boston; Brian Callery and James Marchetti, formerly of the Dorchester Urban Court; John A. Calhoun, former commissioner of the Massachusetts Division of Youth Services and a pioneer in the establishment of community justice centers—our appreciation of their wisdom and support.

This book would never have appeared without the devotion and toil of those expert cryptographers who transcribed, and corrected, the manuscript through its various stages. They have been with us down this path before with the same unflagging support; to Lorraine Bone, Alice Close, Shirley Urban, and Sara White, once again thanks.

We are greatly indebted to Larry Ray of the American Bar Association's Special Commission on Resolution of Minor Disputes for furnishing us with information and the national list of dispute-resolution agencies, which is reprinted on page 289.

Introduction

Only a community interest and involvement will bring about major reforms to improve the manner in which crime is handled. . . . It is time for the community to be brought into the decision-making and implementation process.[1]

This book describes a growing movement in the United States to involve the community in the resolution of disputes that would—or might—otherwise be decided in the criminal courts. Five distinct programs are discernible in this movement: mediation, arbitration, restitution, victim assistance and compensation, and citizen panels to advise on sentencing.

Although there is no single jurisdiction where all of these components are found together, there is a wide diversity of such programs, and they are rapidly proliferating. One of the reasons for this growth is the rising realization that the criminal-justice system in our country—the police, the criminal courts, and corrections—is failing to protect citizens against assaults upon their persons and attacks on their property. With rare exception, each succeeding year in the past decade has seen a sizable increase in the number of crimes known to the police. At the same time, the proportion of reported crimes that are cleared by arrest grows smaller. Our jails are overcrowded; our criminal courts jammed; delays between arraignment and conviction stretch into months and years; and the recidivism rate from prisons and reformatories remains steady at a figure seldom estimated at less than 60 percent for inmates released from them.

Our times are marked by a growing sense by the general public that much of government is inefficient, corrupt, and either unable to or uninterested in furnishing the services needed to ensure a stable and healthy functioning society. When the police fail to protect residents in housing projects or in ghetto areas, we have seen the creation of citizen patrols to take up the slack. When prisons fail to rehabilitate, we see a clamor for restoration of the death penalty, for mandatory sentences, for longer terms of imprisonment, and for more prison construction. When prisoners feel that they are being unjustly dealt with, resort to violence is frequently the result. The men at Attica prison demanded that they "be treated like human beings." Five years after the riot there that took some forty lives, more than 60 percent of adult prisons have established some form of formal grievance procedure to deal with inmate complaints, where formerly virtually none existed.[2]

It is a sign of citizen concern and vitality and a hopeful expression of that concern that dissatisfaction with current public safety and court procedures has led to increasing popular intervention. We shall examine here one jurisdiction whose pioneering community program evolved out of a

court-watching program some years ago, which led to the removal of a corrupt judge and his replacement by one who welcomed the introduction of a
multiservice community-justice program into his court.

The idea of community involvement in the settlement of disputes is as
old as the first families of humans who came together to form a clan.
Responsibility for the resolution of conflict and the dispensation of justice
is the cornerstone of any society. In our own, the judicial is one leg of the
three-part structure of state power, which also includes the legislative and
the executive.

In ancient times, private vengeance was the innate right of every person
who had been outraged in his person or property. It was expected that such
a person would seek revenge or at least compensation. When groups of
people came together in the earliest form of social organization, the family
or the clan or the tribe took part in the process of settlement of disputes,
with fines or restitution or the meting out of penalties of corporal punishment or death as an expression of the group's concern for its offended
member.

The notion that the crown, and later the state, was the only entity that
could resolve disputes and impose penalties was a later outgrowth of what is
called the social contract. According to this principle, when one member of
society is outraged, the entire membership of the group has been hurt. It is
thus both their responsibility and their right to avenge the wrong and to do
justice. In exchange for receiving the protection of the state, the citizen
became a party to a contract that now enjoined him to forfeit his right to
seek private vengeance. But when the state fails to protect its citizens—or
they feel they are not being protected—it is to be expected that they will
revert to a private mode of righting wrongs and will take justice into their
own hands.

In a sense, that is what this book is about, except, of course, that the
programs described here are in no way reminiscent of posses or lynch mobs
or vendettas. Current programs are conducted in the best tradition of community concern for justice to its members, to the offender, to the victim, to
those who administer as well as those who serve as volunteers in these programs. Those who seek to set the balance right, to see that victims are compensated to some degree for their loss, that offenders get somewhere near
their just desserts, are those involved persons who live in the communities
where these acts take place, who have concern for their neighborhoods and
for their neighbors.

The small-claims court for civil disputes, a feature of our courts for
many years, provides a precedent, for its features—informality, the willingness to mediate and to concede, the waiving of formal rules of evidence,
and, above all, the willingness to substitute goodwill and compromise for
the adversary process, which normally marks both civil and criminal

cases—are also features of the neighborhood justice centers as they are the
hallmark of the precursors of those same centers.

Although a program of arbitration may incorporate some elements of
the mediation process and restitution may be a factor in very different programs, each scheme may contain more than one main element. The thread
that binds them together is that they are all community based and represent
a process of informal justice that has little in common with the usual
criminal court proceeding.

Each chapter in this book describes a distinct type of community program, any one of which could have been expanded to book length. Our attempt has been to illustrate in each component the best that can be found, in
the opinion of workers in the field. Where relevant, details of additional
programs are also included, so as not to lose sight of worthy variations on
the theme. The underlying philosophy, purpose, and method of operation of
each program are given in sufficient detail to provide readers with information to enable them to initiate or engage in programs in their own communities. Whenever possible, addresses of current projects are given for this
purpose.

The examples we use are drawn from various parts of the country and
from abroad, for the principles and practice of community-dispute resolution and community justice are international. Space limitations do not
permit us to consider all the related developments that provide further
evidence of the universality of the theme of this book. For instance, lay
judges now participate in the courts of many European countries, including
socialist nations. For many years now, the Scandinavian countries have entrusted the hearing and adjudication of children's cases to child-welfare
boards composed of elected lay persons from the community, which take
the place of the juvenile court as we know it. The British magistrate's courts
continue to operate in a fashion similar in many respects to our American
justices of the peace. We see the emergence of special courts for labor
disputes, as in Israel.

The approach of community-justice bodies is also being used on an increasing scale in family courts and in the juvenile courts now found in every
major country of the world. Housing courts and special tribunals for the
hearing of consumer complaints are two additional specialized tribunals
coming into their own.

In various ethnic groups we find modern application of a procedure that
dates back to biblical times—for instance, the Beth Din found in Jewish
communities in the United States, whose roots go back to the Sanhedrin
courts. Today's Gypsies, whose origins are lost in antiquity, continue to
practice their ancient procedures for resolving disagreements between individual members of their group. The Panchayat courts of India, supplanted during the centuries of British colonial rule by the common-law

procedures of the home country, are gradually replacing this alien imposition on their historic ways of administering justice. The socialist countries,
none of which has a common-law precedent, especially those whose court
procedures are more likely to be derived from Roman or Napoleonic
precedents, resolve the greatest proportion of their disputes in so-called
people's courts, where lay persons, whether as prosecutors, defense coun-
sels or judges, supplant the legally schooled professionals who administer
the courts in our country.

Our focus is also fixed on issues and controversies in the areas of community justice and dispute resolution that are likely to remain significant
and relevant for some time to come. Essential sociological and social science
concepts and ideas are put forward in suggestive and nontechnical fashion
in order to illuminate the presentation, to stimulate analysis of the facts we
present, and to place community justice in as broad a context as possible.
For example, the idea of community, a basic concept in sociology, is being
rediscovered, as a recent book suggests,[3] at the same time that we hear and
read a great deal about the eclipse of community and the "pursuit of
loneliness" as characteristics of contemporary society.[4] Concomitantly, we
are witnessing in the area of justice and dispute resolution a broad movement toward the emergence of building and rebuilding of community.

The community dispute-resolution movement is closely linked to related
movements that emphasize citizen involvement and participation. The proliferation of neighborhood associations, a key element in policies of urban
revitalization, is a case in point. These are paralleled in other areas of social
concern; there are citizen crime-prevention programs, community schools,
health centers, food cooperatives, and community corporations for the
rehabilitation of deteriorated housing. The diversity and vitality that
characterizes the operation of these community projects may help to give
credence to and confidence in the general feasibility of the community
approach to dispute resolution and correction. We believe that this work
appears at a propitious time, when citizen and official reaction toward an
increasing crime rate tends to be expressed in hardened and repressive attitudes and policies for dealing with apprehended and convicted offenders.
The almost universal call for harsher and longer prison terms, the spate of
proposals for uniform, mandated sentences, however slightly modified by
presumption, the repeal of parole laws, and the passage by at least thirty-
seven states of new legislation to restore the death penalty all bear witness to
these new attitudes.

This book aims to set forth the theoretical and policy considerations, as
well as the details of program alternatives to traditional adversary proceedings and to the retributive processes of court and corrections. We look
forward to some reversal of today's reactionary trend in criminal justice
and to the restoration to citizens in our communities of their rights and

duties to participate more fully, as they did in an earlier time, in the resolution of the conflicts that now divide them, in the process restoring to victims their historic roles and at the same time helping to strengthen community ties.

The literature in this field is so voluminous, ephemeral, and scattered as to merit its own bibliography. Without in any way laying claim to comprehensiveness, we aim to respond to a need for a single volume that will assess the present state of the art and incorporate in one place the best features of some of the innovative and imaginative experiments being conducted in community justice today.

A preponderance of the programs we discuss are located in Massachusetts. We offer in explanation (though not in apology) that we have followed many of these over a period of years and are personally acquainted with their initiators and staff. Additionally, some of the program alternatives to traditional criminal-court procedures in this state are the natural outgrowth of the pioneering steps that Massachusetts has taken in the area of community justice. In 1971-1972 it closed down its training schools and released all but a small percentage of their juvenile residents into alternative facilities, many of them privately operated under purchase-of-service contracts with the Department of Youth Services: halfway houses, schools, camps, foster homes and group homes, and a wide diversity of specially designed and innovative programs.[5] Today, almost ten years later, close to 90 percent of the delinquents committed by the juvenile courts to the state youth agency are in the community. In contrast, many states continue to incarcerate 100 percent of their committed young offenders; the state that comes closest to Massachusetts reports that only 59 percent of its committed juveniles are in community-based facilities.

In 1976 the Urban Court was established as a division of the district court of Dorchester (part of the city of Boston), which combined several of the component programs described in this volume—mediation, restitution, victim assistance, and advisory sentencing panels. Its policies and procedures have been widely studied, reported, and evaluated, and it has been observed by visitors from many states and from abroad. In addition, it has given impetus to the formulation of national schemes for extending the basic functions in which it has pioneered to numerous jurisdictions throughout the country.

In extenuation of this seeming overrepresentation of Massachusetts programs, we offer examples drawn from sixteen other states and twenty-three foreign countries. Our aim is to provide as broad a picture as possible of the vast number and diversity of these community conflict-resolution schemes and efforts that may enlighten some as it may encourage others to take the initiative in and give leadership to the establishment of similar programs in their own communities.

We may yet see in the years ahead an extensive network of community-justice centers of all kinds effectively returning to the people in their communities responsibility for, and control over, their own destinies in the dispensation of justice. In a period of shifting values, of national and international tensions and upheaval, we may yet be able to bring "peace upon our house," in the words of the parting benediction, pronounced by today's successor to the tribunals of biblical days.

Part I
Justice, the Courts, and the Community

1 A Note on Community

> The greater familiarity among contending participants in the areas where a sense of community is shared does not eliminate the conflicts, but it may make them less intense.[1]

The primary analytical concept in this book is community, a term that virtually everyone knows and employs although it may be impossible to find two people who interpret or define it alike. It is hardly surprising in times like ours, with the constant news of conflict, violence and destruction, and the never-ending threat of total war, that the idea of community should exercise a tremendous appeal and draw upon our deepest longings for peace. Community provides a vision of unity and so helps to maintain the hope of a desperate world. For these reasons, community tends to become all things to all people, an ideal and an ethical obligation, as well as an objective description of social arrangements. The more powerful the normative, visionary, and emotional aspects of community become, the greater the urge to see it in the Dulcinea of our most impossible dreams.

Its attractiveness is further enhanced when community is combined with the ideal of justice, the central theme of an array of contemporary differences to be settled in the therapeutic and supportive setting of the community. The appeal of community as an idea involves the distinct danger that we become so taken with the notion that we begin to romanticize it and thus make it appear as a sure solution to the problems of the official systems of criminal and civil justice. In this we would not be alone, for the tendency to idealize what is meant by community extends back at least a hundred years, to some of the major thinkers of the nineteenth century. It is, in fact, due to their contributions that community has long ranked among the most fundamental and important of sociology's unit-ideas. The historical importance of the term has not been accompanied, however, by a clear specification of its meaning. Instead there has been confusion bred by the emotive overtones that the word consistently carried with it. Additionally, the nostalgia surrounding the concept has resulted in an intermingling of what is and what should be in social relations.

The elusive idea of community is well summarized in the comparative analysis presented by Hillery, who attempted to identify the essential elements of the term. In a wide-ranging content analysis of published studies, Hillery identified ninety-four separate definitions of community.

He was able to reduce these to sixteen conceptual units and twenty-two basic combinations, but the concept continues to be an enigmatic one, whose numerous and diverse meanings continue to present barriers to full communication among scholars.

The idea of community has long been a fascinating one within the field of sociology. Nisbet's perspective places community at the center of recent intellectual history, for the "rediscovery of community is unquestionably the most distinctive development in nineteenth-century thought."[2] The place of community within sociology has been assured by some of its most important theorists.

Early Definitions of Community

Auguste Comte, the father of sociology, did not employ the term *community*, but he had a vision of it that assumed global proportions within his grand design. For Comte, community meant the love of humanity, which would take the worshipful form of a religion of humanity and would indeed provide the key to the meaning of life itself:

> To live in others is, in the truest sense of the word, life. Indeed the best part of our own life is passed thus. As yet this truth has not been grasped firmly, because the social point of view has not yet been brought systematically before us. But the religion of Humanity . . . will make it intelligible to minds of every class.[3]

Realization of such a social order would, however, require a long process of education, especially the "slow and difficult training of the heart," the prerequisite for the victory of social feeling over innate self-love.

Much the same approach may be said to constitute the core of Karl Marx's thought, although he expressed it in dramatically different terms. For Marx the question was always how the present polarization of humanity (which takes the form of opposed socioeconomic classes) could be overcome. His revolutionary answer is so well known that it may have obscured the community vision that lies beyond the revolution:

> When, in the course of development, class distinctions have disappeared and all production has been concentrated in the hands of a vast association of the whole nation, the public power will lose its political character. . . . If the proletariat during its contest with the bourgeoisie is compelled, by the force of circumstances, to organize itself as a class, if, by means of a revolution, it makes itself the ruling class, and, as such, sweeps away by force the old conditions of production, then it will, along with these conditions, have swept away the conditions for the existence of class antagonisms and of classes generally.[4]

This evolutionary conflict will clear the way for the emergence of community, "an association in which the free development of each is the condition for the free development of all."

The global analyses of Comte and Marx were followed by the classical treatment of community by Ferdinand Toennies, in which he identified the concept with specific social groups. Community was to be found in certain structures, especially kinship, friendship, guild, neighborhood, village, and nation, but not in others like contract, class, market, and city.[5] Toennies perceived a fundamental human need for community but did not see a historical way of turning back to a social order where community groups predominated.

Georg Simmel contributed a very different perspective, which distinguished the analysis of community from the general analysis of history, to be pursued in terms of abstract or purely formal social processes.

For Emile Durkheim, community became an interior reality, which he referred to as solidarity, "a completely moral phenomenon" that does not lend itself to exact observation. The basis of solidarity was shared values, the collective conscience of the people, whose clearest outward manifestation was to be found in law. As he expressed it in his seminal *The Division of Labor in Society*, the common or collective conscience is the "totality of beliefs and sentiments common to average citizens of the same society," which can also be spoken of as the "psychical type" of a society, the binding force that embraces successive generations in an ongoing and enduring social unity.[6]

A more recent contribution shares the same broad perspective as these classical sources. Robert M. MacIver with the possible exception of Toennies, did more than any other theorist to place the concept of community at the forefront of sociological inquiry. From the time of his first major work, *Community*, MacIver saw community as the source or matrix from which all specific groups—families, business organizations, armies—emerged. Community was holistic or "integral," "the greater common life out of which associations rise, into which associations bring order, but which associations never fulfill."[7] His approach encompasses a spiritual or mystical note that sociology can never fully comprehend, the mystery of how and why human beings choose to be involved with and identified with their fellows.

Conceptual Difficulties

Some of the intractable conceptual difficulties in clearly defining community have been pinpointed by Sorokin, who speaks of the term as an amalgam of two separate qualities—territory and high solidarity—which do not combine on any logical, factual, or causal basis. A collection of persons occupying a certain territorial area are not necessarily together in a close social bond; they might, for example, be armies locked in combat. Nor do all persons who share strong bonds necessarily possess a common territory. A religious congregation such as the Jesuits, who might qualify as a community on the basis of a shared life, consists of thousands of members scattered around the world, possessing no common territory. Sorokin therefore concluded that community, moving always in two directions, could not serve as a useful sociological construct.[8]

Because the concept of community occupies a central place in the programs we examine in this book, we shall share MacIver's view that we "must accept the terms of everyday life"[9] even though these "carry with them into the scientific sphere the varieties and ambiguities of popular usage."[10] Consideration of several major variants on the concept of community developed over the past several decades will help in understanding why community has become an area of specialization in the discipline of sociology.

We have singled out three primary orientations to serve as the basis of this presentation. According to the territorial tradition, community is connected with particular structures and places. And by the processual view, community signifies a way of interacting independent of place. The third approach is a broader, societal one in which community is identified with a very general social bond upon which all social organization rests.

Territorial Model

Toennies spoke of village life as the epitome of community (*gemeinschaft*), and the city as the most fully developed example of impersonal togetherness (*gesellschaft*). The former could be likened to a large family, while the latter was a collection of strangers, characterized by actual or potential conflicts between upper and lower strata. The town was seen as an intermediate form, having some of the features of both polar types.[11] This dichotomy that Toennies developed has served as a starting point for a host of territorially oriented community studies, which carry on the tradition that he initiated.

Among the best-known representatives of this tradition are the community classics *Middletown* (1969), the Yankee city series (1940-60), and *Deep South* (1941). These studies selected towns as the subjects of detailed investigation, with status and stratification as major concerns. *Middletown* documented the central role of one predominant family in all the basic activities of the town, while the Yankee City studies were based upon a classification of townspeople into nine social strata, from "upper-upper" to "lower-lower" classes. *Deep South* analyzed the process by which the dominant group of whites excluded blacks from the town's power structure. All of these works assumed that the towns formed local social systems that could be regarded as complete (composed of all basic social institutions), a point of view borrowed from anthropology. This local-social-system approach has been extended in recent years to investigations of suburban communities, such as *The Levittowners* (1967) and *Crestwood Heights* (1963).[12]

These researches have been complemented by a series of studies that focus on smaller territorial units, such as neighborhoods or districts of large cities, exemplified in the unexcelled series produced in the 1920s and 1930s at the University of Chicago. Taking the metropolis as their laboratory, several generations of students, trained by Robert Park and Ernest Burgess, produced such works as *The Gold Coast and the Slum* (1929), *The Ghetto* (1928), *The Hobo* (1925), and *The Taxi Dance Hall* (1928), sociological novelettes that still fascinate contemporary readers.[13] The organizing principle of these books was the idea of natural areas—central business districts, exclusive residential areas, industrial sectors, slums and ghettoes, immigrant colonies, and bohemian quarters—as the basic social units of cities. This sociological tradition has been carried through in more recent community studies like Whyte's *Street Corner Society* (1955), Gans's *Urban Villagers* (1962), and Liebow's *Tally's Corner* (1967).[14]

Networking Model

The perspective of community as a network of relationships can be traced to Georg Simmel, a sociologist and philosopher who was fascinated by the subtle and easily overlooked processes of social life. The most essential of these was sociation, the process by which persons enter into social relations with one another. For Simmel, this very process was society; whenever two or more persons were engaged in sociation, society itself was immediately present. With this as his starting point, Simmel authored a series of brilliant essays on social life at the microlevel (1890-1918). Among his best known are his writings on the processes of small groups, such as the dyad, the triad, and the secret society. He also probed the peculiarities of sociation in modern settings in studies of the city and the stranger.[15]

This nonterritorial approach remained a minor current within sociology. Among early works, Wirth's essay "Urbanism as a Way of Life" (1938), is particularly important in terms of dissociating the concept of community from locale or specific geographic entity. Lately this approach has been gaining wider acceptance with the growing realization that social relations do not neatly correspond to conventional physical boundaries but have a geography all their own. Scholars like Karp and Yoels have urged the study of "personal communities," while others have looked for somewhat larger units called "networks."[17] Stack, in her book *All Our Kin* (1974), analyzed community in terms of the mutual aid relations that enabled black residents to survive in an environment of harsh poverty.[18] The focus on networks in recent years has been coupled with a quantitative approach, sometimes under the heading of mathematical sociology.[19]

Social Bond Model

The most fundamental sense of community equates it with the elementary human urge and readiness to be involved with other persons. Here the reference is not to the "Italian community" in a large city, or to the "community of scholars" in higher education, or even to the community of nation-states in the United Nations, but rather to the entire human family. All mankind is the community that has been directly threatened and torn apart by such historical tragedies as the Holocaust. In the end, it was the policy of conquest and extermination that was found to be less than human. The Nuremberg and Tokyo trials and continuing war-crimes prosecutions proceed not from statutory law, constitutional law, or international law; they proceed from a higher law, a common law, the law of human community.

This sense of community has been developed within the sociological tradition by some of its most influential thinkers. Comte and Marx, in very different ways, wrote of the fullness of community. Durkheim and Weber devoted themselves to the problems that modernization posed for community life. In the twentieth century, many voices have echoed these themes. Parsons drew from them when he pursued "the problem of order." A similar influence can be seen in the works of Fromm, Marcuse, and the Frankfurt school, especially when dealing with the reification and alienation of contemporary social life. Sorokin's studies of "the crisis of our age," the "reconstruction of humanity," and "the power of creative love" are ideas of community that vibrate with a passionate note. The same motifs have been prominent in the recent work of Nisbet.

To capture this tradition in a single passage, we turn to Robert MacIver, who of all twentieth-century sociologists, has most fully embraced the community perspective. He speaks of community as that common togetherness from which all special social relations emerge:

> Wherever the members of any group, small or large live together in such a way that they share, not this or that particular interest, but the basic conditions of a common life, we call that group a community. The mark of a community, then, is that one's life *may* be lived wholly within it. One cannot live wholly within a business organization or a church. . . . The basic criterion of community, then, is that all of one's relationships may be found within it.[20]

Loss and Rediscovery of Community

The theme of community has been featured in some of the most melancholy passages by recent scholars who, following Toennies, mourn the passing of intimate and personal social worlds. As early as *Middletown in Transition* (1937), this emphasis appeared in the body of community studies. Anthropologists continue to restate it in studies of rapid social change, and philosophers, especially the existentialists, make loss of community a central issue.

Reisman, Glazer, and Denney wrote of the "lonely crowd," expressing the view that a genuine sense of community is disappearing amid the production of a standardized, dehumanized mass. Individuals, increasingly incapable of creating fulfilling personal lives, were seen as involved in a desperate search for acceptance, even at the price of complete, "other-directed" conformity, trapping them in a futile, even tragic search, for he who seeks autonomy "cannot achieve it alone. He needs friends."[21]

Recently Philip Slater referred to "American culture at the breaking point" and wrote of "the social and psychological forces that are pulling our society apart."[22] In Slater's vision, American culture frustrates three of the most basic human desires:

(1) The desire for *community*—the wish to live in trust and fraternal cooperation with one's fellows in a total and visible collective entity.

(2) The desire for *engagement*—the wish to come directly to grips with social and interpersonal problems.

(3) The desire for *dependence*—the wish to share responsibility for the control of one's impulses and the direction of one's life.[23]

Slater perceives America as having reached a tragic limit of competitiveness and loneliness from which we must draw back into renewed community life if living is to regain its flavor, its values, and its worth.

Maurice Stein, pursuing much the same theme, attempted to interpret the phenomenon in terms of the three large-scale processes of urbanization, industrialization, and bureaucratization. In his view, each of these dynamics was working to strip humanity of its distinctiveness and togetherness, reducing us to a faceless mass. Urbanization, especially through its standardizing influences, has worked to "prohibit real intimacy."[24] With the coming of industrialization, "every institutional area—the home, the church, the school, recreation, and politics—accommodated to the requirements imposed by industrial work roles. . . . All of this emanated from the outside . . . so that the sense of local autonomy declined."[25] This spreading anonymity has been intensified by the process of bureaucratization. Under its influence, people increasingly find themselves becoming embodiments of collectivities under the control of remote power centers that determine their relationships to each other far more than the factors arising in local life.[26] These controls operate to prohibit real intimacy, to destroy any sense of local autonomy, and to reduce humans to members of impersonal collectivities. These views are bleak; they call to mind the grim pessimism of Max Weber as he reflected on the progressive rationalization of the world.

If the processes that these theorists so tellingly describe are in fact transforming contemporary life, how are people responding to them? How aware of these great issues have they become? What have they done to cope with them? Are there any encouraging signs?

Within the last decade, some more hopeful views have been put forward. In their study *Being Urban* (1977), for example, Karp and Yoels spoke of the rediscovery of community:

> Although the conditions of urban life may seem conducive to impersonality and rationality, persons can tolerate only so much of this impersonality. Perhaps at the height of feelings of depersonalization and lack of integration, persons will seek out alternatives in the environment to provide them with just the kinds of relationships that seem denied them.[27]

They believe that "community is alive; it is our old conceptions of community that no longer have viablity."[28] Their conclusion is based on the perception that "human beings are eminently capable of transforming their environments in important ways." If this is indeed so, then "we find it reasonable to characterize urban life in terms of a number of individual, personal, or intimate communities. Persons, we think, owe allegiance less to a particular territory than to a network of social relationships that is without boundaries. This idea leads us to see that there are as many urban communities as urban persons."[29]

Community as Relationship

We have sought to clarify the notion of community but have not yet specified its usage in this book. Several choices are available. The most important is whether to view community as a group or as a type of relationship. As Sorokin has pointed out, these two notions do not belong together logically or factually. A warm, intimate relationship does not imply a territorially defined group nor vice-versa. Experience teaches that such territorial groups as small towns may be characterized by intense conflict between or indifference toward fellow townspeople. We know, too, that groups scattered around the world—religious congregations and political sects, for example—may be characterized by warmth, trust, and love.

In this book, community will be understood as a relationship, a way of interacting. Sorokin has provided three concepts of interaction. Familistic ways of relating are voluntary, informal, often long-standing, and with a minimum of social distance between the parties, such as in religious orders or congregations. Contractual relations are voluntary, formal, tending to be of limited duration, and marked by a moderate social distance, such as are found in commercial organizations. Compulsory relations are distinguished by the involuntary participation of one of the parties and by maximum social distance between the participants, such as in a military system.[30]

The three concepts prove valuable in summarizing the overall quality of group life, for they weave the various strands into the fabric of community life. Each of the three types may be regarded as ideal types, or segregated pure types; actual social life is a blend of them all. The notion of community that we have adopted is based primarily on familistic relations, with some allowance for contractual or even compulsory forms of interaction.

These conceptual distinctions may be illustrated by what ordinarily takes place in the criminal-court system. Lingering problems between a married couple erupt suddenly into open conflict when the husband assaults his wife. Feeling that she can endure such treatment no longer, the wife files a formal complaint with the court, which responds by ordering the husband to appear to answer to the complaint. The initial contractual interaction has been followed by a compulsory one. If the matter comes to trial, a second contractual and compulsory situation arises, as guilt or innocence are determined within formal rules of procedure. Throughout the court process, the two parties remain strangers and antagonists, a far cry from their original familistic relation in marriage. Eventual decision by the court resolves the issue in its narrow sense but does not touch upon the total relationship between members of the family group.

This same case is much differently handled by a community-justice scheme. Here an essentially familistic orientation permits the disputing parties to become directly involved in informal processes of dispute resolution. This approach looks toward compromise rather than the win-or-lose approach that characterizes the adversary process, having proceeded in a natural sequence (ideally) from compulsory to familistic. More importantly, community justice looks beyond immediate problems to the longer-term relationships. There are certain risks, especially in the area of due process, but these may be offset by a significant creative potential, an ability to leave the situation better than when the parties came seeking justice. This potential currently is being explored and developed in a variety of community programs: neighborhood justice centers, ombudsmen programs, and small-claims courts, dealing with problems ranging from family matters, medical malpractice, prisoners' rights, labor and employment disputes, to consumer grievances and housing conflicts.

These considerations appear to argue that dispute resolution has a great potential role to play in bringing justice into the community, for the value this process has for reviving and even strengthening a sense of living community. The potential of such processes for building and maintaining community is argued by those who conduct such programs within a socialist ideology. If the state is indeed to wither away, they feel, affairs will have to be turned over to average communities in the maner of the comrade courts or other people's courts. Such optimistic views have been disputed by those who raise the question whether the social and cultural bases for such community approaches really exist in the United States or warn against hasty assumptions that we can easily replicate what we admire elsewhere.

Granted that such warnings are to be heeded, we take the position that the potential of community justice and community-dispute resolution merits serious exploration. Popular dissatisfaction with older methods of handling criminal acts and minor disputes is so pervasive that immediate creative initiatives are called for. In the process of exploration, many programs no doubt will be found wanting and thereafter rejected. But the search for viable community approaches to these issues may begin a needed restorative process to many of the fractured and alienated communities throughout our country.

"Justice by the community" as used throughout this book means: (1) a very localized kind of justice, as opposed to one that involves police, courts, and other elements of state power; (2) justice accomplished by familistic-contractual relations; (3) justice that takes place within a familistic-contractual setting, as opposed to a contractual-compulsory setting within the criminal-justice system; and (4) justice familistically interpreted rather than contractually understood, in which the reestablishment of a harmonious relationship is considered more important than the fixing of guilt or a finding of innocence or the imposition of compensation for damages, or other penalty.

When community justice is successful and conciliation has been achieved, cases are not ended by such formal expressions as "the defendant will rise" or "the case is indefinitely postponed." Instead contending parties may make restitution, tender apologies, shake hands, even wish one another well.

2   Our Troubled Courts

> But for a handful of persons, we are making no effort to escape a legal doomsday; many of our most justly respected leaders at the bar and in the universities are like the crowd in Samson's temple before he pushed the pillars, unconscious of the impending surprise and headache.[1]

Popular dissatisfaction with the administration of justice has been increasingly voiced in recent years. Citizens who can agree on little else concur in their complaint that the courts are not working effectively. Liberal groups have expressed concern over such civil-liberties issues as negotiated guilty pleas and demands of judges for reporters' notes. Conservative factions are incensed about the steadily increasing power of the courts to shape social policy in areas traditionally controlled by other branches of government. And radical groups indict the courts for continuing to dole out only so much justice as litigants can afford, while safeguarding the interest of the powerful and the wealthy.

The National Court Reform Act (1968), the National Conference on the Causes of Popular Dissatisfaction with the Administration of Justice (1976), and the National Victims of Crime Act (1977) reflected citizen concern and sought to provide remedies. At the same time, campaigns for court reform have been waged in individual states.

Some Basic Problems

Our courts are public institutions intended to be available equally to all for the resolution of conflicts and the affirmation of rights. In practice, however, a series of factors, long and increasingly familiar, hinder the full realization of these goals. Despite diversity of opinion and ideology, a number of basic issues can be identified. The most important are: inaccessibility of the courts due to delay and rising costs; inefficient procedures; fragmented administration; neglect of the victims of crime; an expanding role for the courts in the area of social policy; political influence and favoritism; and a general failure on the part of courts to keep up with the changing times.

Inaccessibility

To the degree that the courts are inaccessible, the privileges of citizenship are thereby diminished. Some authors have argued that effective access to the courts is the "most basic requirement" of any political system that strives "to guarantee and not merely proclaim, the legal rights of all."[2] In the American court system today, this fundamental right is jeopardized, particularly by the effects of cost and delay.

The costs of litigation have become an increasingly difficult burden for every segment of our society. Not surprisingly, the poor are hit hardest of all. According to a recent study, despite expanded legal-aid provisions, "it is the lack of money that alone or with other factors has separated the poor from lawyers."[3] This obstacle is so fundamental that its removal is *"sine qua non* to making legal services available to the poor." The poor are not alone. Middle-class citizens have found that the expense of retaining legal counsel rivals that of a college education for their children or adequate family health care. Results of a recent American Bar Association survey indicate that average Americans are increasingly unable to afford to pursue legal claims unless these are covered by insurance, and so they are being "deprived of access to our legal system."[4] The high cost of litigation in such areas as medical malpractice claims exemplifies how even the affluent experience difficulties of access. Small wonder, then, that a variety of proposals for prepaid legal services are being developed.[5]

A second barrier to court access is delay. It arises from many sources and produces many types of negative results, due in part to a tremendous increase in the volume of litigation. Americans are said to be the most litigious people in the world. Over the past decade, district courts have witnessed increases of 55 and 25 percent in civil and criminal matters, respectively.[6] As a result, "there is more than double the lapse of time from the charge to the date of the trial," and "once the trial starts it takes about twice as long to try a criminal case today as it did ten years ago."[7] The Supreme Court's docket of cases tripled between 1952 and 1972. The problem of delay has become so severe that it has prompted rethinking of the jury system, one of the pillars of American justice. Understandably the resolution of relatively minor disputes and lesser offenses must be slighted by a court process so heavily overburdened, cumbersome, and time-consuming.

Delay can also be measured in terms of case backlogs, some of them startlingly large. Research in Massachusetts revealed that in nearly half of the counties, there was more than a three-year wait between the entry of a civil case and a jury trial. One county experienced an average delay of five and one-half years.[8] In criminal matters the consequences, though shorter, can be even harsher, since defendants who cannot make bail must be incarcerated until trial. Studies conducted within the last few years report that the time spent in jail prior to trial ranges from two weeks to over four months; the median is almost two months.[9] Release of such findings has led to a predictable outcry and has provided an important impetus for many reform efforts. The problem, however, continues to be intractable; "attempts to reduce delay through special programs, conferencing devices, diversion and other procedural tinkering have seldom proved themselves in practice."[10]

The full dimensions of the problem become clearer when we consider that the costs of delay are not confined to the justice system and the litigants immediately involved. On the contrary.

> The costs of delay extend to everyone. Taxes increase every hour a policeman waits for a case to be called. Taxes increase every time a policeman must go to court only to have the judge grant a continuance. *o* Other costs are less tangible. Police officers are discouraged from making arrests. . . . Continuances and postponements teach that the administration of justice is clumsy and inefficient, indifferent to the needs and feelings of those caught up in a creaking machine.[11]

Considerations like these account for recent administrative and legislative efforts to guarantee the right to a speedy trial.

As few basic or far-reaching changes have yet been made, the net result of the problem of inaccessibility is a profound degree of alienation of the community from the procedures, personnel, and performance of the local criminal court.

Administrative Problems

A second source of major difficulties in the courts is the fragmented organizational structure that has emerged in haphazard manner in the course of two hundred years of American history. Prior to the court-unification drives of the past decade, most state judiciaries were characterized by a bewildering array of specialized tribunals. In New York State, for example, a variety of courts functioned largely independent of one another; they included the court of general sessions, the country court, the surrogates' court, the city court, the municipal court, and city magistrate's court, and the domestic relations court.[12] The Texas judiciary experienced no general reform from the 1890s until the 1970s. Within that period, forty-odd courts operated above the justice of the peace level, with little coordination among them. In one county, 24 district courts existed side by side with 5 courts of domestic relations, 3 juvenile courts, 2 county courts at law, and 1 constitutional county court.[13] Michigan boasted 246 courts grouped into four segments: a state supreme court, a court of appeals, circuit courts, and a mixture of lower tribunals (a common pleas court, a court of claims, municipal courts, probate courts, and a superior court).[14]

Growing dissatisfaction with this state of affairs has resulted in campaigns for court unification, or, at the least, more streamlined administration. Certain basic measures called for include the consolidation and simplification of court structure, centralized rule making, centralized management, centralized budgeting, and state financing. Some observers predict that all states will have achieved some form of lower-court unification by 1990,[15] despite the reservations of those who find little evidence of the superiority of unified over nonunified systems.[16]

At the level of everyday operations, case-flow management of defendants through the arrest, bail, jail, trial, and disposition process is a central issue.[17] Current operations are also characterized by the poor treatment received by many participants, especially victims, witnesses, and jurors who must take time off from work and travel to court, only to have the case continued. Small wonder that so many witnesses refuse to return, and many citizens seek to avoid jury duty.[18]

There has been no lack of suggestions and programs forthcoming for reform of the court system and for alleviating the problems that in some jurisdictions seem about to force the courts almost to a halt.[19] Among these are bail reform, provision of legal counsel, acceleration of the trials of defendants charged with serious crimes or with long criminal records, the free transfer of judges among the various types of courts, and similar tinkering with procedural aspects. But most of these proposals fail to touch on the traditional adversary process, which pits the two parties (with the state representing the victim) against one another in what is, in practice, a duel between opposing attorneys.[20]

For example, a carefully argued plan by an eminent Harvard professor of law would seek to ameliorate some of the most frequent criticisms of our criminal courts by importing from continental Europe the procedure whereby accusation and investigation of criminal charges are done by a judge from the court instead of parceling out, as we do in this country, the two responsibilities: accusation to the police and investigation of the facts to the prosecution. Given the highly political character of our judiciary, the lack of a tradition of trained professional civil service in the appointment and elevation of judges, and the tremendous opposition that such a plan would arouse on the part of the establishment, the proposal remains where it originated—in academic conjecture. Yet it is worthy of consideration if only for the accuracy and comprehensiveness of the criticisms of existing roles of police, prosecutory staff and judges.[21]

One of the most regrettable aspects of current court practice is that it is divorced from the life of the communities that experience the greatest amount of crime—assaults against persons and the theft of property, which bring the bulk of defendants and accusers before the criminal bench. Our courts are not always situated where these persons live; the sessions are scheduled during the hours when most people work; incessant case continuances needlessly take the time and waste the funds of those least able to afford them. Most critical of all the charges that can be brought against our courts is the almost complete exclusion from the hearing or trial of the person most aggrieved by a criminal event: the victim.

No amount of minor procedural changes or rearrangements gives the individuals most closely involved an opportunity to participate in an "accessible, fair and effective means of resolving disputes. Without access to such a mechanism, disputes are invariably destructive, and people are deprived of the chance—and the basic right—to work toward the fulfillment of their just goals and desires with some measure of security and stability."[22]

Political Factors

Political issues present persistent problems in terms of the quality of judges, specifically on the manner of their election or appointment. One Chicago-area commentator has referred to judgeships as the "terminal positions to which warriors retire . . . political veterans with long records of public service who grew up in the service of the organization and who serve as the ethnic representatives of their constituents on the bench."[23]

The political character of the judiciary derives largely from the electoral process, since until quite recently the great majority of judges had to face election campaigns, which required fund raising. In Wisconsin, for example, the cost of getting elected to the state supreme court in the early 1970s ranged from $100,000 to $150,000, and in neighboring Michigan one candidate for the bench spent over $180,000.[24] Such election costs present an ominous message: "judges must indebt and obligate themselves to persons to whom they will owe fulfillment of obligations after they attain the bench."[25]

Limits of the Adversary Process

At the center of contemporary criticism of the judiciary is the rapidly spreading perception that the adversary process is no longer adequate to handle the tremendous burden that has been placed upon it. Critics of the process typically begin by attacking the premise that "the truth can best be discovered if each side strives as hard as it can, in a keen partisan spirit, to bring to the court's attention the evidence favorable to its own side."[26] Basic flaws are found in the withholding of relevant information, the inability of some parties to discover and present evidence that would benefit their side, and the passivity of many judges. The adversary model is said to tend to glorify competition and conflict while its supporters are accused of clinging to outmoded laissez-faire, free-enterprise doctrines that the optimum level of equity is attained when each party promotes its own interests.[27]

Judge Marvin Frankel's perception is that "our adversary system rates truth too low among the values that institutions of justice are meant to serve."[28] Partisanship requires that the primary loyalty of the attorney be to the client rather than to truth, which emerges as a by-product of the contest, a convenience, or an accidental approximation. In Frankel's opinion, the difficulty is that "the truth and victory are mutually incompatible," especially when conbatants possess vastly unequal levels of skill.[29] Frankel implies that our justice system rests upon pious hypocrisy; the state glorifies the adversary process in public proclamations, while simultaneously practicing plea-bargaining on a vast scale to circumvent the process.

Plea-bargaining (used in more than 90 percent of all criminal cases dealt with in certain courts),[30] a unique American practice unknown in any other country that derives its procedure from the common law, brings into question our commitment to the basic principles of the presumption of innocence and the due-process rights regarded as the hallmark of our Anglo-American legal heritage. The resulting cynicism engendered during the court process leaves its mark upon many who pass through it, a mark that sentenced persons often carry with them, broodingly, into the places where they serve their bargained-for terms of imprisonment.

A blatant instance of the extreme limits to which the abuse of plea-bargaining can be pushed is reported in a 1978 Supreme Court decision.[31] The case involved a forged check for $88.30 by a man who was found to have had two prior convictions for which he had served time in prison and a term of probation. If found guilty of the check fraud, he could, as a thrice-convicted felon under Kentucky law, be legally sentenced to imprisonment for life. He refused the district attorney's offer to plea-bargain "to save the court the inconvenience and necessity of a trial" despite the threat of indictment under the habitual-offender law if he refused. The defendant insisted on a jury trial, which resulted in his being found guilty. The jury then recommended, and the judge imposed, a sentence of imprisonment for life. The Supreme Court, on appeal, refused to reverse this decision by the Kentucky court. This decision recently was confirmed by another Supreme Court decision that upheld a Texas court's imposition of a life sentence for a "habitual criminal" found guilty of three thefts totaling $229.[32]

Inadequacies in the Handling of Minor Disputes

Symptomatic of the inadequacy of our system of justice is its handling of a class of problems referred to as minor disputes. Minor in this connection does not signify that the matters in question are unimportant, but rather, that compared to such felonies as homicide, rape, and armed assault, they are of lesser import. Nevertheless such disputes, if left unresolved, can frequently escalate into very serious conflicts.

The mounting resort to litigation for the resolution of citizen disputes, the soaring resort to malpractice suits in all areas, especially in medical practice, together with the proliferation of law and administrative regulation, has resulted in an avalanche of minor disputes between landlord and tenant, producer and consumer, bureaucracy and citizen. The bulk of such cases are ill-suited to traditional formal adversary procedures, with the result that many persons rely on informal avoidance measures in order to accomplish what the courts cannot, or do not, provide.

Inevitably the result has been a growing demand for reform that takes a new look at how the courts deal with victims of crime. As the modern nation-state took over the function of prosecution, thereby preventing persons from exacting private vengeance, victims of crimes found that in order to claim damages for their injuries, they had to find recourse to civil tort proceedings. As such recourse became prohibitively expensive and so removed from everyday life, many persons had no knowledge of how to press a claim for compensation.

Consideration of victim rights emerged from the intense social conflicts of the late 1960s with widespread protest against what was perceived as excessive leniency of the courts toward the accused and the convicted. Police groups across the country lobbied for "the tools necessary to collect evidence and get convictions," a fight that won wide backing in public opinion and editorial comment. Emotions were further intensified by occasional sensational accounts of violent crimes committed by persons while on recognizance or out on bail.

Chief Justice Warren Burger, an advocate of alternative methods of resolving minor disputes, notes that "people with problems like people with pains, want relief, and they want it as quickly and inexpensively as possible."[33] People also desire solutions that are personal, direct, and informal, qualities unlikely to be found because of the inappropriateness of the courts for the handling of minor grievances. Judges may impose on the accused a warning, a suspended sentence, probation, a fine, or a term in prison or jail, but none of these is effective in resolving the conflicts that brought the contestants to court.[34]

A Reorientation of Justice

A significant national conference was held in 1976 at St. Paul, Minnesota. Its site and theme were selected to commemorate a famous address by

Roscoe Pound seventy years earlier on "the causes of popular dissatisfaction with the administration of justice." In attendance were some of the most eminent members of bar and judiciary, scholars in law and social science. The purpose of the gathering, called by Chief Justice Burger, was "candid and constructive self-criticism,"[35] which was to take as its point of departure Pound's 1906 complaint that "our system of courts is archaic and our procedures behind the times."[36] Topics ranged from the workload of the courts through the selection and tenure of judges, problems of the adversary process, and alternative dispute-resolution mechanisms.

Recommendations that emerged from the conference were entrusted to a follow-up task force designed to oversee their further development.[37] The report of the group, published in 1978 dealt, among others, with the following topics that fall within the scope of this book: better means of dispute resolution, alternate forums, neighborhood justice centers, small-claims courts, arbitration, elimination of the adversary process, interests of victims, witnesses, and jurors, and in-prison complaint procedures.[38] National organizations working toward the implementation of the final proposals include the American Law Institute, the American Bar Foundation, the National Conference of Commissioners on Uniform State Laws, the National Judicial College, the National Center for State Courts, the Office for Improvements in the Administration of Justice (U.S. Department of Justice), and the Federal Judicial Center.[39]

One of the most important results of the conference and subsequent activities is the recommendation that neighborhood justice centers be set up around the country ". . . to improve the resolution of minor disputes by studying and surveying existing resolution mechanisms, to encourage the development of effective mechanisms at a local, community, or state level, and to provide access to justice for individuals with disputes not readily resolvable in the existing justice system."[40] These recommendations were embodied in a bill to establish a dispute resolution resource center within the Department of Justice to serve as an information clearinghouse, to provide technical assistance, to conduct research, and to make grants to prospective neighborhood centers.[41]

This Act, passed in 1980, may someday appear as a beacon indicating a reorientation of justice in a community direction, expressed by the federal government, especially the Department of Justice. The lines along which such a national program may well develop have been indicated by two original and thoughtful proponents of basic court reform, Richard Danzig in 1973 and Eric Fisher in 1975.

Danzig's plan calls for "the creation of a complementary, decentralized system of criminal justice," directed toward returning responsibility for the administration of justice to citizens within a neighborhood context.[42] The overall design is quite ambitious. It advocates a network of neighborhood police and attorneys, as well as a neighborhood legislative body. The key idea in Danzig's proposal is decentralization, which he views as the basis of community control, increased autonomy, or "empowerment." Decentralization allows for local discretion in peacekeeping, especially as it develops out of local standards of behavior. Danzig questions, for example, why playing the numbers should be prosecuted in the inner city when friendly poker games are tolerated in the suburbs, or why loitering should be penalized when the alternative is to spend time within a slum tenement. Under local control, such practices might be tolerated, or at least handled more flexibly. In Danzig's view this would not constitute a great departure from normal American practice, especially since policing is much more decentralized in the United States (which has no national police force) than in many other countries.[43] The author's overall conclusion is that certain purposes of the justice system could be more effectively served if they were to be decentralized and transferred to local communities.

Danzig believes that serious crimes against the person should not be under the jurisdiction of local community groups. Instead a broad category of offenses relating to order maintenance would be suitable for their consideration. Order maintenance includes a wide variety of routine tasks that often take police time and effort but that seldom lead either to arrest or conviction. Examples include drunk and disorderly charges, intervention in domestic quarrels, and petty or juvenile offenses. Order-maintenance tasks, in short, might be appropriately handled by paraprofessionals or nonprofessionals rather than by trained police officers.[44]

Within this context of decentralized community justice, Danzig proposes that community courts, which he labels "moots," be established to settle disputes and to resolve grievances through conciliation and mediation. The proposed moots could operate in a variety of locations and might even move from house to house as the occasion demanded.[45] Procedures would be simple and informal. Intake, for example, could be handled by a counselor who would schedule mediation sessions at the convenience of the disputing parties. When all relevant persons had been assembled, the complainant would state the grievance, the accused would respond, and all those present would have an opportunity to join in the discussion. Mediators would facilitate communication and help disputants to shape the terms of a settlement. In this way community courts would keep the peace, restore and strengthen bonds among members of the community, and simultaneously avoid the criminal labels and records that result from formal court action.[46]

The second proposal, by Eric Fisher, advocates community courts as "an alternative to conventional adjudication."[47] They are neighborhood forums with sanctioning powers that they exercise by virtue of their exclusive jurisdiction over selected issues or conflicts. With such jurisidiction, community courts possess real crime-deterrent value rather than serve as "an unnecessary appendage to the formal courts." Meaningful sanctions would ensure respect and support in cases where conciliation proves impossible.[48]

The ideal community court envisioned by Fisher would spring from the community to be served and rely upon that group for support. The product of specific legislation granting it exclusive jurisdiction over minor interpersonal disputes and certain misdemeanors, the ideal community court would adjudicate as well as conciliate; it would impose meaningful and appropriate sanctions and thus present a real alternative to present criminal court procedures.

Fisher concludes with a series of stipulations regarding the operation of the community courts. Proceedings could be initiated by any member of the community; complainants would assume the responsibility of prosecution and accused persons would defend themselves; hearings would be held after working hours and might include public access; procedures would be informal, with records kept only of the proceedings and decisions, in order to facilitate possible review by the court. Due process would follow the guidelines set out by the U.S. Supreme Court in the case of *Goss* v. *Lopez*.[49] Defendants would be guaranteed advance written notice of accusations; decisions with stated reasons would be in writing; the right to call witnesses would be assured. The regular courts would be called upon when needed to guarantee due process and to remedy abuses arising in the community bodies.

Danzig's and Fisher's proposals embody two basically competing

Table 2-1
Comparison of Mediation and Arbitration

Dimension	Arbitration	Mediation
Relation to official system	Closer to adversary process; involves adjudication	Further from adversary process; does not involve adjudication
Relation between disputants	May have equal or unequal power	Should have roughly equal power
Underlying process	Compromise and adjudication	Compromise
Degree of formality	More formal	Less formal
Role of facts	Establishing facts more important	Establishing facts less important
Role of sanctions	Authoritative; enforcement more important	Not authoritative; enforcement less important
Model of justice	Reconciliation and affirmation of rights	Reconciliation

themes in community justice: conciliation and the enforcement of rights. Conciliation occupies a central place in mediation efforts; enforcement of rights plays an equally important role in arbitration. The two proposals provide a standard for assessing the values and priorities of particular programs and their significance for citizen access to dispute-resolution mechanisms in any community.[50] The relationship between arbitration and mediation is set out in table 2-1.

Court Monitoring

Citizens who are dissatisfied with the day-to-day operations of the criminal-justice system have few outlets for effective expression with regard to the functioning of the police and even fewer opportunities to influence the course of corrections. But they do have an unlimited opportunity to observe and criticize the courts. The courts by common-law tradition are free and open forums for any citizen to observe and make note of what goes on.[1] In practice, some limitations are placed upon this privilege when the courts exercise their broad discretion to close proceedings when a victim might be unduly embarrassed (as in sex cases), or to forbid picture taking or tape-recording of proceedings).

The courtroom, especially during criminal trials, has long been a favorite haunt of people who have little else to occupy their time, for it is a rare session that does not furnish some dramatic episode to compensate for tedious hours of waiting. But except for a relatively small proportion of the general public that has contact with a court as defendant, witness, victim, or juror, most citizens have little precise knowledge of what goes on in a criminal trial (excluding what television presents in simplified or distorted form). Few of us base our criticism of the courts on knowledge gained through direct personal experience, yet few of us are without an opinion as to what is wrong with our courts and what should be done to improve them.

The general public is affected by and is aware of the continuing increase in the number of cases that the lower criminal courts must handle each year, with consequent long delays and the postponement of the resolution of disputes. The courts' isolation from informed public scrutiny and the almost complete lack of restraints on the powers of sentencing judges frequently result in wide disparities in sentences, as well as judicial procedures that can be at times inconsistent when they are not inequitable, with adverse effects on certain classes of defendants.[2]

As a consequence of inadequate legal advice to clients or none at all, or of the racial origin and class status of certain defendants, court actions directly and disproportionately affect the poor, the elderly, and members of minority groups.[3] A study of the operation of a large municipal court in Massachusetts reported that 55 percent of defendants classified as nonpoor had a 50 percent better chance of appearing under a summons than by an arrest warrant, which is the experience of persons below the poverty level.[4]

Whether one is arrested or not before appearing in court seemingly depends upon one's financial status.

As a result, public esteem for the courts has steadily deteriorated. Popular perception of the criminal process has been described in this way:

> Scarcely anyone believes that this process is a good one, although the main grounds of objection vary. Judgments of guilt are reached haphazardly and aimlessly, without either the deliberation or the urgency that they merit. Both in substance and appearance, they lack the qualities of rationality and consistency. For no reason other than the inadequacy of the process, persons who have committed serious crimes are not convicted at all or are convicted of a minor offense having no relation to what they did. Standards of individual dignity and liberty that we regard as fundamental are pointlessly violated. It has been our habit to acclaim our noble pretensions at the same time that we lament the failures in practice. The pretensions sound increasingly empty and unconvincing; and our actual expectations fall far beneath them.[5]

In order to document such criticisms and to attempt to correct them, civic, political, and religious organizations have undertaken to monitor sessions of the criminal courts and to present their findings and recommendations for remedial action. This process involves the direct observation and recording of cases, especially when violations of law are discerned or when unjust and discriminatory acts on the part of court officials are suspected to have occurred.

Over the past decade, several types of court-monitoring programs have emerged in response to such citizen concerns.[6] Among the earliest of these initiatives were a series of projects focusing on the rights of defendants. These programs were generally based on some perception of arbitrariness or discrimination in particular court settings, which the court watchers hoped to expose and, ultimately, to eliminate. Libertarian groups were active in these efforts, especially members of the American Civil Liberties Union and the American Friends Service Committee. In Seattle, the Friends attempted to document undue harshness against women accused of prostitution, and in Chester, Pennsylvania, they investigated the treatment of minority defendants. A citiziens' group in Schenectady, New York, looked for irregularities of a more general nature in court practices, and monitors in Rochester, New York, concentrated on the difficulties faced by defendants who could not afford bail. In Boston, a group of monitors were successful in having a sitting judge impeached and removed from the bench, on the basis of his mistreatment of accused persons.

A second type of monitoring has proceeded from opposite value premises. The citizens who scrutinized the behavior of court personnel believed that the law was not being strictly enforced. The best-known effort of this type appeared in Oakland, California, where a group of interested persons decided to evaluate the sentencing patterns of local judges and to publicize their findings. The ultimate goal of this project was to support the election of judges who practiced strict sentencing standards and to oppose the election of judges who were considered to be too lenient.

Another variety of programs concentrated on the collection of information, usually of a statistical nature, in the interests of diverse local campaigns. The Connecticut Citizens for Judicial Modernization gathered data for presentation before a state commission on court reorganization. The American Friends in Allegheny County, Pennsylvania, developed statistics on the bail system and utilized these as a basis for bail-reform proposals. In Brooklyn, New York, other monitors did a time-cost analysis of the family courts.

A fourth type of program is best described in general terms because its goals have been less clearly articulated. The significant characteristic of such efforts seems to have been a concern for the increased involvement of citizens in the court system. The Alliance for a Safer New York devoted itself to providing the average citizen with firsthand information about the courts, in the interests of future activism. The Women's Crusade against Crime in St. Louis, Missouri, observed the courts in order to pinpoint specific weaknesses, whose characteristics were not identified in advance. And in New York City the Task Force for Justice pursued the objective of maintaining a public presence in the courtroom.

The actual work of court watching, and much of the direction of its progress, is usually done by lay citizens, for their volunteer services are in plentiful supply. Legal professionals are not so readily available and may hesitate to antagonize judges or other court personnel with whom they must continue to have a working relationship. Such attitudes may appear to be expedient and self-serving, but they may also be more conscientious than one might expect, for lawyers know that it is the clients who suffer when judges are offended by the attitudes or actions of attorneys. Counsel are retained to represent the best interests of their clients and may feel, understandably, that it is wiser for them to ignore issues of reform of the system in which they practice.[7]

Persons selected for court monitoring begin by learning the basic rules of criminal procedure. They generally receive training in the courtroom from lawyers and judges or experienced court monitors, and they visit jails and police stations in the course of their preparation. It is important that they understand as well the roles of other personnel in the criminal-justice system, especially bail bondsmen, clerks, bailiffs and other court officers, police, sheriffs, public defenders, and prosecutors. A court-monitoring group can gain community acceptance and support by sending speakers to neighborhood meetings to explain their purposes, distributing printed materials, issuing press releases, and making radio and television appearances.[8] Monitoring groups that are trying to persuade officials to observe proper procedures use a number of tactics. They might appear in court every day to observe procedures, publish reports with recommendations for reform, confront and initiate a dialogue with judges at special meetings, and occasionally take part in acts of disobedience reminiscent of civil-rights groups of the 1960s.

At least seven states have organized citizen groups to recruit and train volunteers to serve as unofficial court monitors. Their duties include the observation of trials and court proceedings, the identification of problems, and the making of recommendations to appropriate authorities with regard to their findings.[9]

Illinois League of Women Voters Project

One of the best-known of these groups was initiated by the League of Women Voters in Illinois in July 1974 with funds granted by the State Law Enforcement Commission. The program aimed to identify problems in the courts that might be responsible for the loss of respect and noncooperation on the part of citizens in the areas served by those courts. Projects were established in four counties within the state during the first project year, were extended to three additional jurisdictions in the second project year, and further enlarged to include ten projects in the final year of the study. In three years, the project trained over nine hundred volunteers and assigned them to record information in several areas: continuances, victimless crimes, physical facilities, and the conduct of judges and court personnel. Each study group submitted confidential reports to the chief justice of the respective court, as well as to other court officials and the local bar associations. The Illinois program was unique in seeking a close working relationship with the judges involved and in gaining their cooperation in training the monitors, providing seating arrangements in court, furnishing court calendars in advance, and so on. The court sessions monitored ranged from misdemeanor cases and preliminary findings in felony cases to special hearings in women's cases, jury-selection proceedings, and small-claims matters.

When a project site had been selected, the local league chapter took responsibility for setting up an advisory committee of six to twelve persons and hired a project coordinator. The advisory committee assumed responsibility for recruiting and training monitors, selecting specific courts to be observed, tabulating results, and drafting preliminary and final reports. Paid staff were kept to a minimum throughout, with volunteer monitors assigned by local coordinators to handle daily observation and reporting. Recruiting of volunteers for the court-watching programs was the responsibility of each of the local committees and was accomplished in a variety of ways. They placed articles in local newspapers, posted news stories in the bulletins and the newsletters of various civic and religious organizations, and arranged with local colleges and universities for students to receive course credit for participation in the programs. Additionally committee members made personal efforts to find recruits.[10]

Because most courts are open only during the daytime, the great majority of the court watchers drawn into the program were housewives (50 percent), students (25 percent), and retired persons (14 percent), as revealed in a breakdown of the first three hundred volunteer recruits. Over one-half were between the ages of thirty and sixty; almost all were white; and women outnumbered men by three to one.

The same local committee that recruited the court monitors also directed their training, which took place in two sessions. The first session required study of the league manual, *How to Watch a Court*, which was divided into two parts, the first covering misdemeanor proceedings and the second felonies. At the first training session a local volunteer lawyer and the local committee coordinator explained the rules and procedures prevailing in the courts to be observed, and gave information regarding court personnel, where to sit in the courtroom, and how to complete the appropriate forms.

The monitors were then free to observe courts on their own. After a while, the work of the monitors was reviewed and assessed. Those volunteers who were found unacceptable were given less demanding assignments, and a second training session, devoted to questions and answers, helped to resolve individual doubts and problems. Thereafter assignments were made by the local coordinator; they required an average of one day every two weeks over a four- to five-month period, for a total maximum number of ten court observation sessions per monitor.

Each court observer completed two simple forms for each day in court. One sought information for each case heard during the day, including the individual characteristics of the case, type of offense, and disposition. The second form evaluated the physical facilities of the courtroom, the conduct of the judge and other court officers, the length of court sessions, and the promptness of court proceedings. This information was collected and tabulated weekly by the local coordinators, who maintained a running picture of the operation of each of the courts being observed and evaluated.

The resulting data, summed up in the final reports of each of the projects, were based on close to eighty-two thousand lower court proceedings observed in ninety courtrooms in twenty-two separate courthouses during the league operation. The initial tentative reports was sent to the judges who had presided over the observed proceedings. After receiving the reaction of the judiciary to this preliminary report, the local committees then held conferences with the judges leading to negotiation between the two groups before the final recommendations were published. The process finally resulted in a number of specific modifications and changes in the operation of the courts.

1. Adequate information. Judges in the four counties ordered that the daily calendars of cases to be heard that day be conspicuously displayed. In addition, a bailiff was posted in or near busy courtrooms fifteen minutes before the start of the session to answer questions and direct defendants, witnesses, and others. A special red telephone for information was installed on each floor of the courthouse, answered by specially designated secretaries. One county appointed a roving bailiff to act as information officer.

2. Information about rights and procedures. Monitors reported what many lay persons have noted on their first appearance in court: confusion with the proceedings, augmented by the technical legal language used by court personnel. Only two of the twenty-two courts that were monitored observed the state statute requiring that defendants' rights be posted in all criminal courts. These rights are now posted prominently in all courtrooms, some of them in languages other than English. Non-English-speaking defendants were also aided by a recommendation for certifying qualified interpreters and the distribution of a list of the interpreters to all juges who preside over criminal trials.

3. Delays. One of the rules of the Illinois Supreme Court states that requests for continuances should be considered "so as to expedite the disposition of matters before the court." The court-monitoring project, if it did no more than remind judges of this rule, rendered the court a valuable service. Although comparable figures from other jurisdictions are not easily found, the readiness with which continuances were granted in the courts that were observed—from a low of 58 percent to high of 74 percent—confirms the observations of any lay person who happens into a criminal courtroom for even a few hours.

4. Inequities. Two areas in which the practice of judges in the various courts varied considerably were observed and reported on by the court watchers: pretrial release and the assignment of public defense counsel. Based on over seven hundred bail-bond hearings in three county courts in the state, it was discovered that whether a defendant was released on bail or on recognizance varied enormously with the county in which the arrest took place and with the judge assigned to the case. The percentage of releases on recognizance ranged from 16 to 61 in one court; in another court in the same county, the range was from 0 to 48 percent. In a third county, 19 percent of the defendants who were represented by counsel were released on their own bond as against only 6 percent of those who were without legal representation. As a result of the court-watching project and its reporting, the Illinois Supreme Court Judicial Conference convened seminars for judges on the proper conduct of bail-bond hearings. In the interest of more-uniform and equitable assignment of public defenders, a further recommendation of the project urged that the state supreme court establish standards for determination of the indigency of defendants in criminal hearings.

5. Poor physical facilities. Court monitors were asked to assess features of the physical facilities that directly confronted citizens in the courts—defendants, witnesses, jurors, and the general public. Frequent criticism was voiced with regard to poor audibility; lack of space for conferences between lawyers, their clients, and other related individuals; discomfort in the accommodations for jurors and witnesses; and poor holding facilities for defendants brought in from the jail. The project recommended that courtroom doors be closed during sessions, that conference and small meeting rooms be provided for counsel and client, and that higher levels of courtesy and propriety be extended by clerks and other court officials in their dealings with the public.

As of January 1977, ten demonstration projects were set up to carry on the work initiated by the league, which also issued informational kits on the twelve steps that were to be taken, in every phase of court-watching project development operation.[11]

Other Court-Watching Programs

A major court-watching program, nearly identical to the Illinois program, was funded by a grant from the New York Division of Criminal Justice Services. In one year (1975-1976), this project placed 338 volunteer court monitors in twenty-three local courts in four cities in the state, including New York City. Lay citizens in the program contributed an average of over forty-five hundred hours per month in each area. There were certain differences between the New York and the Illinois experience. The New York group covered night sessions in one city where this was a prevalent practice, and it received an unusually high degree of cooperation from judges and court personnel, ascribed to the cooperation of the state administrative judge, as well as the continuous efforts made by the local groups to keep the judges whom they were monitoring informed of progress.

As a result, a number of significant positive responses were noted throughout the state. Cases were heard in open court much more consistently; judges were becoming more conscious of explaining the proceedings to defendants and the public; longer sessions and extra sessions were held to deal with the backlog of cases; court was convening on time more frequently; defective sound systems were repaired or replaced; and a judicial directive was issued that presiding judges wear their judicial robes.[12]

The next phase of the court-watching activity took place in the juvenile session of the family courts in five cities. This was regarded as almost a revolutionary step, given the legal requirements for protection of the privacy of juveniles during hearings in courts for children. At a time when much criticism is being directed against the juvenile court process and with the movement in many places to transfer more-serious charges against minors to the adult criminal court, there would appear to be a greater need than ever to permit trained and objective observers to monitor court proceedings involving children.

Other court-watching projects have been conducted in Arizona, California, Ohio, Pennsylvania, and the State of Washington. In California, an organization calling itself Citizens for Law and Order published a monthly newsletter containing a list of sentences imposed for a broad classification of offenses. A Chester, Pennsylvania, project centered its attention on disparities in sentencing and revealed that black and Puerto Rican defendants were receiving harsher treatment than whites; that the majority of them were unrepresented by counsel and were unaware of their legal rights; and that these minority-group members were frequently the recipients of demeaning attitudes by court personnel. A Seattle program took more drastic action. It rated observed judges as unacceptable, acceptable, or recommended. These ratings were intended to influence voters in the 1976 elections. The distribution to voters of leaflets containing these ratings resulted in the defeat at the polls of the judges rated unacceptable.

The American Friends Service Committee, the most active organization in court-monitoring projects in New England, regards the victories won to date as relatively ineffective, however. The meting out of justice according to the financial and social status of the defendant is reported as persisting largely unaffected by the scrutiny of court monitors, and traditional criminal-court procedures continue to be inadequate to resolve any large number of community conflicts. The AFSC now recommends that effort be expended toward the creation of alternative, noncourt, community-justice programs for the resolution of local disputes.[13]

"Scrubbing" the Bench

In some instances court watching has gone far beyond the recommendation of changes in procedures or other details of court operations.[14] One of the most dramatic of these took place in 1973 in Dorchester, Massachusetts (part of the city of Boston), in what has been described as a pioneering example of community action. Here a group of concerned citizens who had been outraged by the injustices being committed by the judge of their local court took action that ended with the removal of the judge from the bench and his ultimate disbarment.

The effort was initiated by an organization of local residents who called themselves People First. Its members were largely young adults with a critical or radical orientation who were representative of other activists during these same years. The People First published a newspaper and operated a storefront from which they ran a neighborhood food cooperative, a post of the Vietnam Veterans against the War, and a successful campaign to remove the presiding judge of the Dorchester court from the bench. This campaign was the result of recurring complaints by the community against the presiding judge's conduct: overt bias against minority and welfare defendants; his failure to inform defendants of their rights with regard to bail and the appointment of defense counsel; and the assignment to indigent defendants of lawyers who were former associates, relatives of court personnel, and others doing private work for him. The judge was observed reading his mail during court sessions, told lawyers to "shut up," and frequently imposed bail as high as $50,000 on offenders who were members of minority groups.

Members of People First volunteered their time to monitor Judge Jerome Troy's court and took notes on the court transactions. They were assisted by volunteer law students and practicing lawyers. Affidavits signed by these observers testified that the judge frequently offered young defendants charged with minor offenses the opportunity of enlisting in the armed forces in exchange for his dropping the charges against them. Evidence was also provided that the judge repeatedly used coercive methods and threatened welfare recipients who appeared before him (on unrelated matters) in an attempt to force them to become complainants in criminal actions against their husbands for nonsupport or to coerce them to stop receiving welfare assistance.

Eight years after his appointment to the bench, in the last hours of the administration of the then governor of Massachusetts (all Massachusetts judges are appointed by the governor, with the consent of the Executive Council, rather than elected), the citizen group had gathered ten thousand signatures from Dorchester residents on a petition calling for the judge's removal. A large public rally called by the group was held in a neighborhood park. Support was freely forthcoming from a number of persons who had contact with the judge in his court, which heard an average of fifteen thousand cases annually. In the following year the group addressed a formal petition to the chief justice of the state district court system (local courts of first instance) to suspend the judge and simultaneously sought the offices of the Boston Bar Association in having him disbarred. Some six months later and after extensive hearings, a three-judge panel, including the chief justice of the district courts, issued a report strongly critical of Judge Troy's conduct, his exercise of discretion, and his administrative practices in a number of cases that were detailed by the panel.

Meanwhile evidence had been accumulating with regard to irregular conduct in the judge's personal life. A few years earlier, he had purchased waterfront property, which he was intending to convert into a marina. To this purpose he had illegally filled in wetlands adjoining a public beach in such a way that sewage from the area had polluted the swimming waters, partially because of his failure to construct a culvert that would have carried the sewage away. All of these actions were in violation of state warnings and sanitary regulations. After four years, a cease-and-desist order was issued by the superior court. The judge was charged with taking time off from his judicial duties, along with other court personnel, in order to supervise his marina operation and with having regularly used the publicly paid services of his court officers to operate a bulldozer on the site of the project.

Although these revelations did not directly involve his conduct as a presiding judge, they added to the controversial campaign for his removal from office. One year after it had been petitioned by the People First, the Boston Bar Association accused Judge Troy of "gross judicial misbehavior and a pattern of conduct prejudicial to the administration of justice" in his handling of criminal cases. A short time later, the supreme court ruled that Judge Troy was guilty of improper conduct. Six serious charges against him had been proved: lying under oath on at least two occasions; neglect of judicial duties; using the services of lawyers without paying them; using the services of a court attendant on his marina project; illegally filling the marina site; and trying to pressure a lawyer into contributing to the campaign of a gubernatorial candidate. The court disbarred him as a lawyer and enjoined him from further sitting on the bench. After he refused to resign his position and salary, a petition for the judge's removal was filed in the state legislature, which voted against him—first in the senate and then in the house—by overwhelming majorities. The final step was a hearing before the Executive Council (the same body that approved appointments to the bench), which voted seven to one for his dismissal. One of the attorneys who represented the People First in their initial round of actions said of Judge Troy's removal from office that it "was the first time a judge has been brought to task for his treatment of poor people."

The implications for the constructive community program that ultimately emerged, rather than the irregularities in the conduct of the occupant of the bench, is the prime lesson to be drawn from this dramatic affair. The result was a clear victory for the community, a result that could not have been foreseen by those who had initiated the drive.

With the momentum generated by the grass-roots campaign and the subsequent elevation of a member of the Dorchester court to the presiding judgeship, the time was now ripe for positive action that would continue to involve community members in the affairs of the criminal court. Under the expert leadership of the Justice Resource Institute, a Boston-based nonprofit agency interested in designing and providing community programs within the criminal-justice system (modeled after the Vera Institute of Justice of New York City), a proposal was developed with the advice and support of the Advisory Committee to the Dorchester Court, the probation department, the office of the county district attorney, and the two police districts that served the area.

In March 1974 an invitation was sent to every group in the community to attend a presentation of a proposal concerning the establishment of a neighborhood justice program. Included were civic and neighborhood associations whose members had formed vigilante patrols in reaction to the area's rising problem of crime and vandalism, black community organizations, and the federation of neighborhood houses, which included organizations serving youth. The two justices of the court, together with the director of the Justice Resource Institute, presented the proposal for the creation of the Urban Court and its basic components before a large audience. Their enthusiastic response to the proposal resulted in concrete action: the formation of three committees, each to assume responsibility for one of the program components of mediation, service to victims, and advisory sentencing procedures.

Only one year after the removal of the presiding judge, a proposal for funds was made to establish as part of the court, but physically separated from it, the Urban Court to promote notions of humane justice. In the words of the proposal, "The court system must become more comprehensible to all participants by involving the community, it must recognize that beyond the role of legal arbiter, the court must act as healer in the community and that there are often more effective ways to solve problems than those built into court procedure."[15]

The concerned people in the community who had originally come together to monitor the court and to expose the injustices of its operation were also aware of the high proportion of offenders who are unemployed at the time of the commission of the offense that brings them to court attention. The original Urban Court proposal called for provision of gainful employment as a prime requisite in assisting defendants to lead law-abiding lives. For these reasons the court included a fourth component that serves the other three. All three components refer clients in need of employment to the job-development team, which also accepts carefully screened referrals from the district court probation department.

The job development staff members are trained to deal with persons who have drug, alcohol, mental, or physical problems, and they are familiar with the agencies and programs available in the community for treating these people. Before being referred to a possible employment opportunity, the client meets with a trained job-placement interviewer, fills out a questionnaire, and is asked to participate in a job-preparedness seminar, which helps him to perceive his assets and weaknesses and to see his potential employment opportunities in a realistic light, and (in at least one simulated employment interview) to prepare him to meet successfully with prospective employers.

The team monitors clients after they have been placed on a job to help them to gauge their progress concerning work habits, skills, and general reliability. This follow-up service provides a support system that is especially helpful to persons who are working at their first responsible job or who may have a history of casual and irregular employment. In addition, the team seeks work for its clients among local employment resources whenever possible, on the principle that a community that is sufficiently concerned to help its erring members lead crime-free lives has a responsibility to help such persons find and keep gainful and satisfactory employment. At the same time that the services to be rendered by the urban court were expected to ease the burden on the district court, it was also intended to "re-establish the moral force of the law in the context of a busy, inner-city court where the sheer volume of activity has often caused 'state interests' to appear more prominent than those of the victim, the defendant and the community."[16]

The basic aim of the proposal was to involve the community in the actual operation of the court by dealing with selected cases that were to be referred by the court to the four community components. Since its inception, the Urban Court has been widely hailed as a national model at the forefront of the court alternative movement. At the peak of its operation, the program was unique in combining these four diverse yet interconnected components. Its outstanding performance has been acknowledged by the Department of Justice, which framed its model three-city Neighborhood Justice Centers on many of the distinctive features of the Urban Court.

Court Alternative Sentencing Program

The court-monitoring process that spread across the country in the early 1970s had a recent sequel in the district court of Waltham, Massachusetts, which serves a population of approximately 100,000 people in suburban Boston.[17] Under the auspices of the Massachusets Law Reform Institute, a group of Brandeis University students, members of a volunteer group who had run social-service programs in the city for the preceding eleven years, undertook to monitor the court. They first enrolled in an intensive training program designed to acquaint them with the role of the judge, prosecutor, and defense counsel, as well as with the rights due to defendants charged with a criminal offense and the degree to which court procedures and court personnel were expected to respect those rights.

The student monitors attended court sessions for thirty-eight days and produced a report on their observations, which included recommendations regarding reduction of noise in the courtroom; the desirability of reducing lengthy court recesses; the needs for a court interpreter for Spanish-speaking defendants and for clear instructions to defendants regarding their right to counsel; and the postponement of the reading of the probation report and criminal record of a defendant until after a finding of guilt had been made by the court. From their court experience, the students had realized the need for a program of restitution and provision of a job-placement service for young offenders. In the summer following their monitoring experience, they engaged in research into alternative sentencing programs.

In spring 1977, a restitution program was established in the Waltham court as a result of this student initiative; it was guided by the Political Science Department of Brandeis University with the full support and cooperation of the judge of the Waltham court and the local chamber of commerce. Office space was provided by the court, and a private foundation gave the project its initial finding to begin operations. A year later, the project was fully established, having received a grant that assured its continued operation for some time into the future.

The details of the Waltham operation are not as important as the history of the project itself, representing, as it does, another example of what a community can do within its own boundaries when it voices its critical concern for the way in which the criminal court is operating and thereafter develops an organized plan to correct some of the court's inadequacies.

4 Pretrial Diversion—An Emerging Approach

Diversion, a recent and promising development in criminal-justice reform, is winning increasing acceptance in its application to the areas of police, courts, and correctional institutions. We shall consider here only its application at the pretrial stage of the criminal process.[1]

The pioneering efforts of the Vera Institute of Justice in establishing the Manhattan Court Employment Project in New York City in 1967 and the National Committee for Children with its Youth Project Crossroads in Washington, D.C. in the same year, created prototypes for pretrial diversion projects, which were later funded by the Department of Labor in eight large American cities.[2] Comparable progressive programs are currently found in scores of other cities throughout the country.[3] In any one year, more than 15,000 defendants participate in them.[4]

A basic definition of diversion is "the practice by criminal justice officials—police, prosecutors, and judges—of channeling out of the criminal process offenders who, as a consequence of their probable and assumed guilt, would normally be handled by the criminal process."[5] Within such a definition, pretrial diversion may be seen as a tempering process, an intervention that tends to deformalize rather than increase the importance or severity of the acts and circumstances that brought the offender to book. In this context, diversion may be regarded as a process of decriminalization that aims to reduce recidivism and the likelihood of extended criminal careers.

Some diversion projects focus on young offenders, usually between the ages of 17 and 26, since persons in this age group are the most likely to be successfully influenced. Defendants accepted into pretrial diversion programs include those charged with a wide gamut of offenses; petty larceny, auto theft, drunken driving, receiving stolen property, use of a false identification, forgery, solicitation or prostitution, attempted burglary, simple assault, unlawful entry, destruction of property. Defendants charged with violent crimes, that is, rape, homicide, or armed robbery, as well as persons on probation or dependent on drugs, are generally excluded because rehabilitation for such offenders would rarely be effective within the limited time span of the initial diversionary period. In the future, comparable programs may be instituted to focus attention on the truly serious offenders, but such a step will have to await further experience with current programs. The ultimate fate of participants at the hands of the court is directly related to their evident success in meeting the obligations they have agreed to assume. After sufficient facts to warrant the intervention of the court have been adduced, and enrollment in the diversion plan has taken place, the court is petitioned to extend the hearing of the case for approximately 90 days. Reevaluation then takes place to decide which of three alternatives shall be selected.

If the offender has successfully completed his part of the agreement, the charges originally brought may be dropped and the case closed. If it is believed that the time allotted has not been long enough, the court may be petitioned to grant a 30-to 90-day extension to allow the defendant to continue in the program. Finally, if it is found that the offender has not cooperated with or benefitted from the project, he can be brought to trial for his original offense as if he had not been diverted, with no prejudice to his case by reason of failure to abide by the conditions of the program.

As an alternative to a prison sentence or to a term of probation, diversion represents a choice to selected offenders who express a willingness to cooperate and thus to be dealt with noncriminally. Pretrial diversion gives such defendants the opportunity to be helped through rehabilitative services that confront and help resolve their basic difficulties. It may be viewed as a bold deviation from the traditional criminal process. It uses the court as the source of its referrals and also as the authority for imposing sanctions or penalties for noncompliance by the defendant with the conditions that he has agreed to accept.

One of the basic aims of diversion is to instill a sense of responsibility in the program participants. It tries to achieve this goal through intensive counseling, job placement, vocational and educational services, referrals to appropriate community agencies, and creative, individualized conditions of sentencing. These may require monetary restitution to victims and community or public service, known as "in-kind" restitution. Participants usually stay in the program for four months. The first weeks are devoted to an initial assessment. The participant and an assigned advocate draw up and agree to a service plan, which is then committed to writing and submitted for the approval of the judge. This plan outlines the responsibilities of both the client and the program personnel. The exact terms of the service plan, or contract, vary with the needs and conditions of each individual enrolled in the program. The areas covered in the case of juveniles, for example, may include educational testing and assistance such as tutoring or work with the youth's school, and counseling, which may be with the individual, the family, or a group.

Diversion encompasses a recognition of the seriousness of official concern for certain offenses in a process that avoids the traditional adversary process and at the same time aims to resolve conflict through conciliation and problem settlement. If solutions are available in the community to resolve certain disputes between neighbors, among family members, between landlord and tenant, school and pupil, such incidents are drained of their criminal content and recognized for what they are: disagreements or misunderstandings between individuals that arise from the fact of their living and interacting closely with one another. Socially concerned judges have always sought alternatives to the limited range of sentencing measures available to them for disposition. Diversion provides such judges with the broadest possible spectrum of sentencing measures at the pretrial stage of the proceedings.

It is important to understand the differences between plea-bargaining and entry into the pretrial diversion by a defendant after admission of sufficient facts. In the former instance a defendant faced with the apparent inevitability of conviction and a sentence of imprisonment bargains his guilty plea in return for a reduction in the length of sentence. In diversion the threat of imprisonment is non-existent—unless and until the diverted offender fails to fulfill the terms of the agreement he has made with the court, which by accepting his admission of sufficient facts renders the question of his guilt no longer moot.

Pretrial intervention benefits the defendant, the prosecution, the court, and the community. Its programs are staffed by professionals, nonprofessionals, and community volunteers, some of them with backgrounds similar to those of the defendants. These people in particular provide offenders with role models with whom they may have much in common, yet who have managed to work out a lifestyle outside of the criminal context. Staff members are contemporaries concerned with helping diverted offenders to implement their programs successfully. Such help may be extended by staff at the screening stage, in counseling, and personal assistance. Available statistics indicate that a lower percentage of young first offenders charged with minor crimes and theft who are diverted at the pretrial stage go on to repeated criminal activity.[6]

Prompt intervention at the pretrial stage enables the diversion staff to influence the offender at a time when he is psychologically best prepared to accept the idea of mending his ways. Feelings of guilt and contrition as well as a willingness to cooperate in plans for restitution or reparation to the victim and to perform community service are more likely to be strongest immediately after arrest. Securing the offender's cooperation in a supervised program tailored to his needs when he is of this mind can be expected to be more effective than trying to get his cooperation after months of jail detention and court appearances have drained away any constructive impulses he may have had when arrested.

At least part of the court diversion process operates on the assumption that although the offender brought before the court may in fact not be guilty of the offense for which he is charged, there is a strong likelihood that in his past he may well have committed an offense for which he was never apprehended, charged, or punished. The largely unspoken reality is that a large proportion of the population at one time or another has committed an offense for which they could have been apprehended had a police officer been present. When a person is summoned into court to answer to charges brought against him, if his guilt in the instant case cannot be conclusively proved, he may know—and he may suspect that the prosecution knows, too—that his past activities include offenses for which he was never brought to account. This is not put forward in any cynical sense, but as a highly likely consideration in the minds of many persons involved in criminal justice.

In a related vein, instances may occur in which the offender may be more harmed than benefitted by a failure to confront him with the fact of his guilt. Failure to punish may, in fact, make it more rather than less difficult for him to acknowledge his culpability and help him to resolve the feelings associated with it.

Any suggested procedures for setting aside or overriding civil-liberties safeguards can never be regarded as simple tinkering. Properly conceived and administered, the diversionary approach and procedures must respect, not undermine, these principles.

Most important of these is the basic presumption upon which our system of justice is founded: an individual is innocent until proven guilty. Before alleged offenders may be subjected to the diversionary process, the question of their guilt must be confronted. There are bound to be instances where a defendant may be truly innocent of the charges against him, but the difficulty of procuring competent counsel or the circumstantiality of the events surrounding the alleged offense may be such as to make proof of innocence difficult to establish. In such instances injustice may be done by diverting a blameless offender from a regular court trial.

To the extent that it carries no immediate penal sanction, diversion is a mitigating process, not a punitive one. It makes provisions for alleviating the plight of the victim. It also leaves the defendant free of any criminal record, if he succeeds in the program agreed upon. At the same time, the services that are made available—in counselling, educational or vocational training, medical or other treatment, help in finding a job—might have been difficult for him to secure had not charges been made that brought him into court, and thence into the diversion process.

Whether to emphasize the offender or the offense is one of the never-ending controversies of modern criminal jurisprudence. Indeed, it provides the basis for today's debate over the desirability of punishing specific offenses by specific sentences, whether fixed, mandatory, or presumptive. Did diversion come into existence full-blown or can precedents be found for it? How much of the weight of the criminal-justice system falls on the offending act and how much on the offender? And if persons can be diverted from official court handling, what happens to the alleged criminal charge that set the procedural train into motion?

A brief look to the past will help to place these issues in perspective. Under Roman law, persons were excused from full responsibility for their acts if they were under the age of seven or were mentally inadequate or deranged. These remain the prime exceptions to full criminal responsibility and may be said to have opened the way to later modification of responsibility by reason of other circumstances in the life and condition of persons charged with crime.

During the Middle Ages the moral or spiritual state of the offender largely determined both his fate and the process by which he arrived at whatever that fate dealt out to him. Guilt or innocence was largely a matter of the condition of the offender's soul, whether he had entrusted it to God and was mindful of His laws or whether he was a nonbeliever. An offender suspected of heeding the underworld could be delivered up to be exorcised, or made to do penance or otherwise impelled to cast his lot again with God, even if he had to be tortured to make him confess, or to burn at the stake to ensure his salvation.

We have come a long way with the secularization of dealing with criminal behavior and with the contributions of the Enlightenment to the reduction in the number of offenses punishable by the death penalty and the ultimate abolition of transportation of convicts overseas as a not uncommon penalty.

Probation as a form of sentence began in Boston in 1841 and has since spread throughout the United States and to many countries abroad. Its purpose is to give the convicted offender a supervised opportunity to be diverted from a term of imprisonment to a program designed to help him adjust in the community at an acceptable level. It is worthy of note that the same probation staff who administer the postconviction supervision of an offender also play an important role in the pretrial diversionary process.

The juvenile court has had a parallel expansion around the world from Illinois where it started in 1899 and may be called the first truly diversionary procedure to be instituted within the court system. Now for the first time, children were to be dealt with on the basis of their "need and condition" and not on the gravity, or even the facts, of their alleged illegal behavior. Thus, those acts that would have been crimes if committed by adults, as well as such conditions as waywardness, stubbornness, truancy, even neglect and dependence, were to constitute grounds for bringing a child within the protective care of the children's court, there to be granted "aid, encouragement, and guidance."

Nevertheless, as recently as 1975, a fifteen-year-old boy received a sentence of six years confinement for an offense for which an adult could have received no more than thirty days.[7] Currently, several state legislatures are acting to limit the jurisdiction of the children's court to acts truly "criminal" in nature, that is, to those for which an adult could be charged with crime.

A parallel movement attempts to decriminalize or divert from the criminal-justice process, certain adult offenses such as drug involvement (notably marijuana) prostitution, gambling, sexual acts between consenting adults, vagrancy, and public drunkennness. It is a commentary on our times that many of these behaviors which came onto the criminal calendar by religious proscription are now being decriminalized or no longer prosecuted or punished.

Bail reform is a related diversionary measure. Because fully half of all persons held for trial are ultimately released for one reason or another back into the community, an easing of bail requirements has helped to reduce jail populations, and congestion in the courts as well.

The poor and those charged with victimless crimes, misdemeanors, or minor felonies are well aware that certain other groups, the highly placed, students, children of the well-to-do, are in a sense self-diverted. The weekend jail sentence, the fine in the thousands for the swindler in the millions, the middle-class boy or girl shoplifter driven home to parents by the police, may be taken for granted by many but are resented by those whose low social status does not make them beneficiaries of such preferential treatment.

A sizable proportion of all disputes—and this includes quarrels as well as homicides—take place between and among people who are known to one another, even close neighbors. Not a few of these criminal acts, especially by the young, may be committed as much out of frustration, boredom, or mischief as out of malice. Many of those hailed into court by reason of a criminal complaint themselves have valid grounds for protesting the level on which their lives are led. Diversion aims to extend to defendants such as these the skills of social inquiry, of knowledge of behavior, as well as of resources. Diversion attempts to assist them to steer their lives into individually and socially constructive channels, while sparing them from imprisonment. Throughout any review of our historic trial process, through all of the schemes for its amelioration, runs a profound and eternal pair of opposing concerns: for the protection of the rights of the individual counterpoised to the concern of citizens that they be protected in their persons and property. This conflict is integral in any consideration of basic changes in criminal court procedure and is even more cogent when diversion is projected.

Furthermore, diversion has not yet fully met the criticism that it may run counter to the inherent right of the public to know. A basic tenet of our criminal court is that except under extraordinary circumstances, criminal trials shall be open to the public. Any procedure that seems to smack of the star chamber must be avoided. The citizenry has the right to know who among them has been charged with a violation of the law, to observe the procedure by which guilt or innocence is determined, and to hear the sentence that is imposed. Diverting offenders from formal trial necessarily withdraws their cases from public view and public knowledge. The full implications of this absence of open disclosure have not yet been fully explored.

Diversion at the same time conveys a note of criticism of the traditional court procedures it would supplement or supplant. Of what other major institution in our society can it be said that among its most knowledgeable and concerned commentators and practitioners, impatience with its workings has reached the point where they are devising new procedures to reduce the entrance of persons *into* it?

Increasing reliance upon the courts for the resolution of many of the problems that arise in our complex society requires a note of caution at this point. Any measure put forward as an improvement on present dealing must not result in drawing in a number of persons who might otherwise never appear in court.

Enlightened present day attitudes recognize that violations of the law are not restricted to any one socioeconomic class and that the total number of offenses known to have occurred are far in excess of those known to the police. Unless we deal effectively with law breakers, especially those who do not resort to force or violence, with greater understanding and skill we may soon be overwhelmed by the tide of disruption of our common life, security, and well-being. Our changed attitudes toward and awareness of the social and individual origins of behavior must now be reflected in basic alterations in our procedures. By diverting from formal court action youthful, occasional, or first offenders, we shall free the courts to devote their personnel and procedures to the more swift hearing of the cases of those offenders whose small number are disproportionate to the gravity and repetitiveness of the crimes that they commit.

Roscoe Pound repeatedly asserted that the law fails to take into account the contributions to an understanding of human behavior made by the behavioral sciences. This failure is somewhat compensated for through the diversion process. By shifting the emphasis from the act to the actor in appropriate instances, society removes selected defendants from the realm of retribution. This makes possible a level of understanding that tends toward effective resolution of human conflict not in defiance of but rather consonant with the intent of the penal law to hold individuals responsible for their behavior and to mete out the kind of dispositions that will restore to balance the scales of injustice, pay heed to the just claims of the victim, and thus provide a greater measure of protection to our communities.

**Part II
Remembering the Victim**

Restitution

From Private Satisfaction to Public Prosecution and Communal Justice

Resolution of disputes by compromise, arbitration, mediation, and restitution rather than by confrontation, adversary proceedings, or direct conflict is one of the most ancient approaches to the settling of interpersonal strife and the dispensing of justice. Restitution is perhaps the best example of this, if only by reason of its very long history, dating back to the code of Hammurabi, Mosaic law, and the Twelve Tablets of Rome.[1] Scattered references to restitution are found among other ancient writings, including the Greeks of Homer's day and the Hindus of the Sutra period. Restitution continues to be found among many contemporary peoples, especially in so-called simple societies. In such groups it is understandable that compensation or reparation would be resorted to in favor of victims and members of their families because of the severity of the struggle for survival engaged in by group members. The value of restitution is obviously more vital in such societies than in other more-affluent places or ages.

That this is still true today is exemplified in the fact that whenever true community solidarity exists, restitution appears to occupy a natural place.[2] In the mass society of the United States, religious and sectarian groups such as the Mennonites and the Amish, American Indian tribes, and ethnic communities in scattered areas of large cities provide contemporary working examples. The appeal of restitution is clearly strong and seems to persist over time. Although restitution has declined from its former level of prominence, the concept is being rescued from obscurity and again being promoted as a community alternative to formal court action.

Contemporary historians of crime and punishment are in general agreement that the earliest form of conflict resolution and administration of justice was private revenge.[3] Victims of crime were expected to seek direct satisfaction from those who had wronged them. Among societies organized by tribes or clans, the right to wreak vengeance was generally shared by the kinship group; members were responsible for avenging harm done to one of their number and, reciprocally, were often collectively liable for wrongs committed by their kin. Thus the earliest type of law was not criminal law at all but simply revenge for personal injury. The community, with its respective subgroups, was directly involved in dispute resolution under this procedure. The manner of group involvement was a problem, however. For example, the so-called blood-feud system worked to perpetuate and even to escalate interpersonal conflicts rather than to end them or to effect a reconciliation among the parties. In this sense, the famous Hatfield-McCoy feuds of Kentucky kept alive the enmity between the families involved until very recently.

During the Middle Ages in Europe as interaction among large groups increased, the settling of disputes by blood feud gradually developed into a system of reparation payments in money, in kind, or in other equivalents. This transition is well illustrated by the following:

> In the tenth century, a group of Norwegian lords and their dependents sailed to Iceland, where they established a system of communal justice whose method of claims settlement remained the blood feud as it had been in Norway, but with one improvement. A payment of value could be offered and accepted without shame for an injury done to the complainant and his family. Once a payment had been made the blood feud came to an end and the victim had no further right to exact vengeance upon the offender until he committed a fresh wrong against him.[4]

This system of communal justice spread south across most of Europe where it came to be known as "composition," in the sense of "rebuilding" or "making whole." Reparation payments were defined by the councils of tribal elders who based their decisions on the age, sex, and social status of the victim, as well as on the seriousness of the grievance done. Some tribes constructed quite elaborate scales of standardized payments where compensation was determined, for example, by the number of wounds inflicted on a victim and even the size of such wounds.[5] The lives of all persons, moreover, were assigned a value, called the *wergild*, which had to be paid as compensation in the event that death resulted from the commission of a crime against a member of the tribe. The value of the wergild depended on rank, from serf to king. Originally the family of the slain victim could refuse or accept the wergild; later acceptance was made compulsory. Ultimately it was left to public justice to impose the penalty, which made its way to the king's coffers or, as in today's court practice, to the state, in the form of fine and/or court costs.

Such arrangements may seem crude, but they constituted a rule-of-thumb justice that worked to achieve restitution and compensation and to discourage personal or private revenge, in the process tending to dampen or defuse the emotions to which it gave rise. During the Middle Ages, restitution also included provision for the support of the victim's family, an expression of a concern for the long-range effects of criminal acts on the victim, which was not to reappear until very recent times.

As centralized monarchies began to develop out of feudalism, the system of justice in Europe again changed to reflect the new order. The *bloodwirt* made its appearance as a fine for the shedding of blood, but payable now to the king, lord, or other superior rather than to the kin of the person who had been harmed. It was distinct from the wergild in that it constituted a penalty for murder. The crown had now become officially involved in settling interpersonal disputes and repairing injuries, acting in the capacity of mediator, arbitrator, and, increasingly, judge and executor of sentences—whether money payments, the imposition of pain, or death. Now the monarch rather than the tribal leaders was party to interpersonal disputes among his subjects because such conflicts violated "the king's peace." An offense came to be seen as an affront to the entire realm, and the king as the supreme ruler moved against the offender in the name of all of his subjects.

Thus began in the thirteenth century the practice of describing cases as the crown versus the alleged offender. As a consequence, a revised system of payments for injury was instituted, specifying that all reparations were to be divided between the monarch and the victims of crime. One portion (which the Anglo-Saxons termed the *bot*) went to the victims as compensation for their losses, while the rest (the *wite*) went to the crown as combination settlement fee, court costs, and penalty for the breach of the peace. With this practice, the principle now prevailed that victims were indebted to the state for services rendered in their behalf.

This system of split reparations endured for some centuries. As state power continued to be centralized, however, the victim's share in the settlement steadily declined. Exactly why or how this transition took place remains somewhat unclear to scholars who have investigated it, although Schafer claims that on the Continent, the right of the injured party to receive restitution diminished around 850 A.D., being gradually replaced by the State's imposition of a fine. The majority view seems to hold that "it was chiefly owing to the violent greed of feudal barons and medieval ecclesiastical powers that the rights of the injured party were gradually infringed upon, and finally, to a large extent, appropriated by these authorities."[6] Whatever the reason, it ultimately became a matter of judicial discretion in criminal proceedings whether the victim would receive any reparation. That the practice of victim reparations survived at all may well have been because certain judges proved more receptive to traditional claims for restitution and because a small percentage of victims stood on their ancient right to such compensation.

The inclusion of some reparations to victims in criminal proceedings at the discretion of judges crystallized in Europe around the beginning of the seventeenth century. In Germany it became known as the "adhesive procedure" (*Adhäsionsprozess*) because of an old phrasing of consent in which victims agreed to allow such procedures to attach or "adhere" to the criminal trial. While still affording victims some relief, it provided a dramatic illustration of the ever-increasing predominance of the state. The punishment of offenders and the payment of reparations to the state had gradually come to displace concern for victims and their plight.

There finally arrived a point when victims were prohibited by law from settling matters privately; they were now obligated to bring offenders before the authorities and to be subject to penalties for striking private bargains with offenders in return for nonprosecution.[7] Such private settlements became known as the crime of *theftbote* in England and were prosecuted under other designations elsewhere on the Continent.

Criminal justice had now become the monopoly of the central state power. It had started with private and collective vengeance, went through the process of negotiation and composition and the adoption of codes setting forth rates of restitution to the feudal stage, when local rulers served both as mediators and collectors of part of the restitution awards; and finally arrived at complete state takeover of both the process of administration of justice and the pocketing of any money penalties. In the process provision for recompensing the victim disappeared, or was abolished.

Those victims who sought compensation for their losses now had to look to emerging civil procedures, generally known as torts in Anglo-American jurisprudence, which at least theoretically accorded victims the right to recover losses through civil rather than criminal suits. In practice, however, most victims found this avenue difficult and costly, marked by a tedious adversary process and, frequently, long delays. Also the victim was now expected to pay for professional legal assistance. And even when a favorable judgment was given, there still remained the problem of collecting any settlement. The offender might well have been indigent at the time of the crime and would certainly remain so during imprisonment, making it impossible for the victim to achieve any gain at all, even after a lengthy and costly suit. With the increasing specialization of the courts and the corresponding growth and specialization of the legal profession, victims were bewildered by, or even discouraged from, their search for reparations that might fairly compensate them for their losses. Fortunate, and rare indeed, would be the victim who succeeded in being fully compensated for the losses suffered as the result of the crime against him.

Late-nineteenth-century awareness of the cumbersomeness and want of justice in this process led to a return to restitution as a means of settling disputes and of making reparation for criminal damages. In a series of conferences between 1878 and 1900, prominent American and European authorities debated the question at length. Sir George Arney, chief justice of New Zealand, and William Tallack, a penologist, provided an early initiative at the International Prison Congress at Stockholm in 1878 by proposing a more general return to the ancient practice of restitution.[8] In 1885, at the International Prison Congress in Rome, Raffaele Garofalo, a noted

Italian criminologist, again raised the issue. The delegates at the International Penal Association Congress in 1890 adopted a resolution holding that modern law does not sufficiently consider the reparation due to injured parties; in the case of petty offenses, time should be given for indemnification; and prisoners' earnings in prison might be utilized for this purpose.

At Paris five years later, the question of restitution was again placed on the conference agenda: "Is the victim of a delict sufficiently armed by modern law to enable him to obtain indemnity from the man who injured him?" Six papers were presented, urging various forms of compensation and restitution by offenders, but no final conclusion was reached, except to refer the matter once more to the next conference. In 1900 at Brussels, delegates to the Sixth International Penitentiary Congress discussed restitution at great length, the noted Belgian penologist Prins pressing for a decisive statement on the matter. But the other participants could agree only to reaffirm the motion of an earlier Congress regarding reform of the civil procedures in order for victims to receive some form of reparation. With this stalemate, the matter of restitution seems to have disappeared from these international forums for many years.

A new initiative in behalf of restitution was provided by the criminologist Hans von Hentig with the publication in 1941 of an influential article on the interaction of offenders and victims. This was followed in 1948 by his well-known *The Criminal and His Victim*, which called for renewed attention to victims of crime, with specific advocacy of restitution. A year earlier, Benjamin Mendelsohn had utilized much the same approach in a paper read before the Rumanian Society of Psychiatry, "New Bio-psycho-social Horizons: Victimology." This paper qualified Mendelsohn as one of the founders of the emerging discipline of victimology, and he is generally acknowledged to have coined the term.

In the next several years as a result of such important writings, the topic began to attract a following. The psychologist Henry Ellenberger discussed psychological relationships between the criminal and victim. Margery Fry, a British magistrate and noted penal reformer, called for "justice for victims" and led the movement in England for a new awareness of the plight of victims and the need to provide more effective remedies for injuries than existed under tort law.[9] The public response was so strong and favorable that the British Home Office commissioned a study of the entire question. The result, in 1960, was a book by Stephen Schafer, *Compensation and Restitution to Victims of Crime*. With this publication, restitution had reemerged as a major issue in criminology, penology, and public policy in the criminal-justice field.

Since then the study of victimology has become an accepted professional specialization. Based on the assumption that crime cannot be adequately studied or correctly understood as long as the role and rights of the victim are ignored, the discipline raises questions about criminal-victim relations and about societal responses to them. Punishment as the final focus of criminal-court proceedings has been severely criticized; the role of the state has been brought into question; and a wide diversity of schemes for compensation and restitution to victims has been advanced.

These scholarly developments have led many jurisdictions to appropriate funds to provide compensation to victims of crime, especially those marked by violence. A number of state jurisdictions have followed this example and created compensation funds before federal legislation on the matter was proposed in 1979. Victimology as a discipline solidified its claim to recognition in 1973 with the holding of the First International Symposium on Victimology in Jerusalem. Five volumes of papers emerged from the conference, which provided further impetus to the movement.[10] Shortly thereafter, the first Institute for Victimology was set up in Tokyo, utilizing an interdisciplinary approach to the subject. Restitution became a specialized area of victimology when the First International Symposium on Restitution convened in Minneapolis in November 1975. With the second international victimology conference held in Boston in 1976, the third in Muenster, Germany, in September 1979, and the fourth planned for Japan in 1982 the role of the victim and the concomitant development of other than adversary procedures for the settlement of disputes has become an important specialized field of inquiry, no longer subordinate to the broader areas of criminology and penology. Restitution serves to join this concern for the victim with the twin concern for punishment of the offender, to the end that true justice is done to both. Recent years have seen the reemergence of this ancient and universal practice in legislation, policy, and program.

The first statewide laws mandating its use were enacted in Iowa in 1974 and Colorado in 1976. Iowa requires that restitution be a condition of the disposition order in probation and deferred sentences, after approval by the court. The Colorado legislation is more comprehensive: "that restitution be utilized wherever feasible to restore losses to the victims of crime and to aid the offender in reintegration as a productive member of society," in conjunction with a jail or prison sentence, fine, probation, or parole. National bodies, such as the Advisory Commission on Criminal Justice Standards and Goals, the second revision of the Model Sentencing Act by the Council of Judges of the National Council on Crime and Delinquency, the American Bar Association, the American Law Institute, and the 1972 Annual Chief Justice Earl Warren Conference on Advocacy in the United States have all recognized the principle of restitution as a desirable and applicable sanction in lieu of, or in conjunction with, other forms of disposition available to the sentencing judge. The Law Reform Commission of Canada has also advocated the diversion of offenders from traditional criminal disposition by means of restitution programs.

By 1975, no fewer than nineteen restitution programs were identified as operating in the United States and Canada, and their number has steadily increased since. These programs were found in thirteen of the states and two Canadian provinces and served both juvenile and adult offenders. In recognition of this growing movement, the Law Enforcement Assistance Administration in 1976 provided funds for pilot restitution programs in seven states, and the Office of Juvenile Justice and Delinquency Prevention of the Federal Government allocated $2 million in 1977 to initiate restitution programs for juveniles at the postadjudication level in ten jurisdictions. Its intent is to apply restitution after the juvenile has been found delinquent in an attempt to determine the pertinence and effectiveness of such proceedings in the cases of more serious offenders.

Car thefts by youths are among the most frequent offenses to come before the criminal courts, and the most troublesome to resolve to the satisfaction of the victim or the reclamation of the car thief. The following case from the files of a juvenile restitution program shows how such cases can be dealt with in constructive fashion through the use of restitution.

A boy of sixteen took and did twelve hundred dollars worth of damage to a car belonging to a lawyer who had left it to be fixed at a local body shop. The boy had been walking home from school when he saw the car in the garage, the keys dangling from the mirror; the doors were unlocked.

After the boy had been apprehended and the victim informed, a confrontation session was arranged by the court restitution program. The victim's initial reaction was one of extreme anger. "You stole my car, you stole my car," he kept repeating. When he learned that the body shop had been somewhat at fault for its carelessness, he relented slightly but continued his outrage against the boy. His severity somewhat mollified by the boy's ready admission of his guilt, the victim began to inquire about the boy himself. Discovering that the boy came from a broken home and had no father, the victim proffered the fact that he himself had no sons. In the course of their discussion, both man and boy discovered that they shared an interest in boating. The boy agreed to work off the loss that he had inflicted on the victim, and the court procured a job for him after school. The entire amount was repaid within the year after the occurrence of the incident. The boy went on to enroll in a maritime course, to which he never would have been admitted had he been found guilty. Instead his case was continued without a finding, to be finally discharged, and the record sealed. During the course of the year, the man frequently invited the boy to go sailing with him on his boat.

Today restitution is widely supported as an appropriate sanction for criminal offenses. It is often used as a condition of probation for first-time offenders and is also used in conjunction with parole. Community service is increasingly resorted to as a form of restitution. Because of the relatively small amount of damages sustained in the average property crime, full restitution is feasible and is widely employed.[11] Nearly all states have recently passed laws authorizing restitution as a penalty for a variety of offenses.

Some Theoretical Considerations

Self-Determinate Sentence

In 1965 Kathleen Smith advanced the far-reaching concept of the self-determinate sentence, presented under the ambitious title of "a cure for crime." The plan has been since revised and updated but its core—restitution in a correctional setting—has been retained.[12] The measure is designed to provide simultaneously for the needs of both victims and offenders, with indirect benefits for society as well. Victims would receive compensation for injuries from a national fund, while offenders would be allowed a greater degree of autonomy and be treated with greater dignity than has historically been their lot. Smith has expressed the fundamentals of her proposal in this way:

> The self-determinate sentence is so named because the length of sentence an offender serves under this system is to the greatest possible extent his own responsibility. It is determined firstly by the seriousness and type of crime he commits, and secondly by the effort he makes during his sentence to compensate for his crime.
>
> Under this system prisoners would be required to work a minimum forty-two hour week, at full union rates, until their crimes were paid for out of their earnings, and their victims compensated. Instead of assessing offenses in terms of time to be served in prison, the Courts would assess them in terms of money to be earned in prison. All offenses necessitating a prison sentence would be assessed by this means.[13]

The notion that prisoners should be paid full union rates addresses a long-standing problem in corrections, for prisoners historically have been paid so poorly that full restitution to victims has been impossible. For example, until very recently many federal prisoners have been paid only thirty-five cents an hour and some as little as fourteen cents, a small fraction of the minimum wage required of all firms in interstate commerce. Even more shocking, these underpaid federal prisoners were actually a favored group, since state prisons paid even lower rates.[14]

Smith's ideas have been demonstrated in practice at a recently established reformatory near San Jose, Costa Rica, where for a forty-hour work week prisoners receive the same minimum wage as is paid to workers on the outside. One-quarter of their earnings go to their victims, one-quarter to the state, one-quarter to their families, and one-quarter to their individual account, part of which may be spent in the institution and the balance turned over to them upon release. Reports from the program indicate that prisoners work a full eight-hour day and are as productive as outside workers in both quantity and quality of output.[15]

As Smith outlines it, the self-determinate sentence has several basic purposes. It is designed to provide greater justice for victims by focusing on the injuries they have suffered and by supplying them with timely relief. It should transform the prison experience of offenders in a positive direction at the same time that it lessens the stigma placed upon them. Hence it should work to reduce the total volume of crime.

A specific mechanism, a national compensation fund, suggested by Smith would accumulate discretionary fines from which some repayment could be made to victims in cases where their assailants were unable to provide restitution by reason of ill health, old age, or death. Revenues for the fund would derive from fines levied on offenders in proportion to their persistence, intent, menace, and nuisance value, as well as from fines imposed for such crimes without victims as breaches of the peace, drunkenness, gambling, and the like.

Although victims are cited as the prime beneficiaries of the plan, its impact is directed largely toward offenders. Smith is primarily concerned that incarcerated persons should find some meaning in their prison experience and that their dignity should be safeguarded. The initial task, then, is to overcome the prevalent neglect of the work-related needs of prisoners. As she argues:

> No one doubts the desirability and value of useful employment for non-prisoners. To prisoners, it is far more vital. . . . A prisoner has only those prospects and actions that prison allows him. Every important attachment, choice, possession of normal life is reduced for him to a minimum. . . . If he is not permitted to displace his energies and frustrations in the satisfaction of work, there is a low probability of his recollecting enough of the habit, interest, and confidence of normal life to fit into it again when the time comes.[16]

In order to facilitate such work-related satisfaction, Smith proposes the full union rates, plus piecework incentives, group bonuses to promote productivity, some personal property, an annual two-week vacation from confinement, and a final incentive of early release when three-quarters of the restitution has been paid. Under this last provision, the remaining restitution would be accomplished in the course of normal work in the community after release.

The most controversial portion of the plan undoubtedly is the contention that restitution by means of the self-determinate sentence will reduce the volume of crime. Smith believes this will happen in three ways. First, there would be an increasing awareness that crime is not a paying proposition; there would no longer be the luxury, for instance, of pulling off a large robbery and enjoying the proceeds after a short period of incarceration. Second, there would be a rehabilitative effect, especially on first offenders. For these persons, "The encouragement of their ability as wage-earners and their restoration to respectability by their own efforts would fit them both psychologically and practically to renounce crime."[17] Finally, restitution would break up the solidarity of offenders and would encourage them to reveal the identity of accomplices, since otherwise one person might have to repay the damages caused by a whole group.

The strong appeal of Smith's proposals rests largely upon her emphasis on practicality. In her view, the self-determinate sentence is workable because it directly satisfies the interests of all parties—victims, offenders, and the state. While the appeal to victims and to the authorities might be generally granted, the attractiveness for offenders is likely to remain a matter of doubt. For skeptics, Smith has these final comments:

> The self-determinate sentence makes work as attractive as possible to prisoners. The overriding factor that would persuade most prisoners to make an effort would be that on their work would depend their pay, and on their pay would depend their release date. Few would consider it worthwhile to sabotage a system that settles the length of their sentence in their own hands.[18]

Admittedly Smith's proposal is not put forward in the context of community justice. Despite this limitation, it is worthy of consideration for several reasons. First, it looks toward the needs of victims, who are characteristically neglected by the present criminal-justice system. Second, it supports the workability of restitution as a practical alternative to older penalties. Finally, it seeks not merely compensation for specific offenses but the reintegration of offenders into normal community life.

Creative Restitution

A sharp contrast to Smith is presented by Albert Eglash, who emphasizes the creative potential of restitution by reason of its power to leave the situation better than it was at the time of the offense.[19] Although it is not as detailed as other plans, this proposal has a fresh and provocative quality, which merits the attention of those interested in the development of restitution schemes.

Eglash begins by suggesting that restitution be placed in a more general context, that it be related to larger models of justice as a social process. He identifies three basic designs of the justice process. Retributive justice responds to offenses with various types of punishment; distributive justice provides the remedy of treatment; and restorative justice reacts with restitution to victims. Thus, restitution is to be distinguished clearly from both punishment and treatment, as illustrated by the following specific contrasts:

(1) Punishment and treatment focus on the behavior of offenders, while restitution looks to the consequences of their behavior.
(2) Punishment and treatment overlook the victims.
(3) Punishment and treatment place offenders in a passive role, while restitution gives them an active part to play.
(4) Punishment and treatment remove offenders from the situation of the offense; restitution keeps them in the situation, while reversing their behavior.
(5) Punishment and treatment expect misbehavior to stop; restitution does not expect that future errors will disappear, but begins a learning process.
(6) Punishment and treatment choose between the principles of necessary determination and free will. Restitution is able to admit both.[20]

Having set out the general features of restitution, Eglash distinguishes four important subtypes. There are two criteria employed in this classification:.whether restitution itself is mandated or free and whether the specific form of restitution is mandated or free. The four resulting variants are shown in figure 5-1.

	Form Determined	Form Freely Decided
Restitution Freely Decided	Ritual	Spontaneous
Restitution Determined	Mandatory	Creative (guided)

Based on Albert Eglash, "Beyond Restitution—Creative Restitution," in Joe Hudson and Burt Galaway, eds., *Considering the Victim* (Springfield, Ill.: Charles C Thomas, 1975), pp. 93-94.

Figure 5-1. Four Variants of Restitution

Eglash personally advocates the creative or guided type of restitution as an innovative response in criminal matters. His argument rests upon a fundamental concept, referred to as the "second mile," whereby:

> The reparative effort does not stop at restoring a situation to its pre-offense condition, but goes beyond what our own conscience requires of us, beyond what a court orders us to do, beyond what family or friends expect of us, beyond what a victim demands of us, beyond any source of external or internal coercion, beyond coercion into a creative act, where we seek to leave a situation better than it ever was.[21]

Eglash's proposal may not have a direct or practical appeal, but some of his insights are valuable in the determination of the philosophical and theoretical bases of any design to introduce the principle of restitution into the existing criminal-justice process.

Punitive Restitution

The late Stephen Schafer presented a restitution proposal based on the synthesis of several concepts. Of these, the most important is his concern for victims, not surprisingly, since Schafer was among the pioneering scholars in this area. His concern for victims was linked to the key idea of offender responsibility, which Schafer viewed as the central principle of corrections. The overall goal of his proposed measures was the reaffirmation of the rule of law, the basis of all civil liberty. He looked especially to the courts to realize this goal and confronted the problems created by the dual system of criminal and civil justice.

In Schafer's view, modern systems of criminal justice focus on the responsibility of the offender, a responsibility unfortunately defined solely toward society or toward the state rather than toward the specific persons who had been victimized. One study Schafer conducted found that most inmates serving time for violent offenses had no sense of having harmed identifiable individuals, an especially surprising finding in this assaultive crime.[22] Restitution, Schafer felt, addressed the deficiency that (in the words of the British penal reformer, Margery Fry) "to the offender's pocket it makes no difference whether what he has to pay is a fine, costs, or compensation. But to his understanding of the nature of justice it may make a great deal."[23]

Reaffirmation of the rule of law vindicates society as a whole and renews the guarantee of the rights of its individual members. At the same time, Schafer's approach embodies a vital psychological purpose: the provision of "spiritual satisfaction." When a crime has been committed, its victim understandably desires to see the offender called to account. Failure to do so leaves the victim with the feeling of having been cheated or outraged with impunity, which might encourage the pursuit of private revenge. That these feelings are very deeply rooted in our nature is evident from the routine workings of the criminal court where only rarely will victims appear to ask that charges against an offender be dropped or a sentence reduced. Where the rule of law is reasserted and offenders are required to repay their victims, there is the satisfying sense that enough has been done and the conflict need not be extended or escalated.[24]

Schafer urged that civil and criminal procedures be combined in restitution for considerations of both economy and precedent. The state would save time, expense, and the need for repeated hearings if restitution were made a component of criminal sentences. Other important economies would result since the unified procedure would eliminate the problems arising when the civil and the criminal court reached different decisions based on the same evidence. As to precedent, Schafer noted that the use of fines as penalties made the state the recipient rather than the victim. The practicability of the procedure could be seen in the operation of German criminal courts, which retained authority to combine both civil and criminal penalties in the one proceeding known as adhäsionsprozess.

Schafer outlined the actual operation of the unified court procedure:

1. Restitution to the victim of crime should be entertained within the scope of the criminal procedure by the same criminal court which deals with the criminal case, and the sentence should be a combined one, of which restitution should be a part.
2. Restitution should be claimed by the victim; but in default thereof, the court should deal with restitution as part of its concern.
3. If the question of restitution may cause considerable delay in deciding the sentence, the court should pass a partial sentence concerning punishment, and postpone the decision concerning restitution.
4. A decision on restitution should state the amount of restitution and order the installments as a percentage of the offender's earnings, to be paid by him after release from the penal institution, or after he has paid the fine, if this were the only penalty. The court's decision should be based on a consideration of the offender's social position, personal circumstances, and reasonable, minimum standard of living.
5. Restitution should be collected in the same way as taxes, to be deducted from earnings by the offender's employer, or collected by the tax office from his income and paid over directly to the victim.
6. With the aid of fines or related sources of revenue, the state should set up a Compensation Fund, and victims compensated from it when the total restitution proves to be irrecoverable, or if the offender is not known.[25]

Schafer hoped that through his synthetic approach, the very concepts of punishment and restitution would be transformed. No longer would punishment be vengeful and impersonal; on the contrary, it would be restorative and educational. In exerting themselves to make good the losses of their victims, offenders would come to understand the consequences of their acts and would begin to be liberated somewhat from their burden of guilt. At the same time, restitution would not offer a convenient escape from responsibility, especially for those who might have the resources to buy their way out of punishment. On the contrary, all offenders would experience the legitimate disapproval of society in more direct ways, especially through incarceration. The transformation that Schafer hoped to achieve is reflected in his terminology, where *punitive restitution* alternates with *the restitutive concept of punishment*. The influence of these ideas is exemplified in some of the programs that have been developed.

Policy Issues

When principles are translated into programs, certain basic choices must be made. The variables or questions involved will differ according to the context of planning, but in all cases a limited set of choices will define the essential character and structure of the operational project. In the area of restitution, a group of these key issues has been identified by the Institute for Policy Analysis:

Goals:	Will the program be primarily victim oriented, or offender oriented, or both?
Type of restitution:	Will restitution be primarily monetary, or service, or both?
Eligibility:	Will eligibility for participation in the program be relatively broad, or will it be restricted in some way, such as to first-time offenders or nondangerous offenders?
Planning:	How will specific restitution plans be developed? Will victims have a large or small role? How much negotiation will be involved? Will offenders and victims meet? What role will the community play?
Services:	What sort of services will be available to offenders? Will these be required or voluntary? What services will be provided to victims in addition to restitution?
Control:	Who will monitor the individual cases and specific restitution plans? What role will the courts play? How much administrative autonomy will the program have?[26]

The decisions taken on these issues will decide a range of alternative program types. In theory, the range could be very large; in practice, the number of models is relativley limited. The Institute for Policy Analysis sees the following types as most significant.[27]

Basic Restitution: The program consists entirely of a procedure for handling financial transactions from offender to victim. The victim is notified that restitution may be available if a statement is sent to the court documenting losses from the offense. Prosecuting attorneys (and possibly judges) ask for restitution. Offenders make payments to the court, which reimburses the victims. Other activities to provide assistance to victims or offenders are not included. Offender rehabilitation and victim assistance receive roughly equal emphasis as stated goals.

Expanded Basic Restitution: Programs are identical to those for basic restitution, with the exception that assistance is provided for lower-income offenders to find employment, either through placement or through subsidized employment. The goal tends to be to provide as much repayment as possible for as many victims as possible.

Victim-Assistance Restitution: Programs of this sort extend a variety of services to victims to assist them in obtaining full restitution. Such efforts include the provision of information and transportation, advocacy during proceedings, and aid in documentation and in the recovery of property. Such programs typically have well-developed employment components to facilitate the repayment process.

Victim-Assistance—Offender-Accountability Restitution: In this model there is increased emphasis on helping offenders, as well as victims. Restitution is viewed largely in terms of its therapeutic value. Considerable attention and resources are often focused on victim-offender interaction, such as when face-to-face meetings are held between these parties to determine the type and amount of restitution. In addition, offenders may be encouraged to apologize to victims or victims to permit offenders to work directly for them to make good the offense. Arbitration is sometimes used in these contexts to decide the actual restitution plan. Employment assistance is also widely available.

Employment Restitution: Here the primary emphasis is on finding employment for offenders. The rationale is that employment will facilitate repayment to victims and reduce the potential for recidivism among offenders. Job development and job placement therefore become the focal point of staff activity. In handling individual cases, staff look toward long-term employment opportunities and the development of job skills.

Social-Service Restitution: Programs of this sort concentrate primarily on helping offenders deal with their personal problems, which may have motivated the offense in the first place. Offenders are required to participate in such service-oriented efforts as counseling, special education, or job training. Less emphasis is placed on obtaining full restitution or on assistance to victims.

Community-Accountability Restitution: Projects under this heading have several distinguishing features. They are located within the neighborhood or community where the offender lives, and a panel of community volunteers actively participates in the planning of restitution. Offenders are led to an awareness of the consequences of their acts on victims and on the community as a whole, whose disapproval is expressed through the panel. Finally, a concerted effort is made to deter offenders from a repetition of their crimes, especially by sentencing to some kind of community service.

Other models may emerge in this area in the course of time, but currently these models dominate the field. Figure 5-2 diagrams the models.

Figure 5-2 sets out the range of policy issues, but each of the major decisions requires a whole set of more-limited or more-detailed choices to be made. These include legal problems such as due process in restitution, involuntary servitude considerations, the factors that may legitimately be weighed in determining a restitution order, legal limits on the scope and amount of restitution, and legal questions relating to the enforcement of restitution agreements.[28]

Adult Restitution Programs

Proposals that emphasize a community component in restitution are found in a variety of current experimental programs operating in the adult correctional field. By reason of their potential for rehabilitation, for reducing prison terms, and for lowering correctional costs, the Law Enforcement Assistance Administration has supported many of these programs and may continue to do so in the future. The following three programs, originating and operating in conjunction with a correctional service or facility, a halfway residence, and the probation service of a court, dramatically illustrate the originality and diversity that their sponsors bring to the problem of dealing with convicted adult offenders.

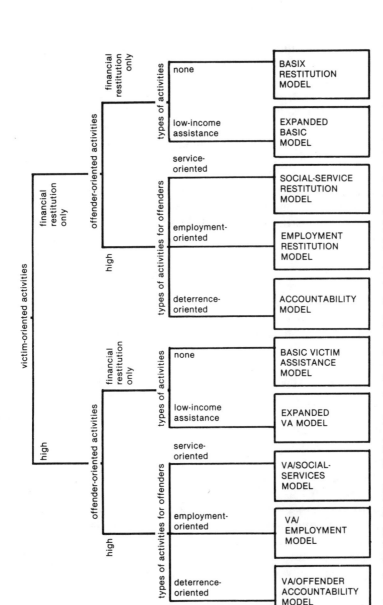

Source: From Anne L. Schneider and Peter R. Schneider, *An Overview of the Restitution Models in the Juvenile Justice System* (Eugene, Ore.: Institute of Policy Analysis, 1979), p. 35.

Note: The three dimensions from which these ten models are derived are victim-oriented activities, offender-oriented activities, and type of offender activities (social service oriented versus deterrence oriented). Although the dimensions have been treated as categorical variables (for example, "high" versus "low"), these are, in fact, continua and are displayed categorically only to permit the development of a typology of restitution models. An actual restitution program could mix and combine the various activities in several ways not shown here, thereby creating mixed models or entirely new models.

Figure 5-2. Derivation of Restitution Models from Three Dimensions of Restitution Programs

Minnesota Restitution Center

The center began operations in 1972 in the Minneapolis-St. Paul area and has since served as a national model.[29] The program operated in an adult halfway house, with the important provision that release to the house serve the explicit purpose of restitution by the offenders to their victims. Residents had to be serving time for property offenses, to have had no past history of violent offenses, and to have been out of prison for at least five years prior to their instant conviction. These criteria were designed with an eye to community response, in the belief that people would be more receptive to the program if it excluded violent offenders.

The process of selection of inmates was a random lottery. Those whose names were chosen were given the option of entering the program or of serving time in the traditional manner. After having served three months, those who chose the program were released from prison directly into the minimum-security residence. A restitution agreement with their victim was then worked out, including a face-to-face meeting when both parties were agreeable to it. Residents received assistance in job placement from staff at the center and agreed to meet a schedule of payments to their victims. When this had been accomplished and the terms of the restitution agreement had been met, the residents were released from the halfway house.

This program provided valuable insights into some of the difficulties that any prospective restitution program may face; the greatest has been keeping restitution as the focus of the residential experience. When their urgent needs and personal problems intruded upon their restitution activity, participants in the program often demanded so much attention that treatment rather than restitution was likely to predominate. Drug dependency, absenteeism from the house, and other violations of the center's rules confronted staff with continual challenge and frequent crises, circumstances that often relegated restitution to a secondary consideration. Another major difficulty resulted from the parole board's attitude that the center should not be permitted to provide an easy way for prisoners to complete their obligation. Limits were accordingly placed on restitution payments so that residents could not depart too much in advance of the date when they would have been released under routine parole procedures. This rule tended to make the center a substitute prison with an increased custodial function rather than the usual halfway house and thus deprived the restitution effort of some of its incentive. It was difficult to avoid the understandable tendency for restitution to become mechanical and even superficial in its day-to-day operation.

Although a resident might meet personally with his victim at the outset of his involvement with the center, actual repayment consisted of little more than mailing a check, with no further relationship necessarily taking place between offender and victim. This approach appears to resemble closely the restitutive concept of punishment. Offenders were kept together in the residence, just as they would be in a prison setting, their fate still largely determined by the state parole board. Community participation was also limited. Residents lived and worked in the community because the center required them to do so while making their restitution payments, but the men felt segregated from their neighbors because of their custodial restrictions. In the end, considerations other than these forced the closing of the program, which nevertheless deserves recognition as the seminal forerunner of other restitution programs, many of them nonresidential.

Victim-Restitution Parole Program

This program was designed in 1974 by Sheriff John Buckley of the Middlesex County House of Correction, Billerica, Massachusetts, for two ends: victim restitution and what is called "mutual agreement parole planning," modeled after the American Correctional Association parole contract.[30] Successful completion of the terms of such a mutually individualized plan results in release from prison at the date specified in the agreed-upon contract, a date that is generally well in advance of what would have been granted through ordinary parole procedures. The combination of victim restitution and mutual agreement planning involves Billerica inmates and correctional personnel in designing individualized correctional programs in which restitution is the key element.

Eligibility for entrance into the program is determined by the parole officer at the time the inmate is received at the institution, after an examination of his record. Those who are sentenced to at least one year and are not serving time for such offenses as assault, drug peddling, violation of public trust, or escape, are eligible for entry into the program. Inmates who agree to participate, work out their individual plans with their correctional counselors and parole officers, to include three components: an institutional treatment program, a parole plan, and a parole release date. Completed plans are submitted to the full parole board for final approval, which is granted at a hearing at which the inmate is present and in which he participates fully.

Restitution agreements worked out to date have been in rather modest individual amounts, ranging from one hundred to four hundred dollars. These figures may not appear impressive, but this county house of corrections receives persons under relatively short sentences. Its inmates are confined for less-serious offenses, usually involving smaller losses for their victims. But even such relatively small amounts may constitute a large loss to those victims who may have had little at the time they were robbed. Additionally even such modest repayments would be very unlikely to have been made in the course of the usual criminal-court procedures. Restitution agreements are worked out between offender and victim, with a parole officer acting as go-between. When possible, face-to-face meetings are arranged between offender and victim. When victims cannot be located or for some reason do not wish to receive repayment, the inmate is allowed to name a social agency to be the recipient of restitution. To date, at least one community drug program has thus benefited.

Inmates participating in the program are released an average of two months earlier than they would have been otherwise. In addition to this real incentive, the shorter terms served saved the institution approximately eighteen hundred dollars on each participant, at a daily per-capita cost of thirty dollars.

The Billerica victim-restitution parole program incorporates several of the restitution principles discussed previously. It follows Schafer's notion of punitive restitution by allowing restitution to serve as an addition to, rather than as a substitute for, imprisonment and by emphasizing offender responsibility. It also follows Smith's proposal in that it permits inmates to have some voice in determining the length of their sentences. In a limited sense, the plan may be said to also involve Eglash's idea of creative restitution in that it emphasizes the participation of individual offenders in designing and implementing plans for their own correction. Overall the Billerica project may be characterized as an experiment in the restitutive concept of punishment.

The following incident drawn from the file of the Billerica House of Correction illustrates this approach. The record began on a spring Saturday afternoon when three young adults, under the influence of alcohol, decided to settle an outstanding score. After cruising the streets of their neighborhood, they spotted their man mowing his front lawn. The three stepped from their car and beat their unsuspecting victim severely. Shortly thereafter they were apprehended. At the arraignment, it was learned that they had been mistaken in the identity of their victim. Convicted of assault, they were sentenced to the house of corrections. When the sheriff reviewed their case, he felt that they might benefit from participation in a restitution program, particularly if they were to confront their victim. The three inmates agreed to meet with him in the sheriff's office. The victim had serious reservations initially, but after receiving assurances that the assailants desired to make some amends, he agreed to participate.

The confrontation was an emotional experience for everyone concerned. As the victim entered, using a cane and still showing bruises about his face, the room became hushed and tension mounted. After a minute of silence, the sheriff requested the young men to study their victim closely. He then showed them a photograph of the victim before they had brutally assaulted him. Two of them began to weep. Slowly a dialogue developed between the victim and his three assailants, resulting in apologies to him. At the meeting's close, the participants agreed that restitution would be made at the rate of ten dollars a week from each of the inmates for a period of one year, a sum sufficient to cover the victim's medical costs. The money was to be drawn from their work-release salary. Jobs were found for them, and they were released each morning to go to work, returning to the house of correction at night and spending their weekends there as well. Upon fulfillment of this commitment, all three were released from custody.

In the four years since, none of them has been reconvicted.

This experiment, as well as similar models currently operating in Oregon, California, Colorado, Georgia, Maine, and Connecticut, will in the years ahead test in practice the restitution concepts brought forward by the theories. The work-release program combines several features: it makes it possible for persons in confinement to work on the outside at prevailing rates of pay, to serve out their sentence, and to spend their evenings and weekends, when they might have got into trouble on the outside, under custody.

Ontario Victim-Offender Reconciliation Project

This project is an interesting example of an effort on the part of a community group to cooperate in setting up a restitution project for adult offenders.[31] Sponsored jointly by a community group and the Mennonite Central Committee and working in close cooperation with the local probation office, the project had its beginnings in the volunteer probation program attached to the local court. As the result of volunteer experiences, the court decided to give offenders an opportunity to be confronted by their victim, the two together to work out an agreement for restitution of the loss that had been suffered, and effecting reconciliation between the two parties.

The first case referred to the program by the court probation office involved several offenders and twenty-two victims, with a total damage of over two thousand dollars. The offenders met with their victims and agreed to accept responsibility to repay approximately one-half of the damage that they had done. Upon the completion of a six-month period, full restitution had been carried out, and the offenders were described as having derived great benefit from their confrontation with their victims.

In the following year, a committee was formed from the Mennonite community, the probation staff, and a representative from the Kitchener, Ontario, community. A number of meetings held with persons drawn into the discussion from citizen groups, probation and parole officers, judges, lawyers and prosecutors, and the police were designed to revise the original draft proposal. A grant from the federal government made it possible to initiate the project with the hiring of two workers. Staff also evaluated the reconciliation process and utilized the results of their experience in training volunteers from the community to serve as third-party helpers. One of the most important incidental benefits of the program was the development of close working relationships with agencies in the community, as well as with representatives of the criminal court.

The initiators of this program see it as providing an alternative to the traditional criminal-court process in dealing with offenders in the community. The aim is to bring the victim and the offender together in an attempt to reach a reconciliation between them and a mutual agreement leading to restitution. The fundamental aim of this program is to deal with criminal offenses as a conflict between individuals who are brought together for common understanding and resolution of their disagreement rather than to submit the offense to a trial. Offenses dealt with to date have included mischief, theft, breaking and entering, malicious damage, and minor cases of assault.

The program limits itself to those cases that involve identifiable victims, particularly private individuals and small businesses. In most instances the offender has been placed on probation, and the process is recognized as part of the probation order. The specific terms of it are: "that the defendant come to a mutual agreement with the victim regarding restitution with the assistance of the probation officer or person designated by the probation officer. If agreement is not reached, or is not carried out, the matter will be referred back to the court." Once this is completed, further supervision is not needed.

The program sponsors stress their fundamental belief that conflict does not, and need not, always reach the point of criminal behavior and that lessons can be drawn from this experience that point to the possibility of dealing with many types and levels of conflict through procedures of conciliation, in which restitution is one of the key elements.

Restitution for Youthful Offenders

Court restitution programs originate usually as the result of the initiative of a judge and independently of any overall statewide plan or organization. Given this usual auspice, a proposal recently funded by LEAA in Massachusetts is significant because it is administered by a state agency, the Department of Youth Services (DYS), which receives committed juveniles and administers a statewide network of secure facilities, as well as a wide array of public and private community-based agencies for youths committed by the courts.

When Massachusetts, in an unprecedented move, closed its juvenile training schools in 1972 and sent all but a few dozen of its twelve hundred youthful inmates back into the community, it also created seven regional offices to administer these large and scattered care facilities in order to bring them into closer contact with the communities whose young people they served.[32] In line with this enlightened approach, restitution programs were attached to four juvenile courts in the state. The success of these programs led the DYS to seek approval for a Youth Services Restitution Program, which began operation in spring 1979.

The program describes itself as "a national demonstration project" because of the breadth of its coverage of juveniles in the state and its application of restitution as a rehabilitative strategy for dealing with youthful offenders, an expected five hundred in the first year and a half.[33] Both boys and girls will benefit from the service, which is limited to those between sixteen and nineteen years of age who have been committed to DYS or referred by the court directly to the restitution program. The economically disadvantaged (youths from families whose annual income is $12,000 or less) are to be given preference for acceptance into the program. The service is further limited to defendants charged with an offense against a victim that is deemed suitable for restitution. "The program is designed so that the juvenile offenders will repay society in a constructive, tangible manner . . . [and] to involve the youth, their victims and the relevant communities."[34] It is a work-experience program combined with supportive services that will give the youth enrolled in it the satisfaction of earning the money to repay their victims, and, it is implied, with something for themselves as well.

Additional services of counseling, skill training, education, and leisure-time activities are expected to enhance the prospects of the youth enrolled in the program for long-term employment after they have graduated from it. A not-inconsiderable anticipated benefit is the turning of young people away from antisocial behavior during the years when they are responsible for the largest proportion of serious offenses committed in the state. Victims are compensated at least in part for their loss, and the community as a whole is benefited by the public-service component of the plan.

The program was motivated by "the documented belief that juvenile delinquency and youthful crime in Massachusetts are a major outgrowth of the youth unemployment problem."[35] Studies had also found the youthful-offender population to be characterized by poor or nonexistent work histories, recurrent patterns of family instability, academic failure, criminal associations, social inadequacy, and alienation. As a result, at least one-quarter of the young people from this kind of background are found to follow later criminal careers.

Basic to the program is the confrontation of the offender with the person he has wronged or harmed and the working out of a program of restitution that will be paid out of the earnings of the offender, for whom a job will be found. The jobs offenders do are community-service, public-benefit work, so that at the end both the victim and the community will have been repaid.

The panel that hears and makes the recommendation for restitution is composed of staff of the regional DYS office, community volunteers, and the victim representative and/or the victim. As in other programs, the aim is to make "a significant impact upon youth as a result of being exposed to the human consequences of their criminal actions."[36]

The commissioner of DYS who initiated the restitution program and saw it launched states:

> The story that started me thinking about what justice meant and what it could do is that of a judge in Chicago faced with sentencing 24 Blackstone Rangers. A zealous court shrink or social worker convinced the judge to sentence 12 to the slammer and 12 to "good works", working in a home for the mentally retarded. After 18 months, 11 of the 12 who were locked up were re-arrested (the 12th has disappeared); 3 of the 12 who worked recidivated. When the other 9 were asked why they succeeded, their responses were all variations on the theme of feeling a sense of worth by giving to someone else. A most basic human need fulfilled—that of being needed by someone else.
>
> I do not wish to romanticize all of this. I do not push it as a panacea. But I have seen it work and work dramatically with a number of pretty rugged juveniles and young adults. There is some evidence to suggest that when using community panels, the specific sentences mean less than the process, the interchange between defendant and community/victim.[37]

Lynn Youth Resource Bureau

Another example of the potential of restitution in juvenile matters is provided by the Individualized Restitution Program in Lynn, Massachusetts, set up under the auspices of the Youth Resource Bureau in that community. Its stated goals are to increase the sense of responsibility among offenders, to reduce recidivism, and to provide assistance to offenders. It aims to be creative and flexible in individualizing restitution plans according to the nature of the offense, the characteristics of the offender, and the needs of the victim.[38] The program functions in a sequence of eight related phases.

Step 1: Case Disposition	A judge in the juvenile court makes a referral to the Youth Resource Bureau for restitution.
Step 2: Intake	A worker from the restitution program contacts both the youth and the victim. Both parties are asked to come to the resource bureau to provide additional information. At that point, the remaining steps in the process are explained to the participants.

Step 3: Mediation	Both parties come face to face to discuss the offense and their feelings toward it. A recommended plan is drawn up and signed by both parties.
Step 4: Restitution Board	The board is a group of community persons and professionals in the area of dispute resolution. Within ten days after receiving the mediation report, they meet to review the case and to tailor a plan for restitution. They make specific recommendations, which are sent to offender and victim, as well as to the juvenile court judge. The interests of both parties are safeguarded by advocates who participate in the board's planning.
Step 5: Judicial Review	A hearing is held within forty-five days at the juvenile court to consider the plan set up by the restitution board. If the plan is satisfactory to all parties, it is sent to the Youth Resource Bureau, to be converted into a contractual agreement.
Step 6: Contract	The contract drawn up by the bureau is signed by both parties. Penalties for failure to live up to the agreement are discussed, as are the benefits to offenders of going beyond the stated requirements.
Step 7: Implementation	The offender meets with a counselor in order to find a job. The emphasis is placed upon developing job skills, not merely paying off the particular restitution contract.
Step 8: Follow-up	Upon successful completion of the agreement, offenders are referred to Youth Resource Bureau for other needed services.[39]

This program description indicates the richness and variety of the creative efforts being made in the field of restitution, in this specific program the victim-advocate component. The process of offender-victim interaction, though highly desirable in theory, has often proven difficult in practice, primarily because of the widespread unwillingness of victims to meet offenders. The Lynn program staff believe that they have greatly reduced this difficulty through the provision of an advocate, a specific person who accompanies the victim through the process and speaks for the victim's interests at all times:

> The victim advocate, accountable to the Project Director, is responsible for encouraging the participation of the victim in the restitution process and protecting whatever rights the victim may have. The victim advocate performs the following functions:
>
> 1) Coordinates activities with counselor and mediation staff.

2) Contacts victim as soon as restitution referral is made to the Youth
    Resource Bureau. Fully explains program to victim, including ways the
    victim can become involved.
3) Appears with victim, if requested to do so, at any meeting victim par-
    ticipates in with regard to mediation. Provides counsel for victim dur-
    ing the entire process.[40]

The role of the victim advocate appears to have a special significance
for the restoration of community, for it immediately begins to remove the
anxiety and isolation that many victims experience, emotions that play a
major part in the reluctance of victims to meet offenders, based in part on
their sense that the system provides many more resources to offenders than
to themselves. The resultant alienation does much to extend and even inten-
sify the experience of victimization. In the Lynn program, this element is
greatly reduced by providing both victims and offenders with advocates
(called counselors), allowing the process to take place in an atmosphere of
support, which helps to facilitate the process of reconciliation.

Earn-It Program

Earn-It is an alternate sentencing program for youthful offenders operating
in the district court of Quincy, Massachusetts, since the spring of 1976. It
provides restitution to victims of crime through a job-placement program
for offenders. Its three major goals are to compensate the victim, to deal
more effectively with the offender, and to protect the community.[41]
    These three aims were the concern of the presiding judge, Albert
Kramer, who proposed that first offenders be given an opportunity to earn
a second chance by working to repay the damages caused by their offense.
The court would monitor the progress of individual offenders and at the
same time retain its power to impose fines or other penalties if the agreement was not lived up to. This program comes close to the ideal of creative
restitution though initiated by a judge and run by the court. Offenders
spend most of their time in the community, coming to the court area only
for assistance or to make restitution payments. They therefore have access
to normal social and recreational contacts in the community and the opportunity to behave, and be treated as, members of the community despite their
offense. They have not been completely diverted from the criminal-justice
system, but they avoid much of the labeling and many of the criminal
associations that result from imprisonment. The program represents one of
the best extant examples of full community participation by the court, probation staff, schools, social agencies, and business community.
    In order for the program to be effective, jobs had to be made available,
which meant that local firms would have to cooperate by pledging to pro-

vide work opportunities. An intensive campaign convinced one hundred businessmen, members of the local chamber of commerce, to make an initial pledge of one hundred work hours each to the court. In addition, the chamber organized a court advisory board to help promote the program and to monitor its performance on the employment side.

With this tangible community support now available and with funds from a federal grant, the program began with the judge's abolition of the long-standing procedure of "continuing without a finding" for first offenders, which meant that the court simply overlooked the first offense. Young persons now charged with an offense had to choose between admission of sufficient facts—in effect, a guilty plea—and standing trial. A large proportion of young defendants chose the first option and agreed to make restitution to their victims. Second and third offenders also began to choose Earn-It over other alternatives when the program was extended to include them. Currently these constitute the majority of participants.

Offenders who enter Earn-It are referred for supervision and assistance to a counselor who functions as a combination probation officer and case worker. Urgent needs of offenders before restitution itself can begin may include finding a place to live, enrollment in a drug or alcohol program, family counseling, medical treatment, and job placement. Employment is arranged with the participating firms; other needs are referred to local agencies.

When the offender is ready to begin making restitution, a negotiation session takes place. When both parties assent, the negotiation can take place face to face; if one of the parties prefers not to meet with the other, the counselor serves as go-between. Offender and victim must come to agreement on the amount of restitution and the schedule of payments. One of the most unsettling problems for which the staff was not at first prepared was the presentation of excessive claims by victims.[42] In some instances, victims would submit estimates for automobile repairs and collect restitution money but would never apply it for that purpose. Earn-It counselors require that receipted bills be submitted before any payment is made for damages, and now investigate all claims and make inquiries to verify the purchase price claimed by the victim. The discovery of inflated claims has sometimes resulted in the subsequent repayment to offenders of overpayments they have made to victims. Such instances of fraud can seriously damage the restitution process and result in disillusionment and a cynical attitude on the part of the offender. The program cannot always guarantee that degree of respect on the part of the victim toward the offender, which is required if the restitution and rehabilitation process is to be effective.

Most of the payments for restitution are raised through the job-placement arrangement, which assigns a maximum of one-third of his wages to the offender and at least two-thirds to his victim as restitution.

Other sources of funds for restitution are earned through community-service work, which is ordered by the court when there has been no personal victim of an offense or when the amount of restitution to an injured party is small. An act of vandalism such as ringing a false fire alarm may result in a community work order to replace broken glass in a school building, or to paint fire boxes. In a minor shoplifting incident where the article is easily returned, offenders without prior records may be required to do volunteer work in community agencies such as hospitals or day-care centers. A person who has injured the eyesight of another person may be assigned to devote a certain number of hours to reading to the blind, and a drunken driver who has injured a pedestrian may be ordered to work in the emergency ward of the local hospital.

One of the most dramatic, and successful, cases resolved by the program involved a teenage boy who, without a license and under the influence of alcohol, stole a police cruiser and totally destroyed it, for damages close to ten thousand dollars. The boy was an automobile body worker and unemployed at the time. The city carried no insurance on the car, which therefore represented a total loss. The boy was evidently a skilled body worker and owned a full set of tools and equipment needed for this work. As a result of the mediation meeting, the case was continued for a year. The police department, which was in need of an automobile body worker, had not included in its budget the cost of purchasing the tools necessary to repair its vehicles. It agreed to hire the boy under a contract for the year, during which time he agreed to work for the town repairing police and city-owned trucks, at the standard rate of pay. In exchange for his work and the use of his tools, restitution was lowered to a thousand dollars. Both parties fully expect that at the end of the one-year contract, the case will be discharged and the boy will have won a permanent position on the staff of a city department.

Proceeds of the Earn-It program totaled $407,000 in the five years since the inception of the program, having risen from $37,000 in its first year to $110,000 for the year 1979, all of it earned by offenders and repaid to their victims. Additional thousands of dollars have been earned and used by offenders for their own rehabilitation programs such as the court drunk driver course. Sums earned by participants in the program have been put toward fines, which would otherwise have gone unpaid because of the offender's unemployment. Offender earnings have also gone to pay for shoplifted items, which have been donated to charity. Equally important, a total of 16,505 hours of work by juvenile and adult offenders in lieu of fines have benefited municipal or nonprofit agencies. Many of these offenders have been spared a sentence to a correctional institution, resulting in considerable savings to the county or state, given the 1980 annual per-capita cost of prison confinement at fourteen thousand to fifteen thousand dollars.

Enthusiastic support by the community has been widely expressed in Boston-area media.[43] Reaction of the community was aptly summarized in a radio editorial:

> The system has a number of obvious virtues. It gets young people who've been devoting their energies to law breaking into the work force—where a number of them seem to be staying. It keeps them out of corrections facilities (where rehabilitation is unlikely and the attempt at rehabilitation costly). And, not the least by any means, victims aren't ignored: they're paid back for damages and inconveniences.[44]

The success of the program may be ascribed to the simplicity of both its underlying concept and the manner in which that concept is applied. It fits easily into the existing court structure and from the outset has been integrated with the commercial enterprises and social agencies of the community. It achieves a basic reordering of traditional procedures without demanding sweeping changes. These features of the program were recognized at a national restitution conference that commended Earn-It as a model for other restitution programs.

The program seems also to have commended itself to victims who have benefited from it. One of them wrote to the court:

> I would like to compliment you, the staff and the EARN-IT program for the fine service that has been rendered to myself and to the community. I did not know a program such as EARN-IT was in existence until I received your letter requesting that I contact you. When I read your letter I was surprised and a bit skeptical of the idea; but now after seeing the program in action I am thankful it is here and I hope it will continue for a very long time. This outstanding project has extended justice to all parties and it has renewed my faith in our judicial system.[45]

The rapid growth of restitution programs in Massachusetts is reflected in the 27 percent increase in restitution monies collected by probation officers across the state during 1979, a total in excess of $4 million, up from $3 million in the previous year. These sums were collected from offenders and paid over by the court to victims as compensation for the crimes inflicted on them.[46]

On the national level, the federal government has undertaken to fund, as of January 1980, forty-one programs to enable courts, probation offices, and social agencies to provide for restitution as one of the availabilities in the disposition of adjudicated juveniles. The aims of the program include a reduction in the number of youths incarcerated in each project's jurisdiction and a reduction in the recidivism of youths involved in these projects; provision for some redress or satisfaction with regard to the reasonable value of the damage or loss suffered by victims of juvenile offenders involved in these projects; increased knowledge about the feasibility of restitution for juveniles in terms of cost-effectiveness, impact on differing categories of youth offenders, and the juvenile justice system within these projects' jurisdiction; an increased sense of responsiblity and accountability on the part of participating youthful offenders for their behavior; and greater community confidence in the juvenile justice process within these projects' jurisdiction.

Juvenile offenders to be served under the program are those who have been adjudicated; status offenders are specifically excluded. Three methods of restitution are spelled out in the program announcement: monetary restitution, community service, and direct victim service, any of which may be combined with other sanctions, treatment, or dispositions, exclusive of incarceration. An important feature of the program is the subsidy it provides for youth employment. Although the original grant is for one year, individual projects may be continued for an additional one or two years if they meet the criteria established for continuation.

Conclusions

Some problems of both a policy and an operational nature have arisen in the course of the extraordinary rate at which restitution as an alternative to traditional court dispositions has proliferated across the nation. Although there seems to be consensus that offender-victim meetings are desirable when both parties agree to them, the results have been mixed, and offender confrontations are now reported to be declining in some restitution programs. Individuals involved in either side of the restitution process seem more and more inclined toward the position that it is the payments that really count rather than meetings between victim and offender and a possible resulting relationship. Among possible reasons for this development is the problem of victims' lashing out at the offender during their meeting and as a result alienating him from the restitution process. Jurisdiction is also a problem; offenders can be compelled to attend such meetings but victims cannot. Many victims have no desire to confront offenders, preferring to remain strangers to them and desiring only to receive restitution for damages. As caseloads for restitution program staff grow, this aspect of the program comes to be deemphasized, ultimately affecting the initiation and maintenance of offender-victim relationships.

The decline of offender-victim meetings and interchange results in an essential part of the program being lost, for a major aim of the restitution program is to counteract the prevailing impersonality and anonymity of much criminal behavior by making offenders aware of the personal harm that they have caused. A great deal can be lost if the experiences of the victim must be interpreted to offenders through third parties (counselors, advocates and other staff members) rather than through face-to-face confrontation. The attitude of ordinary citizens toward crime and toward offenders can change little so long as they are able to keep their distance from offenders whose needs and problems they prefer not to hear or attempt to comprehend.

Schafer's position that the proper place for restitution is within the criminal-justice system, especially in cases of violent crime like assault and battery or armed robbery, respects the community's need to be protected from such offenders, at least to have assurance that rehabilitation will be achieved before they are released. Therefore only the criminal-justice system is adequate to handle restitution on a large scale, to provide security from violent offenders, and to impose other sanctions when restitution agreements fail.

Those who disagree with this position point out that the criminal-justice system cannot accomplish the real goal of restitution—the reintegration of the offender into the community—for within that system the offender lives and works in a separate and alien world. Attempts to place restitution in a punitive setting constitute a sham, a contradiction in terms, for there it is merely punishment under another name. Furthermore incarceration is tremendously expensive, an "extravagance," as it has been termed by Milton Rector.[47] In contrast, restitution in the community provides significant savings in tax dollars while offering a more humane approach to dealing with offenders.

Consideration of restitution, whether from the punitive or creative side, regards it as of considerable rehabilitative value for offenders, although this assertion remains largely unproven or undocumented. Both the Minnesota Restitution Center and Earn-It have produced some data indicating that restitution may well be rehabilitative, but the Minnesota program has closed and Earn-It has not yet been fully tested. Results therefore appear as intriguing illustrations or isolated success stories. The Minnesota program experience, which reported that the personal problems of offenders frequently interfered with or sidetracked restitution, would argue against the rehabilitative power of restitution in some instances, especially those where an offender's lack of responsibility complicated the situation.

Until these problems have been faced and resolved, the rehabilitative value of restitution must remain somewhat speculative. Burt Galaway, a leading proponent of restitution, admits as much:

> The rationale for speculating that restitution might be more rehabilitative than other correctional measures includes the notion that restitution is related to the amount of damages done and thus would be perceived as more just by the offender; is specific and allows for a clear sense of accomplishment as the offender completes concrete requirements; requires

the offender to be actively involved in the treatment program; and provides a socially appropriate and concrete way of expressing guilt and atonement. It maintains that the offender who makes restitution is likely to elicit a more positive response from persons around him than the offender who is sent to prison or is subjected to some other correctional sanction. *Restitution is perceived as a sanction that enhances self-respect* [emphasis added].[48]

A simple test designed to assess changes in self-image, and offender perceptions of the justness of restitution, if carried out in the near future, should be helpful in demonstrating whether restitution truly has something to offer that traditional correctional practices, with their acknowledged high rates of recidivism, clearly do not.

Restitution can help to reduce the labeling of offenders by sparing them the usual police and penal records, as well as by changing the community's views about specific offenders or the authorities' view of them. In order for these results to come about, the community and the authorities have to be made aware of the opportunity afforded by such restitution efforts to offenders. Current statements about the effect of restitution on the reduction of labeling will remain rather hypothetical until, like assertions about its rehabilitative value, they are tested.

A lingering issue of some concern is the determination of the offenses that could be handled through restitution. Early proposals recommended that only crimes against the person be included. Currently this line of thought is less widely held, and it is now claimed that it is easier to determine the extent of the damages owed in cases of property crimes than in rape or assault cases, and therefore restitution has been much more frequently resorted to in such instances. Proponents of restitution continue to seek realistic and workable standards for applying it in cases of personal violence. Still unresolved is the degree of seriousness of the offenses where restitution could be utilized. So far it appears that restitution is being used almost exclusively in fairly minor cases.

The value of restitution procedures as preventive of further conflict between the two parties in a criminal encounter, and of recidivism on the part of the offender, should not be underestimated, despite the reservations noted in these closing paragraphs.

6 Assistance to Victims

> Sentencing is obviously important to the defendant but it is also important to the crime victim—often the forgotten person at a criminal trial—and provides a handy barometer of how society is thinking about crime at any given moment.[1]

The role of the victim of crime has come full circle since a much earlier time when he, or his family or tribe, pursued the one who had offended against him and sought revenge by wreaking physical harm or demanding restitution in money or kind for an economic loss suffered as a result of the criminal encounter. As the money compensation originally paid to the victim came to be collected and kept by the state, the victim's remaining satisfaction—seeing the assailant brought to justice—hardly constituted adequate payment for damages done. But until recently this was the sole recompense provided in our courts to victims, beyond whatever damages they might collect by bringing a civil suit. Their role was therefore limited to making the criminal complaint and thereafter testifying as witnesses for the prosecution.

Today courts are beginning to restore their original role to victims, providing them an opportunity to participate in several steps in the court process. In addition, provisions are being made in some jurisdictions to bring them into active participation in arbitration and restitution programs and, in some instances, in the determination of the sentence to be meted out to persons who have harmed them. And some laws provide payment of public funds to victims as at least partial compensation for what they have suffered.

The origins of state payment to victims, quite apart from what the victim may receive in restitution from the offender, may be found in the social contract that the Enlightenment emphasized as the basis for the relationship between citizen and society. Under this concept the victim relinquished his right to avenge himself if attacked or robbed. In exchange, the state undertook to pursue, apprehend, prosecute, and sentence violators of the criminal law.

But if the state fails to protect its citizens, do the latter then have a right to expect the state to reimburse them for the results of its failure to safeguard their persons and property? This line of reasoning and its justification for state regard for victims may not have been that deliberately arrived at. However, as the rate of clearance by police arrest of reported criminal offenses continues to drop to today's estimated one-quarter or one-fifth of all offenses known to the police, the number of jurisdictions that have enacted legislation entitling the victim to some payment from state funds has grown.

Anyone who has had his car stolen, his dwelling burglarized, his pocket picked, or his person assaulted knows the fright, anger, and helplessness that follows such an experience, to say nothing of the monetary loss and the disruption of life which such crimes entail. Aside from whatever such harm the victim may have suffered as a result of a criminal encounter, there is the added consideration that his presence at the trial of the defendant is vital for a successful conviction. One of the unending problems confronting prosecutors, defense counsel, and other criminal-court personnel is that an alarming number of victims and other witnesses fail to appear in court when the incident in which they were involved, or observed, is being tried. The Vera Institute reports that such failure to appear is largely due to frustration with slow and cumbersome court proceedings.[2]

Vera Institute Witness Alert System

As a result of this and other findings, the Vera Institute in 1970 established a telephone alert system for prosecution witnesses. This permitted selected witnesses (both police and civilian) to pursue their normal daily routine at work or at home on the day scheduled for the trial in which they were to testify until they were actually needed. At this point, they were called by telephone or, in the case of police, by radio.

The success of the alert system resulted in the establishment in 1975 of a Victim Witness Assistance Project designed to reduce time spent in court and to provide a range of needed services. Launched originally in Brooklyn, where almost fifty thousand criminal cases are processed each year, it represented a cooperative effort on the part of the district attorney, the courts, police, and the Vera Institute.

The project undertook three objectives: to notify all prosecution witnesses of the date they were due in court, to provide the prosecution with a list of witnesses and their expected availability to appear when needed, and to provide a reception center for victims and witnesses. This center would also provide a children's play center, transportation to court, a crime-victim hot line, a burglary repair kit, and the services of counselors. The project maintained a roster of services available from community resources, its volunteer staff drawn largely from students at high schools and colleges and from senior citizen groups. It is reported that at the end of 1976, five hundred hours of service were being contributed each week by these volunteers from the community.

The reception center and the counselors offered services in areas not directly related to the victim or witness role in the court proceedings. They helped victims and witnesses to complete forms for state compensation, loss of earnings, or unexpected expenses such as funeral or medical costs. Any witness who reported harassment by the defendant would have this brought to the attention of the detective investigative unit in the district attorney's office. The Vera Institute report describes the instance of a woman who had filed a complaint that her husband had abused her and threatened her with a gun. She was referred to an organization for battered wives and was helped to expedite her application for welfare aid.

One of the unique features of this pioneer program is an emergency repair service, which operates seven days a week to fix broken locks, board up windows, repair doors, and otherwise secure the victim's premises against further depredation. The repair crew is equipped with a two-way radio to receive emergency calls for its services through police headquarters.

If the success of the project were to be gauged exclusively by a change in the witness appearance rate, the resultant increase from 54 to 57 percent would not appear impressive. But the saving of $2 million a year by freeing sixty-five tours each day for police patrol duty is clearly a benefit. Two additional benefits resulted from the project. The institute designed an experimental program to offer conciliation and mediation to victims as alternatives to formal criminal prosecution in certain cases where defendant and victim had a relationship prior to the occurrence that brought them into court, and it gave strong impetus to the victim-witness assistance movement in other jurisdictions throughout the country.

Victim-Witness Aid in California

No more dramatic and telling instance of the difference in the lot of the defendant and the defendant's victim has been recorded than an account of a vicious attack on a family by a deranged assailant completely unknown to them.[3] The two-year-old son was stabbed to death, and an unborn child was mortally wounded. At the moment of his arrest, the defendant was read his rights, was housed and fed by the state to await trial, and received legal defense and medical attention for his drug-abuse symptoms.

No parallel protection or service was extended to his victims, whose medical bills totaled more than $30,000 beyond what their medical insurance would cover and an additional $4,000 for uninsured damage to their home. On the day scheduled for the trial, they were subpoenaed to appear in court, to which they had to make their own way, while the defendant was transported. The defendant was shielded from revenge or retribution, but there was little concern for the protection of witnesses. In addition to the potential of encountering the defendant's friends at court, witnesses are intimidated by the criminal-justice system itself. Criminal-justice agencies think of witnesses only as they are needed. As for the victim, "the media sensationalize the criminal while the victim suffers in silence and obscurity."

Although California has enacted a generous compensation law for victims of violent crime, less than 2 percent of the victims of such crimes actually collect state compensation. They must wait from six months to a year to receive payment even though they may need immediate assistance and relief to avert financial disaster.

In response to such occurrences as this, the Probation Department of San Mateo County established a victim-witness assistance program in 1975. Today the program operates with witness waiting rooms in both the municipal and superior courts, staffed by five full-time and two part-time employees, and the assistance of more than seventy volunteers.

Victims of violent crime are referred directly to the program from the police; the process is facilitated by a twenty-four-hour switchboard and a six-day work week. Victims may also be referred by hospitals, community agencies, friends, and neighbors. Police officers at the time of the event provide the victims with a notice written in simple language informing them of their right to apply for state compensation and to prepare them to meet a volunteer from the program. The notices are written in three languages besides English. Witnesses to a crime who are not necessarily victims of it are also informed of the need for their appearance in court and the nature of the proceeding. A map directs witnesses to the courthouse and gives such details as the entrance to be used. When they arrive, witnesses are met by volunteer guides who oversee the services available in the waiting room: hot drinks, comfortable seating, simple instructions, and guide service to the courtroom.

Victims are given such immediate necessities as cash, groceries, transportation, homemaking services, child care, interpreting, crisis counseling, as well as contact with friends, relatives, and employers. "Bloodied or damaged homes or automobiles are cleaned and restored. Funerals are arranged. Victims are relieved of financial burdens—red tape, and pressure from creditors—while they are assisted in recovering from the emotional and physical trauma of the crime." Victims of violent crime in this county recover compensation from the state at a rate far exceeding the state average, due in part to the expert help of trained volunteers in the preparation of claims.

The family of the victims of the brutal assault and murders briefly described previously received assistance from volunteers within hours of the crime. "Volunteers cleaned floors, rugs, walls, appliances and furniture throughout the house. They restored and painted the caved-in walls, and repaired the broken windows. Volunteers also did what they could to blunt the impact of the losses. Nursery furniture was packed and stored. Baby pictures were removed from the mantle. The curious, and the woman who wanted to sell newspaper clippings in a scrap book as mementos of the crime were also kept from the victims.''

This regard for victim sensibilities was matched by concern for the economic effects of the crime. Creditors agreed to take no action against the victims until the family had recovered; the mortgagor consented to post-pone payment of both principal and interest. Applications for state com-pensation for the expenses of the funerals were also processed by the volunteers. Had the program not come to their aid, the family would have been left in permanent debt. Instead arranagements were made for out-standing bills to be paid, the family receiving more than $40,000 in services through the program. This was far less than the cost to the state of the seven-month trial that resulted in the second-degree murder conviction of the defendant and his sentence to state prison.

The experience of the Aid to Victims and Witnesses program has led to a number of conclusions applicable to any criminal court that is desirous of providing community-based programs as supplements to the traditional run of court services.

1. Victim-witness-assistance programs should not be limited, as they are in some jurisdictions, only to victims of certain crimes such as rape but should be made available to all crime victims.

2. Victim-assistance programs should be interagency ones, working with and in behalf of all criminal-justice agencies to create greater support for the program and help to eliminate rivalries between them.

3. The program should be volunteer based. If victims were to receive the level of assistance and services provided by the state to defendants, the cost would be prohibitive. The motivation of volunteers derives from their desire to serve; their presence in the program also represents the concern of the community for the welfare of the afflicted victims in its midst.

4. By making the program a local responsibility, a sense of immediacy and concern for one's victimized neighbors is created that avoids the bureaucratic and time-consuming procedures of statewide programs. Fur-ther advantages of a local program are manifest and numerous. The services it provides do not partake of the nature of a dole but render direct and per-sonal assistance. Victims are given every opportunity and encouragement to assume as much responsibility as possible in order to restore their previous way of life. Localized efforts can effect long-range savings because they are extended immediately. Many of the services are often donated locally.

5. A local program can provide immediate emergency assistance as needed, much more rapidly than could be done by a statewide agency.

The report of the program summarizes its chief benefit in the following words: "Perhaps the most valuable of all services provided to victims of violent crime is simple human contact and comfort at the time of crisis. This is far more rehabilitative than a cash handout months later."

Victim-Witness Assistance in Illinois

A program originating under private rather than public auspices has been in operation in a Cook County criminal court since June 1977.[4] Sponsored and operated by the Junior League of Chicago, its members staff the day-to-day operation of the program under the supervision of a paid director. The budget for the first year was $28,750; the county providing office space, furniture, telephone, mailing, and office supplies.

The program was patterned after a similar program established earlier by the Cook County prosecutor's office in another part of the city after the proven success of this original program in providing for the comfort, convenience, and security of victims and witnesses. The prosecutor's office helped to develop the program, gave it official endorsement, and shared responsibility for selecting the director and training the volunteer staff who were to operate it.

The objectives of the program were clearly set out in the handbook issued to all its volunteer participants. Through cooperation with the prosecutor's office, it would improve communications between victims and witnesses and that office and simultaneously furnish victims with information on the scheduling of their cases in court and inform them with regard to court systems and procedures. It would enlist the cooperation of the police to ensure their informing witnesses of the availability of the service. Employers would be asked to cooperate in allowing witnesses to attend court sessions without loss of pay. The community would be invited to encourage the participation of victims and witnesses in court trials, as well as to recruit volunteers.

The original proposal also anticipated the benefits that would flow from the program: a reduction in delay in court processing between arraignment and final disposition of cases; a decrease in the need for continuances; a reduction in the number of cases closed; and an increase in the number of court decisions based on the merits and the facts of the case simply by ensuring the presence of the necessary witnesses. As each case was disposed of, volunteers sent letters to witnesses informing them of the final outcome of the trial they had testified in and thanking them for their participation.

Volunteers agreed to devote four half-day sessions to training, including study of the court components and procedures and observation of trials with particular reference to the problems confronting victims and witnesses. In-service training would encourage volunteers to analyze their experiences and continue to learn. Thereafter they were expected to work between two and four days a month for one year.

The role of these volunteer paraprofessionals was to complete the data-information card for each witness, based on information gathered from him, the prosecutor's office, and court files. They were prepared to answer questions from witnesses and provide them with their court appearance dates. Part of the training was directed to help them to become sensitive to the needs and problems of individual victims and witnesses and competent to make helpful referrals to other agencies. In the broadest sense, their service was that of liaison with the clerk's office, the prosecutor, police, defense counsel, and neighborhood community organizations.

The first contingent of twenty volunteers was drawn almost entirely from Junior League membership. In their first year of service they devoted over two thousand hours to this community program, serving some eighty-five hundred people with personal contact at the courthouse and forty-seven hundred more through correspondence. As a result of their efforts, the number of no-show witnesses in criminal trials in the court where they served was cut in half. Soon thereafter the project opened a second branch in the city of Chicago and helped to establish similar programs in two other Illinois counties.

In Peoria, for example, directly as a result of a court-monitoring program carried out by a group of local citizens who observed more than three hundred misdemeanor jury trials between 1973 and 1974, a witness information service has been established largely with volunteer services to supplement the small paid staff. The program assists witnesses from the time their case reaches the district attorney all the way through disposition. Volunteers mail to witnesses information on court procedures well in advance of their expected appearance, locate addresses of persons whose mail is returned undelivered, and follow up with telephone calls to witnesses to remind them of the time and place of the hearing.

Thereafter volunteers meet and guide witnesses to the proper courtroom, provide information, answer questions, and, should the witness fail to appear, notify them of the eventual outcome of the case. Local employers have signed agreements allowing their employees to appear as witnesses without loss of pay. These agreements now cover nearly one-half of the area's work force. Witnesses who have been helped by the service had a 17 percent higher rate of appearance than those who did not receive these services.

In its early years, the service dealt only with witnesses in misdemeanor offenses; it has since expanded to include selected felony cases as well. And it has gone further than its original intent by providing victims who are eligible for compensation or restitution with help in completing the necessary forms and following their cases through the necessary channels to completion.[5]

The Urban Court, Dorchester, Massachusetts

This court includes a service to victims whose purpose, not unlike that of other programs described in this chapter, is to help orient victims to the criminal-court process; to schedule cases for hearing; to ameliorate the pain and loss suffered by victims by providing limited services; and to demonstrate to the community the concern of the criminal justice system with their needs. The Dorchester community suffers from a very high crime rate, resulting in much dissatisfaction among area residents who are reported to view the police and the court as not responsive to their needs.

The victim component of the court is staffed by a director and three advocates housed in the Urban Court offices, less than two blocks from the district court. The reliance on volunteers to help staff the program is not nearly so extensive as in either of the other two programs described. Clients come to the program from two sources: the district attorney's office and the local police. While victim referrals may originate from either of these two sources, they are all handled in much the same manner.

Each morning the victim specialists attached to the district attorney's office sit in on the screening of cases to be arraigned in the court. They listen to the victim's story and attempt to assess what needs the victim may have as a result of the crime. If the needs are extensive, the specialist fills out a service-referral form, which is sent to the attention of the victim advocate in the Urban Court for follow-up. These needs may encompass emergency housing, child care, training or employment, physical or mental health, welfare, transportation, crime prevention, consumer information, senior citizen services, insurance emergency funds, alcohol or drug referral, foster care and adoption, interpreter services, and eligibility for state victim-compensation funds. The extent of these needs is an indication of the importance of the service that the component renders as well as a gauge of the inadequacy of court machinery in areas not covered by victim-assistance programs. The list also illustrates the complexity of the situations that confront the victims of criminal acts.

After a victim's needs have been referred to the component's office, an advocate is assigned to the case. The victim is then contacted either by telephone or mail, offered the services of the program, informed of its purpose and an interview arranged at the office of the component or at the victim's home or place of employment.

The advocate during the interview conveys to the victim a concern for his needs and appreciation of the trauma to which he has been subjected. The initial response of the victim is usually surprise that such a service exists, followed by expressions of relief and gratitude for the services proferred—an array of community agencies and services available as supplements to the component's own limited resources.

Very early on, it was realized that volunteer help from the community would be required to enhance the effectiveness of the program, which could not expect to pay for all personnel required to meet all the needs of the victim clients coming to their attention. The initial plan was to enlist and train twenty volunteers to serve in three basic areas. They would develop skills in crime prevention to assist residents to protect their homes and apartments better from break-ins. They were prepared to identify household valuables with special equipment for registration with the police department. They would help to transport victims to and from the court and serve as guides and escorts (especially important for victims who lack transportation or who have had their cars stolen, as well as providing protection for victims who may be fearful of venturing alone away from their homes or loath to leave their premises unguarded). Such volunteers would serve as friends of the victim in court, providing both information and support to the victim, at times and under circumstances when both are vitally needed, as much for the prosecution of the case as for the emotional well-being of the victim or witness.

Dade County Pretrial Program

An interesting variation on the role of the victim is found in Dade County, Florida, where since 1972 a pretrial intervention progam has been in operation.[6] The initiation of this program was at least in part a reaction to the growing criticism of plea-bargaining as a cheapening of the criminal-court process and commonly referred to as "bargain basement justice." The frequency with which plea-bargaining is used may be seen in the fact that in some jurisdictions as high as 90 percent of all serious cases are disposed of in this manner, and without trial.[7] Plea-bargaining permits a defendant, in return for a plea of guilty, to negotiate for a less severe sentence on the basis of a reduced level of criminal charges, in this way reducing trial time and cost, or even making a trial unnecessary. The major criticism of plea-bargaining is that it imposes a penalty on a defendant who may wish to assert his right to a trial but who may be induced to accept the offer to bargain this right against the expected benefit of a reduced charge and a consequently lighter sentence.

Under Dade County's innovative experiment, all negotiations with the defendant take place before trial (instead of after a plea of guilty as in plea-bargaining). With the judge presiding, the defendant and complaining police officer, as well as the victim, are invited to participate in the session.

The unique feature of this procedure is its inclusion of the victim in the bargaining process. In the usual plea-bargaining session, the victim is not present or invited to propose what he may regard as a proper disposition of the case. By reversing the traditional process of a conference before the judge between defense and prosecution—prior to a formal plea of guilty instead of afterward—many of the questionable elements of plea-bargaining are eliminated at the same time that victims are given a chance to take part in matters directly affecting their interests.

Benefits of Victim-Witness Advocacy

Any extension of advocacy services to witnesses will be hastened by demonstrable savings in dollars that they make and in the time of all concerned: complainants, witnesses, defendants, police, defense attorneys, and court personnel. This is well exemplified in an audited evaluation recently made of Milwaukee's Project Turnaround, which combines five units: a victim-witness advocacy unit; a citizen contact and support unit to provide personal services to victims and witnesses, which generally "humanized the system"; a justice-information service, which resulted in improved record keeping and considerable saving of police time; a sensitive crimes unit, to prosecute sexual-assault and child-abuse cases, which reduced court delay by an average of one month for each such case; and a citizens' complaint unit in the district attorney's office. This last unit reduced waiting time of complainants from four or five hours to thirty minutes. An important by-product was a reduction in the number of complaints filed by referral of civil cases, for example, from the criminal court to the local legal aid society.

In a single year $830,000 was reported to have been saved by the introduction of these units under the aegis of the victim-assistance program just for the city of Milwaukee. Later adopted in sixteen jurisdictions around the country, the plan netted a saving of $3.2 million annually, without reckoning the enormous number of hours saved for all the participants in the court proceedings.[8]

A concluding note on the economics of victim assistance may further illuminate the seriousness of the plight of the victim in the current crime scene. A 1978 report states that in the most recent year for which figures are available, more than a million and a half persons were victimized, with resulting physical injury. Of these, more than one-third required medical attention, and almost all of them reported time lost from work as a result of injury incurred by the offenses against them. The estimated total cost of victim-compensation programs, whether partially covered by federal or state funds, is set at $143 million if stringent minimum-loss criteria are applied to the claims of victims, as against almost twice that amount—$261 million—if no minimum loss criteria are applied.[9]

Conclusion

The programs briefly set out here cannot possibly encompass all of the efforts being made around across the nation to give recognition to the role of the victim-witness. The Vera Institute of Justice of New York City has been running such a program for some years. Nationally the District Attorney's Association has sponsored such programs through sixty-eight offices all over the United States.

Speedy trials are among the most effective measures for deterring crime as well as assuring conviction of the guilty, as Cesare Beccaria pointed out more than two hundred years ago.[10] Failure of witnesses to appear in court to testify—because of intimidation or fear of reprisal—is one of the reasons for delays, continuances, and postponements. Mindful of the crucial role of the witness, the federal Department of Justice in 1970 embarked on a Witness Security Program, which cost $62 million in the first eight years of operation.[11] A March 1978 report of the program gives the fate of witnesses and informers who had not been protected by the program in 50 narcotics-related cases: 45 murders, nine attempted murders, nine death threats and assorted physical assaults.[12]

Protective custody of key figures in the prosecution of violent crimes by detention in jail or in special secluded facilities does not constitute sufficient protection for material witnesses. The future undoubtedly will see a much broader extension by our criminal courts of such programs as these, in addition to those concerned with witnesses whose presence is less critical to the successful conviction of offenders on trial.

Compensation to Victims

The care and the support that we give to the victims of crime should be both compassionate and practical. The public response to crime should include the relief of financial distress caused by crime and the provision of medical and psychological treatment to the extent that these are required and helpful.

—Statement of the United States Catholic Conference, approved by the National Council of Catholic Bishops, Washington, D.C., November, 1980.

Compensation as Redress

After centuries of being left to the mercy of both offenders and the courts, victims of crime today are being provided with some means of obtaining reparation for their losses. Realization of the needs and rights of the victims of crimes is neither new nor revolutionary. The code of Hammurabi written some four thousand years ago stipulated a form of victim relief, by providing that "if a man was robbed and the robber not found, the victim [could] make an itemized list of his losses, for which he would be compensated by the city. If it is the life of the owner that is lost, the city or the mayor shall pay one maneh of silver to his kinfolk."[1]

Among the early Hebrews the law granted compensation to individuals for time lost at work, as well as for pain, suffering, and shame incurred by disfigurement.[2] Similarly, in ancient Arabia, the responsibility for caring for the dependents of a homicide victim was placed upon the community.[3] And during the Middle Ages an elaborate code of reparation by the criminal offender was developed within the Anglo-Saxon legal system.[4]

These forms of compensation or reparation replaced the more-primitive methods of personal revenge by the victim or the blood feud by his family, clan, or tribe. The earlier, violent means of redress were the natural result of the *gemeinschaft* social structure of these primitive times where relations among individuals were familistic, involuntary, and emotional. As the early societies evolved into a more *gesellschaft* order, where social interaction was more impersonal, voluntary and secular, a structured, less personally hostile, and direct means of achieving reparation became necessary.[5]

The state, town, or lord provided a centralized, less-violent means of redress against the criminal offender, but "the price of state assistance in bringing the wrongdoer to justice soon became disproportionately high [for the victim]."[6] For example, under the feudal system, as society became organized to the point where it undertook responsibility for the apprehension and punishment of offenders, criminal acts came to be regarded as injuries to the state entity.

Thus the rights of the victim were subordinated to those assumed by the collective society and remained so until the past two decades, when once again official attention began being paid to the needs of victims. The time and expense involved in governmental compensation schemes calls for justification for such legislation, and several theories have been advanced as rationale for this resurgence of victim-compensation plans found today in twenty-four states.[7]

Under the social-responsibility theory, payments to victims of crimes are closely related to the modern evolution of the welfare rationale. As society expands its conception of its role in relation to the individual citizen in the areas of public education, physical and mental health, and unemployment relief, the development of compensation to victims of criminal acts constitutes but a further step. The contention here, as with the individual unable to find work or to pay for needed medical care, is that "an innocent victim ought to be entitled to aid in maintaining that degree of dignity, security and comfort which he needs in order to provide for himself and his family."[8]

Compensation schemes with a strong or purely social-welfare base generally require evidence of need or financial hardship as a prerequisite for state aid. In line with this welfare-extension theory, some jurisdictions locate the administration of their victim-compensation program under the welfare department. A variation of this theme is found in the analogy between victim compensation and workmen's compensation. Without assigning guilt to the state or to society, this theory of risk distribution argues that the most equitable way by which to absorb the impact of the loss borne by an innocent victim is to assess it against that party best able to assume and distribute it: society as a whole.[9]

Another contention for the adoption of state compensation plans argues that the state has an implied contractual obligation to protect citizens against attacks on their person or property. Therefore, when a crime takes place, the state is seen to have failed to uphold its end of the social contract. As summarized by Senator Ralph Yarborough in support of an early federal bill for victim compensation:

> Having encouraged our people to get out into the streets unprotected, we cannot deny this puts a special obligation upon us to see that these people are, in fact, protected from the consequences of crime.[10]

Certain jurisdictions base their compensation statutes on the assumption that they will thereby enhance the effectiveness of crime detection and improve crime prevention. It is well recognized that for a variety of reasons, at least half of all crimes that take place are never reported. Since most statutes allow recovery of victim-compensation funds only if there has been a showing that the victims cooperated with the police, it is anticipated that more crimes will be reported by those who could recover some of their losses. Moreover, the allowance for recovery to persons injured in an attempt to apprehend or to aid in the apprehension of an offender might well be expected to result in greater citizen participation in the prevention of crimes.

Concern for the plight of the innocent victim is implied in all victim-compensation statutes. There is an understandably inherent, if emotional, belief that while the state feeds, clothes, houses, and provides a defense for the rights of the criminal, for too long it has ignored the predicament of the innocent victim.[11] It is only fair, this argument continues, that if the rights of the guilty are safeguarded, so must be those of the victim.

Administration of existing compensation acts has been assigned to one of three types of auspices. Some statutes call for the administration of the program by specially created agencies or tribunals, while others provide for expanded jurisdiction into this area by existing agencies. In other places authority for determining awards of relief is delegated to the courts. Creation of a new agency is the favored option because it encourages the development of procedures specifically designed to carry out the purposes of the act and because it would be less likely than an existing agency to be burdened with improper attitudes at the outset: "The specialized agency . . . would start with the assumption that applicants are citizens with a right to government assistance."[12]

Persons who qualify for compensation usually fall within four categories: the victim, dependents of the victim if he has been killed, conscientious citizens killed or injured in the course of attempting to prevent a crime or assisting the police in preventing a crime, and the dependents of such citizens. All victim-compensation statutes specify that direct pecuniary losses must have occurred due to the personal injury or death of the protected party. This typically includes medical and rehabilitation expenses, funeral expenses, loss of income and support, and certain additional expenses listed in the legislation. Most statutes do not provide for the awarding of payment for pain and suffering or damage to property.

Most compensation plans place a ceiling on the amount of payment to be awarded. One such scheme includes the additional limitation of a minimum injury as a requirement for obtaining relief. The purpose underlying the setting of a maximum limit is to avoid both bankrupting available funds and the possibility of public criticism or rejection of such plans as being overgenerous. Minimum requirements are set by the need to balance victim needs against the costs in money and time required to process their claims. In order to prevent double compensation to a victim, most acts direct the tribunal, judge, or agency involved to deduct from this award any payments that the victim or his dependents receive from other public funds.[13] Methods of payment in compensation statutes vary from the award of one lump-sum payment without any provision for adjustments in accordance with changed circumstances, to awards that permit periodic, reviewable payments.

The types of crimes for which compensation will be awarded range from a general description of crime to a specific list of offenses. Some schemes exclude crimes that have occurred outside the state or country, actions that are not regarded as crimes by the relevant statute, and accidents involving a vehicle, unless such vehicle was intentionally used to cause death or injury.

Federal Legislation

The federal government's concern for the plight of the victim has been expressed in a bill approved by the House Judiciary Committee in June 1979, which would authorize a federal contribution of 25 percent of the cost of eligible state programs of compensation to innocent victims of violent criminal acts.[14] These funds would be used to compensate victims for economic losses resulting from violent crimes against them, including medical expenses, time lost from work, and costs of therapy and rehabilitation not otherwise covered by insurance. Strong support of the legislation has been forthcoming from law-enforcement and criminal-justice personnel and agencies, particularly since its provisions are designed to encourage victims to cooperate with police in securing the conviction of offenders.

Under the terms of the proposed act, the U.S. attorney general is responsible for the administration of the act, for prescribing rules necessary to carry it out, and for the approval or denial of state applications for federal aid.

The act provides for a committee on victims of crime, advisory to the attorney general with respect to administration of the act, and to compensation under the following conditions:

1. Individuals must have been injured as a result of a qualifying crime. Compensation also is to be paid to the surviving dependents of a victim who dies as a result of such a crime.
2. The victim who has assisted and cooperated with law-enforcement authorities in apprehending and investigating the crime is included in the state compensation scheme.

3. The state must require that all law-enforcement agencies and officials inform victims of qualifying crimes of the existence of, and procedure for applying for, compensation.
4. The state must have a law or rule claiming the victims' rights for damages against the offender.
5. The victim may not be required to seek or accept welfare benefits before applying for such compensation.
6. If the victim contributed to the infliction of death or injury, the claim may be reduced or denied.
7. The offender must be required to make restitution to the victim or the victim's surviving dependents.
8. Apprehension or prosecution of the offender may not be made a prerequisite for eligibility for relief.
9. A minimum charge must be assessed on an offender convicted of a qualifying crime, payable to the fund from which state compensation is made.
10. A convicted offender's debtors are required to place any funds owed to him in a fund for the benefit of the victim. The two classes of qualifying crimes set out in the act are any criminal, punishable act designated by the state as appropriate for compensation, and any state crime subject to exclusive federal jurisdiction.

Under the proposed act, the federal government will assume 25 percent of the sums paid to victims of criminal offenses designated as eligible for state compensation and 100 percent of the costs of state compensation to victims of crimes subject to exclusive federal jurisdiction. Computation of these costs is subject to certain limitations, which exclude administrative costs, awards for pain and suffering or property losses, and compensation awarded to individuals who fail to report the crime to law-enforcement agencies within seventy-two hours or to file a claim within one year. Deductions must also be made for payments covered by other sources, such as workmen's compensation or private insurance plans.

Compensation for lost earnings and support may not exceed $200 per week; the ceiling payment to an individual victim is $25,000. The prospect of federal funding is expected to encourage legislative action in the remaining states that have not yet enacted a victim-compensation program.

State Legislation

Twenty-four states currently provide some form of victim relief through individually run programs.[15] Each state has set up its own guidelines as to what parties may be compensated and how much relief they will provide.

For example, while Nevada limits relief to individuals injured in preventing crimes and to rape victims, Maryland additionally provides payments to individuals who have been injured in other types of violent crimes and to the survivors of homicide victims. All but three states place maximum limits on the total amount of compensation available to a claimant, ranging from $10,000 to $50,000. Maryland allows unlimited permanent disability on death benefits but has a $45,000 ceiling on other injuries. New York provides for unlimited funding of medical costs. Washington's compensation plan provides no limitations on funding, but the program is administered under, and is limited by, the workmen's compensation law.

Every state restricts or denies relief where, through negligence or provocation, the claimant is found to have contributed to the commission of the crime. Compensation to victims who are members of the families or households of the offenders is allowed only in California, Delaware, and Tennessee.

Procedural aspects of each plan also vary from state to state. Half of the existing programs are administered by independent compensation boards. Of the remaining plans, eight are handled by workmen's compensation or other state boards, and four require that the claimant directly petition the state court for relief. Sixteen states bar claims that do not meet a minimum damage requirement. Financial hardship or means tests are imposed in one-third of the programs.[16]

Just over half of the states subsidize their compensation programs through tax revenues. The remaining programs are funded either by taking a set percentage of all criminal fines levied or by adding an additional increment ranging from $3 to $21 on fines assessed against convicted persons. The theoretical drawback to the add-on fine is the lack of any direct connection between the victim and the offender who has been fined. The additional amount is set, whether or not the particular crime in question involved injury to an individual. Thus in Montana and Delaware, fines are assessed against traffic violators. The method has proved an effective means of relieving some or most of the tax burden of financing these programs.

In an effort to facilitate victim participation in their programs, the New York, Alaska, California, and Minnesota plans require that police officers inform all victims of violent crimes of compensatory provisions, as well as the procedure for applying for relief. Minnesota allows victims to sue a police officer who fails to furnish this information. Pennsylvania also requires the police to notify crime victims of their rights, including application for state compensation. This includes payment for medical bills, loss of earnings, and loss of support in death claims, up to a maximum of $25,000.[17]

Legislation in Other Common-Law Countries

New Zealand

In 1963 New Zealand became the first country to enact a centralized victim-compensation plan. Protection under its Criminal Injuries Compensation Act is limited to victims of one of the twenty-seven violent crimes scheduled in the act. Although questions of entitlement and the amount of entitlement are essentially decided by the three-member crimes compensation tribunal, a ceiling restricts the amount of compensation that may be awarded, limited to a maximum period of six years.

Beneficiaries of the act include victims of violent crimes and their dependents if the victims die but do not cover bystanders. The beneficiary is compensated for the cost of personal injuries reasonably and actually suffered as a result of an offense, such as medical bills and loss of wages. As with many criminal statutes later enacted in other countries, a criminal conviction or even a criminal proceeding need not have taken place in order for a victim to be eligible.

When the New Zealand act was first introduced, it was noted that the state's obligation did not arise from its failure to prevent crime but was based rather on the propriety of the state's acceptance of some responsibility for innocent victims in order to spread the loss thereby incurred.[18] By this reasoning, compensation in New Zealand is viewed not as a right adhering to the victim but as an act of grace on the part of the state.

Great Britain

The British compensation plan was not enacted by legislation but rather was based on an order of the government in Parliament in 1964. Under this order, the six-member Criminal Injuries Compensation Board was set up to review victim claims. Board decisions are subject to reversal in court upon a showing that the board has abused its discretion.

Although the British scheme does not specify a list of crimes for which a victim will be compensated, it specifically excludes offenses committed within the family setting, as well as motoring offenses. Both victims and their dependents, as well as bystanders who may have attempted to prevent, or aid in preventing, a crime are covered under the order.

Although conviction of an offender or the instigation of criminal proceedings is not required, the victim must fill out a detailed form in order to provide the board with the information required to investigate the claim fully. Awards were initially made on an ex-gratia basis, but recent court decisions have held them to be a matter of legal right.

Northern Ireland

The Northern Irish plan arose out of the Criminal Injuries to Persons (Compensation) Act of 1968. It provides that the county court in whose jurisdiction the offense has occurred shall determine the eligibility of the victim for damages, independent of the apprehension, residence, or acquittal of the offender.[19]

Compensation is paid for injury or death resulting from a violent crime or from aiding in the lawful arrest of a person engaged in such a crime. Determination of the amount of compensation is based on: reasonable expenses incurred as a consequence of the personal injury, loss of earnings, pain and suffering, and other proper and reasonable expenses. Injuries arising from traffic offenses are not compensated unless the vehicle had been used to perpetrate the injury, to facilitate the crime, or to escape following the commission of an offense, or to prevent an arrest. This Act adheres to the general view that compensation is an act of grace by the state and not a right of the victim.

Israel

Although Israel has not enacted a legislative scheme for compensation of victims, restitution can be granted in either civil proceedings or in the course of criminal proceedings. Relief through the civil court is often inadequate and impractical. Relief through the criminal process (aside from the necessity of apprehending the offender who can thereafter be ordered to make reparation) has its own limitations:

1. The court considering criminal cases does not willingly enter into the consideration of civil questions, the extent of the damage, causation, etc.
2. As a consequence of this it prefers to refer the victim to the civil court.
3. The above considerations apply particularly when there is a question of physical injury, which tends to raise complex questions of causation and assessment of damages. In cases of property damage the court reveals more elasticity, and greater use is made of this power.
4. The court views the compensation order as part of the punishment and thus takes into account the personal circumstances and financial position of the offender when considering whether to use this jurisdiction and make an order for compensation.
5. In principle the court uses this jurisdiction in simple cases and when the amount of damage is more or less clear.[20]

Canada

Eight of the ten Canadian provinces have since 1972 adopted crime-victim compensation plans.[21] Although the plans are by no means identical, they are quite similar in many of their essential features. All but Ontario's provide a specific list of the crimes covered by the scheme. Ontario's legislation states that compensation may be paid to any individual killed or personally injured by an act occurring or resulting from a crime of violence constituting an offense against the criminal code. However, offenses involving the use or operation of a motor vehicle, other than assault by means of a motor vehicle, are excluded.

Each province includes within its plan not only the victim of a crime but also those injured while assisting police in their duty, while attempting to arrest an offender themselves, or while trying to prevent the commission of an offense. Moreover, dependents of these parties or those responsible for their support are also eligible for benefits. The majority of claims in these matters, however, are raised by the victim.[22]

In order to receive compensation, a claimant must show that a crime has occurred and that injury or death resulted from it. Apprehension of the offender is not required. Although a conviction is not required under the Ontario plan, registration of a conviction is considered to be conclusive evidence that a crime has in fact been committed. Moreover, the victim need not prove his claim beyond a reasonable doubt, as is required in criminal cases. Hearsay is allowed in determining the existence of the required elements, thus allowing for fewer technical evidential obstacles than are present in most criminal trials.

Although the claimant is not bogged down with all the restraints found in the criminal process, awards will not be made unless a sufficient showing is made that a crime has actually been committed:

> In one Ontario case, *Wlasenko*, the applicant who was intoxicated at the time of the injury, claimed that he had been assaulted by the driver of the taxi in which he was taken home. The taxi driver denied this. His evidence was that the applicant had fallen on the sidewalk while getting out of the cab. Two other witnesses produced conflicting accounts of what occurred. The Board dismissed the application.[23]

Except in Quebec and Manitoba, compensation for pain and suffering is also allowed under these plans. In addition, medication, counsel fees, destroyed clothing, as well as loss of income, of the amenities of life, and of expectations of life are allowed in British Columbia.[24] Compensation may be awarded for reasonable expenses as well as for other pecuniary losses incurred by the victim, such as cost of maintenance of children born as a result of rape.

Double recovery is prohibited under these plans. Most jurisdictions provide for both a minimum and a maximum limit in their compensation plans. Although Ontario, Quebec, and Newfoundland have no minimum damage entry requirement, they have not experienced the deluge of trivial claims that had been predicted by proponents of the limit.

Due to public-policy considerations, claimants can be disqualified from receiving compensation if they refuse to notify or cooperate with the police. A claim will also be denied if the criminal act was committed by a member of the claimant's family or someone living with him.

A one-year limitation for the filing of claims is found in all provinces except Quebec, which limits it to six months. Some provinces, such as Ontario, exclude police and those covered by workmen's compensation from filing a claim. All statutes require that any behavior by the victim that might have contributed to his injury be taken into consideration when determining the right to an award.

Australia

Five of the six Australian states have adopted some form of victim compensation within recent years, although there is no national act.[25] Since the five state plans are largely identical, only the major differences between them will be described.

New South Wales: The New South Wales Criminal Injuries Act, adopted in 1967 as the first such legislation to be enacted in Australia, called for the criminal court to determine victim eligibility for compensation. When such an order is made, the victim must apply to the under secretary to receive the payment from the Consolidated Revenue Fund.[26] If the offender is acquitted or the criminal charge dismissed, the judge may certify how much compensation would have been awarded if the offender had been convicted.

Once the under secretary has received the application, he must provide the treasurer of the revenue fund with a statement of the amount of compensation awarded by the court, together with the amount that the victim has received from other public sources.[27] The treasurer may then authorize payment of the net sum.

Despite the absence of specific language in the statute, the government will make similar payments to victims of unidentified or unapprehended attackers after an investigation, including police reports. Only violent crimes specified in the act are covered by this plan. Loss or injury considered for compensation includes pregnancy, shock, and loss of wages. Such payments are viewed as acts of grace and not as rights.

Queensland: The Queensland compensation plan, modeled essentially after that of New South Wales, differs from it in two respects. The statute expressly provides that victims who have been injured in cases where the offender is not apprehended or convicted may nevertheless apply for compensation, described as ex-gratia payments. In instances where the victim has incurred injuries while assisting the police, the maximum ceiling for compensation may be exceeded.[28]

Victoria: The basic structure of the Victorian statute differs from that of other Australian states, resembling more that of New Zealand and Britain. Under the 1972 Victoria plan, a three-member crime compensation tribunal is authorized to review applications for compensation without being bound by the legal rules of evidence or procedure used in court proceedings. The tribunal may demand information from police and medical records and review such information in private hearings as it deems appropriate. Its decisions are not subject to administrative or judicial review.

Like most other compensation plans, a ceiling is imposed on the amount of compensation to be awarded to a victim, but this may be waived. The Victoria statute is limited to victims killed or injured in the course of a violent crime and to their descendants. Compensation is limited to victims of specific crimes that are punishable by imprisonment rather than by fine. Payments may not be awarded to victims who are relatives of the offender or members of the offender's household. A significant distinguishing feature of this Act is the provision that compensation is not ex gratia or discretionary but is a legal right.

Legislation in Europe

Austria

In September 1972, the Austrian government enacted a victim-compensation plan providing for aid to its citizens injured by any illegal and deliberate act punishable by more than six months' imprisonment.[29] In order to be eligible under this plan, the victim must have suffered bodily injury or damage to health, resulting in medical expenses or a reduction of earning capacity.

Aid from the state is not conditioned on the sentencing of an offender by the courts. Payments will be made if the offender is unknown, dead, or has acted in a state of unsound mind. The victim and his dependents are precluded from receiving aid if they are found to have incited or taken part in the crime or if they fail to contribute to the solving of the crime, the apprehension of the offender, or the assessment of their damage.

Applications for payments are submitted to the National Offices for the Disabled, though the final decision as to the amount of aid to be granted lies with the minister of social affairs.

Netherlands

In 1975 the Netherlands provided for payments from a national compensation fund to anyone who had sustained severe bodily injury as a result of a violent crime committed within the country.[30] Payments were made available to Dutch citizens as well as to resident aliens, to victims as well as relatives of victims who die as a result of criminal acts.

Although the term *crime of violence* is not defined in detail in the bill, acts committed without criminal intent, such as most traffic offenses, are excluded. Compensation is also denied if the victim is partially responsible for the commission of the crime. Unlike comparable plans in most other countries, compensation is permitted if the victim and the offender are part of the same household.

The amount of compensation is determined by what is considered just and fair under the circumstances. Both material economic injury and immaterial injury, such as pain and suffering or cosmetic damage, are taken into account in this determination if they result directly from the offense. The victim's finances are considered, and no compensation is allowed if the victim can bear the damages without excessive hardship. Both minimum threshold requirements and maximum limits payments are specified.

Requests for compensation must be made within six months after the crime was committed or the victim died. Contrary to most other national plans, the crime need not be reported to the police for compensation to be paid.

Iceland

Icelandic law provides a victim with two alternatives when the perpetrator of a crime is known: to claim monetary reparation during the trial of the defendant or to sue him in a court proceeding.[31] The survivors of the family of victims of a crime in which the offender is not identified may receive death benefits through the social security system.

Persons disabled to the extent of 50 percent or more may receive disablement benefits under the national sick benefit fund on a scale that increases with the degree of disablement. Injuries resulting from hit-and-run automobile accidents are compensated by private insurance companies.

Sweden

Since 1971, a new system of compensation for personal injuries to victims of crimes, administered by the Ministry of Justice, has been in operation.[32] In principle, compensation will be paid only where the social and economic circumstances are particularly distressing. The payments are to be ex gratia, and there is no guarantee that full adequate payment will be made. As with most programs in other countries, the Swedish plan sets a maximum limit to amounts that can be given to a claimant. In addition, the plan requires that a minimum amount of damage must have occurred before a claim will be considered.

Luxembourg

The Motor Vehicle Guarantee Fund provides that when accidents caused by an unidentified motor vehicle or when civil liability arising from the accident is not covered by the obligatory motor vehicle insurance law, the victim may press his claims for bodily injuries against the Common Fund.[33]

Turkey

Although the Turkish government provides means whereby the victim of a crime may receive reparation from an offender, there is no government victim-compensation scheme for crimes where the criminal is unidentified.[34]

Federal Republic of Germany

A law on compensation to victims of violent crimes provides benefits for victims and their surviving spouses and dependents.[35] The acts covered must be intentional, unlawful attacks against the person; they exclude offenses against property or those committed through negligence. The law covers German nationals and resident aliens. Compensation may be denied if the victim is found to have contributed to the commission of the crime, if the victim fails to cooperate with the police, or if it would appear inequitable to award payments.

Funds are drawn from the general tax revenue of the government. Benefits of the system are determined by the rates and provisions that cover benefits to war victims (that is, regardless of existing financial need). The war victims' benefits agencies throughout the country receive the claims and determine the benefit payments to be made. These include costs of medical treatment and such measures as vocational rehabilitation. Any economic damages resulting from injury to the victim, such as incapacity to pursue a former trade or profession, will be compensated at rates comparable to those for industrial injury. Seriously disabled victims, whose earning capacity is reduced by 50 percent or more, as well as their dependents, may be paid a pension. No separate compensation for pain and suffering is allowed.

France

Under a plan of victim compensation recently proposed in France, victims of an indictable offense in which the perpetrator is unknown or insolvent will be entitled to benefits from the government.[36] The victim must have no other means of adequate compensation, such as industrial accident or social security coverage. Moreover, the victim's financial status will be taken into account in determining both eligibility and amount of payments. The plan will cover only personal injuries that result in death, permanent disability, or injuries resulting in total incapacity. Payments will be limited or denied if the victim cohabits with or is closely related to the offender or is found to have contributed to the crime.

A board composed of three judges attached to each appellate court will administer the plan, investigate claims, and decide compensation. The board is not required to wait for the verdict of the criminal court before it makes its determination of a case.

Part III
Doing Justice:
Representative Programs

Arbitration

The strength of arbitration for the community court concept is that while its results are coercively imposed upon the participants, they themselves have usually chosen by a private process of negotiation, the manner and the means by which the decision will be reached.[1]

Arbitration has a long and respected history as an instrument for the resolution of disputes. Criminal justice is, in fact, a late arrival as an area for the application of arbitration procedures. Over the years, numerous institutions and agencies have discovered arbitration to be an effective means of settling a wide range of disputes. Recent discussions of the process further highlight its versatility. Various authors have proposed that it be applied in such situations as family disputes, consumer grievances, medical malpractice claims, landlord-tenant conflicts, uncomplicated civil disputes, automobile accidents, attorney-client disagreements over fees, and small-claims courts. The use of arbitration on a large scale originated in the field of labor; its adoption for this purpose dates back to 1913, when the Department of Labor was established by the U.S. government.

The basic premise of conciliation and arbitration as used in labor disputes is set forth in the National Labor Relations Act of 1936 (Wagner Act), which states that private economic rights are not to be exercised in such a way as to interfere with the larger public interests of society as a whole. Arbitration has been an invaluable tool in bringing labor and management to accords that serve the public interest. In essence, the process consists of the submission of conflicts to one or more neutral parties who conduct hearings on the matters and hand down a judgment that is binding on the parties involved. The process can be either voluntary or compulsory, with the former being the predominant variety. Compulsory arbitration is limited to extreme cases, such as those involving essential unions like police and firefighters. This does not mean, however, that arbitration becomes a substitute for collective bargaining. On the contrary, arbitration constitutes an extension of that bargaining process, often serving as the final phase.

Three basic types of arbitration are the most common: permanent arbitration under an appointed arbiter, tripartite arbitration, and ad hoc arbitration. In permanent arbitration, one individual agreed upon by the parties acts as arbiter for all disputes arising out of their relationship. There are certain obvious advantages to this approach, particularly in the field of labor relations. The permanent arbiter will be familiar with the terms of the contractual agreement between the parties, as well as with the history of disputes and judgments arising from it. This assures a continuity to the terms of the initial accord. Sometimes this process is utilized with three permanent arbiters rather than one, each of whom is called upon to resolve disputes on a rotating basis.

Under tripartite procedures, both disputants select a representative to participate in the arbitration process, and these persons choose a neutral chairperson to preside. The three arbitrators then sit as a panel and arrive at dispositions by majority vote. Proponents of this method point to its ability to bring out each party's viewpoint in the course of deliberations. When the two initial representatives are so far apart that they cannot agree on a neutral chairperson, collective-bargaining agreements usually provide that some designated outside agency, such as the Federal Mediation and Conciliation Service or the American Arbitration Association, name the chairperson.

Ad hoc arbitration proceeds on a case-by-case basis, seeking a neutral arbitrator according to the features of particular disputes. When a neutral party cannot be found within some specified period of time, an agency with an arbitrators' roster will be asked to appoint someone. Advocates of ad hoc arbitration argue that it is more realistic than other methods because all negotiations produce some lingering bad feelings that most likely will be directed toward the arbiters considered responsible for unpopular provisions. When arbitrators are selected on an ad hoc basis, it is argued, this problem is avoided and all negotiations begin with a clean slate.

Regardless of the method chosen, the arbitration process is quite simple. A problem is presented, with each disputant stating its view of the issue and its suggestions for a resolution. Individual arbiters or an arbitration panel then conduct discussions and raise questions in an effort to clarify the situation. When all of the relevant material has been heard, the arbitrators hand down a decision, which must be observed by the disputing parties. The legality of such binding was clearly established in 1925 with the passage of the United States Arbitration Act.

Arbitration for Community Disputes

There have been many calls for expanding the use of arbitration as an alternative means of conflict resolution in community settings. Mund is one of those who has made a case for it:

> The positive side of community arbitration far outweighs any drawbacks. It is an institution that should just be there, for those who need it. It is inexpensive to organize and run. It will not compete with the currently established arbitration institutions, will not take clients away from lawyers

or controvert the public policy towards out-of-court settlements. It will give a new class of plaintiffs a forum and operate to lessen the tensions constantly created in a person who must deal with the bureaucracy of the society in which he lives.[2]

In a sense, this is neither new nor radical, for there have long been procedures similar to arbitration that have performed these functions. A good illustration can be found in university courts or disciplinary panels. Such campus courts are generally governed by the regulations of the university at large, congruent with the laws of the state in which it is located. These tribunals exist primarily for the purposes of controlling damage to university property and preventing interference with or obstruction of the educational process. Students or faculty members found in violation of such provisions typically are liable to three disciplinary actions: warning, suspension or expulsion, or termination of employment.

In cases like these, students or faculty members may or may not also face criminal charges after the university sanctions. The campus courts they face usually consist of representatives of students, faculty, and administration. The panels hear testimony, weigh evidence, render verdicts on guilt or innocence, and set penalties. Appeal to the head of the university is generally allowed.

Many due-process rights are respected in university court actions, including access to counsel, notice of charges, hearing before an impartial body, cross-examination of witnesses, the privilege of remaining silent, and the right to receive a written decision.[3] Absent from such protections are the guarantee against double jeopardy and the right to be judged solely by one's peers.

Other serious deficiencies include the nonconstructive nature of the sanctions imposed. Expulsion, for example, eliminates these students as sources of future disruption but does not satisfy the full requirements of community justice.

Community arbitration carries the process much further and displays a number of distinctive features such as have been described by two experienced community arbitrators:

(a) Arbiters are not "neutral," because they consciously advocate a process of negotiation and compromise to forestall other responses, especially the violent.
(b) Community arbitration typically occurs in a situation where rights, duties and expectations must be defined gradually.
(c) The opinions of arbiters are not decisive in the solution of community conflicts, because the parties involved must themselves formulate a solution they can live with.

(d) Arbitrators in community contexts play many roles: as legitimizers, resource expanders, facilitators, and trainers.[4]

Community arbitrators become legitimizers when they act to establish the right of a group to participate in negotiations. As resource expanders, arbitrators work to redefine the situation so that they are not perceived as zero-sum or winner-take-all games. In the capacity of facilitators, arbitrators focus on effective communications by interpreting the claims of each party to the other and by working to keep the discussion moving. Finally, in the role of trainers, community arbitrators teach the parties about the basics of negotiation, formulation of specific demands, development of negotiation strategies, interpretation of the maneuvers of the other side.[5]

Rochester 4-A Program

Among the most significant community arbitration efforts is the 4-A initiative in Rochester, New York, whose name derives from the phrase "arbitration as an alternative" to the criminal courts.[6] The program began in 1973 under the auspices of the American Arbitration Association. In 1979 the project struck out on its own and currently is known as the Center for Dispute Settlement, a not-for-profit corporation. To introduce the 4-A initiative, a representative case history is here related.

A landlord filed a criminal complaint of assault against one of his tenants, alleging that she had kicked him in the knee during an argument over a loud stereo late one night. The complaint was referred to the arbitration program, to which both disputants agreed. At the hearing it became apparent that the problem extended beyond the precipitating incident to include the relationship between the parties, which had been steadily deteriorating. The tenant, a single parent on welfare, was three weeks delinquent in her rent. In a recent and related incident she had asked the landlord to certify her tenancy to meet the requirements of the welfare agency. He had refused to do so, and as a result, the department of social services had not sent her the rent money, and she therefore could not pay the rent.

These problems gradually emerged in an emotional two hour meeting. At length, a solution was found. The tenant reported that she had received emergency welfare money on the day of the hearing and was willing to pay one-half of the delinquent rent. The landlord accepted the offer. Since both parties wanted to terminate the tenancy, a date was set for the tenant to move out. The adversaries worked this resolution out on their own; the arbitrator simply formalized matters by ordering them to live up to their bargain. All criminal charges were dropped, and no further demands made on the resources of the justice system.[7]

This case illustrates the underlying concept of the 4-A initiative: to convert criminal matters into civil proceedings and to resolve them speedily in a nonadversarial setting. Such a procedure may appear to evade the difficulties posed by minor crimes, but the move to a civil procedure is an essential first step to deal with fundamental causes of conflict rather than with superficial symptoms or external manifestations. This comes across most clearly when one considers that most 4-A cases would be handled in the regular courts, with continuances, dismissals, defaults, and warnings, none of them truly effective responses to the conditions that led to the complaint or a deterrent against repetition of the incidents.

The 4-A procedure begins when a complaint is filed with the courts by an alleged victim of a crime, an action which would normally lead to the issuance of a warrant. But if the alleged offense is within a range of misdemeanors and involves parties who have an ongoing relationship, the clerk of court may suggest informal resolution. Should this prove agreeable, the complaining party will complete a form indicating a willingness to enter the program. All such requests are reviewed subsequently by the district attorney's office. Notice is given the accused party at this time that if he will participate in the 4-A hearing, the original complaint will be dropped. Refusal to participate leaves open the possibility of future prosecution. When consent has been secured from both parties, a hearing is scheduled, generally within a couple of weeks.[8]

This referral process is different from that used in pretrial diversion. Diversion is a method whereby accused individuals consent to certain conditions, in exchange for which they are allowed to remain in the community. When the conditions have been completely fulfilled, the original charges are dropped, and a criminal record is avoided. Diversion thus typically involves some admission of guilt on the part of the accused. Arbitration is quite different; it is concerned with compromise and settlement rather than guilt or innocence. Further, diversion may deal with either minor or major offenses, while arbitration has generally been limited to minor cases.

When the disputants appear at the hearing, they are informed of the 4-A procedure's combined use of mediation and arbitration. Mediation is employed first in an effort to allow the parties to fashion their own solution; arbitration is brought in to settle the matter when disputants have not been able to work it out themselves. Thus the initial emphasis is on negotiation and compromise rather than conflict. The 4-A arbitrators begin by seeking to identify the basic needs and issues involved in the dispute, which must be resolved if the parties are to continue their relationship. Once these matters have been clarified, the facilitator tries to establish priorities among the demands of both sides in order to make it possible to agree on trade-offs. Throughout the process, every effort is made to establish or reestablish some minimum of trust between the disputants so as to reduce the likelihood of future problems.

The presence of an authoritative arbiter seems to answer the need for definitive results, especially since the decisions of this person immediately become enforceable. Arbitration thus resembles the process of adjudication that takes place in the courts, but as used in the 4-A program, it is employed only in a supplementary way, to complement and build upon the negotiations of the parties themselves, a reversal of the dynamics of the official system of justice.[9]

The key to the program's success lies in the high quality of staff and volunteer mediator-arbitrators. Some fifty persons make up the available pool of volunteers. Some are lawyers, business people, or teachers, while others are citizens involved in community issues. Some hold advanced degrees, while others are high school graduates. Blacks and whites as well as Hispanics are represented, as are men and women, young and old. Most have close ties to the neighborhoods where disputes originate and a sincere commitment to the nonviolent settlement of conflict. Before being assigned to cases, volunteers undergo an extensive program of training, which includes an introduction to relevant law and the rules of evidence, as well as the dynamics of negotiation.

Such diversity of personnel has opened a range of options and provided a useful flexibility. Some hearings are conducted entirely in Spanish by a Hispanic panelist, thus obviating the need for slow and cumbersome translations. Other hearings have involved deaf mutes, and so a volunteer with professional training in dealing with this condition was chosen to preside, an option seldom available in the courts.

As a result of its success, the center has achieved a high level of acceptance by the local community. It has been invited to provide third-party services in prison disputes, school desegregation conflicts, and controversies involving public employees. Its assistance has also been sought in the design of procedures for dealing with consumer complaints, disputes between tenants and public-housing authorities, and other matters.[10]

Statistics from the first two years of the program's operation give some indication of its effectiveness. Over a thousand referrals were sent to the center, and hearings were held for approximately one-third of them. Some 40 percent of the cases had to be closed because of the unwillingness of one party to submit to arbitration. Such figures may seem to be rather unspectacular, but it is important to note that only a handful of the original thousand cases returned to the criminal-justice system for further processing. Thus, if both direct and indirect effects are considered, the center may be said to have played a very important role in the screening of several hundred cases per year out of the regular system. If the preventive value of the successful hearings is also figured in, the benefits of the 4-A initiative seem impressive indeed.[11]

In the course of the past several years, the 4-A concept has gradually spread across the country, largely as a result of the efforts of the National Center for Dispute Settlement of the American Arbitration Association. At present there are 4-A projects in Philadelphia, the New York City area, northeastern Ohio around Cleveland and Akron, and San Francisco. As the model has spread, some distinctive variants have developed.

In San Francisco, for example, two-person teams rather than single mediator-arbitrators are utilized. One of the volunteers on such panels is an experienced arbitrator-mediator, while the other is a recently trained lay person with no previous background in arbitration. Both members are appointed by the American Arbitration Association Disputes Panel. As in Rochester, the volunteers seek a mediated solution whenever possible and hand down an award where mediation fails. Some twenty-five persons, comprising a representative cross-section of the community, have been serving as arbitrators.

The San Francisco program has reported that of the first one hundred cases processed, almost half (42 percent) had a positive outcome. The others (54 percent) had no formal action taken. Among the positive group, about half submitted to mediation-arbitration, and the rest settled matters among themselves. Very few of the cases referred to the program returned to the criminal-justice system. Some three-fourths of the clients interviewed in the study stated that the program had been helpful in resolving their problems and that the great majority of the negotiated awards were working well.

The San Francisco program stands up well when assessed in terms of financial costs and benefits. The total expenditure for the pilot period was $71 per case referred and $178 for each case resolved through mediation-arbitration. This compares quite well with the court-cost figures for the Los Angeles district attorney's office (the only ones available), which list the cost of processing a misdemeanor at $400. Arbitration, therefore, has produced a 50 percent savings in the 4-A cases for the taxpayers of California. In the current climate of fiscal restraint, these figures provide a strong argument for adoption of the model elsewhere.[12]

Arbitration of Consumer Disputes

Proponents of consumer justice assert that in the current state of affairs consumers cannot assert, or compel resolution of their grievances, as equals with those from whom they buy.[13] Among the most important reasons cited is unequal knowledge or familiarity with the technical details of sales transactions, which may be compounded by disparities in educational background.[14] A related difficulty is documentation. Consumers typically do not retain the essential records, while merchants do, largely as a result of government regulation. It is hardly surprising, therefore, that in the face of perceived injustice the only action that most consumers take is "self-help in the form of refusing to pay amounts which they do not believe are justly due."[15]

Such issues are more fully appreciated when specific mechanisms of redress are considered. Among the most important, in theory, are small-claims courts where consumers can seek satisfaction within a setting of simplified procedures. In practice, despite the suspension of technical rules of evidence and the elimination of attorneys, small-claims courts have generally not measured up to the task. On the contrary, many of these courts have become collection mills where merchants obtain default judgments against consumers.[16] Dramatic evidence of the problem was provided by one California study that found that business and government initiated some 60 percent of all small-claims actions and that individuals rather than businesses were defendants about 80 percent of the time.[17] Among contributing factors cited in this connection are the inaccessibility of small-claims courts and the widespread ignorance of the courts among consumers.

Some of the problems involved in resort to the small-claims court are illustrated by the following incident related to the authors:

> My one and only court experience occurred a few years ago, as a result of a dispute over a security deposit on our apartment. My wife and I had decided to move and gave our landlord (who was also our next-door neighbor) the usual sixty-day notice. He instructed us to apply one-half of our security deposit to the final rent payment and agreed to return the balance to us. Several months later we wrote our former landlord, who told us that he had lost the building and referred us to the new owners. They, in turn, replied that responsibility for the deposit rested with the previous owner, who failed to respond to our letters.

> A tenants' rights group referred us to the small-claims court of the housing court where we could sue for double damages. No one at the court offered any help in filing my complaint or filling out the necessary forms. I later learned that the staff must limit themselves to answering questions directed to them.

> Four months later—now nearly nine months after we had moved—I appeared for the court hearing. My opponent failed to appear, and I was awarded double damages in a default judgment. My wife and I had won, or so we thought.

> A few weeks later I received formal notification of the decision and on the same day, a call from my former landlord's lawyer, who stated that a fire in his office had prevented him from attending. A motion for a new hearing was filed and granted, and a month later I was back in court.

> The second hearing was similar to the first. The lawyer for my opponent (who did not appear) argued that his client did not have to pay because he no longer owned the building. The judge reaffirmed the original decision.

It seemed that we had won again, but on the way out, the lawyer informed me that an appeal would be filed, and that I would not hear anything for some time.

After nine months with no word from any one connected with the case we received a notice that a jury trial would be held in about six weeks. Two nights before the scheduled trial my ex-landlord called to say he would meet me on the following day and pay the money owed. In return, I agreed to withdraw charges.

The most memorable moment in the case occurred over coffee when my former landlord gave me an inside view of the workings of the courts. He assured me that there was nothing personal about the dispute, that his problem was that he had spent the security deposits on gambling. By strategic use of the courts, however, he knew he could buy time—at least two years: "You never show up the first time. The second time, you appeal. If you lose, you ask for a jury trial, and that takes another year. By then most people either move or give up." There had been, he confessed, no fire in his lawyer's office. "But you're paying me *double damages*," I stammered. "Look," he replied, "that's how the game is played. There were twelve tenants in that building; so far, you're the only one who has gotten any money."

Similar difficulties have been identified in another potential mechanism of redress—administrative agencies dealing in consumer affairs. At the national level, the Federal Trade Commission can issue cease-and-desist orders upon discovery of fraudulent practices. But such monitoring powers have little impact on the problems of individual consumers, especially since long periods of time typically elapse between the filing of an initial complaint and the issuing of a cease-and-desist order by the agency.[18] Even if such delays could be eliminated, the FTC is prohibited by statute from involvement in many types of consumer grievances.

Similar obstacles are encountered with consumer fraud bureaus in individual states. The major sanction available to most of these agencies is an injunction proceeding brought by a state attorney general against a particular merchant and a particular fraudulent practice.[19] This can hardly be viewed as a serious deterrent, however, since unscrupulous merchants would not mind having to provide an occasional refund if their improper practices could be continued against the vast majority of customers. Such an outcome is virtually assured by the small staffs and limited resources of the fraud bureaus. Even the compulsory nature of the injunction approach can be viewed as a serious drawback, for it produces a form of justice in which merchants may pay damages when they sincerely believe they have done nothing wrong.[20]

Remedies have sometimes been available to consumers by means of informal procedures created by suppliers. The majority of such actions have been provided under the auspices of the Better Business Bureau, which adopted for this purpose the arbitration rules of the American Arbitration Association's Center for Dispute Settlement.[21] The bureau will arbitrate claims in three types of situation: when a business, in agreement with the bureau, has precommitted itself to arbitration of consumer-related disputes; when both disputants, by contract, have precommitted disputes to bureau arbitration; or when both parties submit the matter to Better Business Bureau arbitration at the time it arises. There are further limitations on the types of claims that may be submitted to arbitration. Disputes involving warranties, defective goods or services, misrepresentation, billing errors, or late deliveries are arbitrable; claims of personal injury, intentional torts, and criminal violation (such as criminal fraud) are not.[22]

Such procedures have been successful in resolving the difficulties of many consumers, but they have been subject to criticism on a variety of grounds. First, because of their voluntary nature, supplier-created procedures cannot enforce the rights of consumers when firms are intransigent or wholly uncooperative. Second, such resolutions take place in private, without written records of arbitration sessions, a procedure that makes it much more difficult for consumers to challenge an award that they consider unsatisfactory, especially in the face of limited judicial review. At the same time, the nonreporting of consumer arbitration eliminates the potential educational benefits and the possible deterrent effect that the procedures might offer. Finally, despite recent modifications, arbitration of disputes in supplier-created forums has typically followed the model developed for commercial disagreements, which is arguably inappropriate for consumer-related matters.[23]

New Proposals for Consumer Justice

A variety of commentators have put forward proposals for fresh initiatives in consumer justice, and despite differences, there are some broad areas of agreement. At the most general level, it has been suggested that a consumer arbitration board or other dispute resolution forum have the following characteristics.

(1) The board must be accessible to consumers in their own communities, ideally, in the same area where the transaction took place.
(2) Membership of the board should be drawn from unimpeachable sources, and consumers have a role in their selection.
(3) The procedures of the board must remain simple and informal.
(4) Some financing method must be worked out to spread the cost throughout the consuming public and business community.

(5) The board's decisions must be capable of enforcement, through the pressure of publicity as well as through recourse to the courts.
(6) The availability of the board must be well publicized.[24]

Implied in this listing is the element of speed, certainly a great virtue for consumers. The ability of arbitration to resolve disputes more rapidly than conventional procedures has been demonstrated in various settings. In Washington State, arbitration was found to clear up grievances six times as quickly as the superior court, with elapsed time averaging only sixty days as opposed to one year.[25]

Financing has raised many issues among proponents of consumer justice, and much remains to be done in this area. It has been suggested, for example, that merchants', trade, or industry associations, as well as consumer organizations, subsidize the operation of dispute-resolution bodies.[26] Under another plan, individual corporations absorb the cost but are allowed to pass it along to customers. It has also been proposed that consumer forums might achieve economy by employing volunteer arbitrators in a "night court" setting, with a panel of arbitrators available to resolve disputes on a regular basis and the use of office space whose rent had already been covered.[27]

Why should merchants agree to participate in such activities, inasmuch as the emphasis of the discussion has been on justice for consumers? The answer is that such dispute resolution is in their own best interests. The willingness of businesses to submit grievances to arbitration can enhance their standing with the general public, and more importantly, can reduce the amount of litigation that firms engage in, leading to substantial savings of both time and money. For example, home remodelers in Cleveland who submitted consumer disputes to arbitration reported a 60 percent decline in litigation after an experimental period of two years.[28] Other reasons for the participation of businesses in arbitration include competitive pressure and statutory requirement. Eventually firms may be legally obliged to submit to arbitration any dispute that consumers wish to handle in this manner, and consumers may be required to exhaust such remedies before appealing to the regular courts.

Magnuson-Moss Warranty Act of 1975

The Magnuson-Moss Warranty Act of 1975 was a major development in the field.[29] This legislation regulates goods sold under a written warranty in transactions affecting interstate commerce. One of its prime goals is to encourage warrantors to establish mechanisms voluntarily for the resolution of consumer disputes. Participating merchants can set up their own programs or utilize existing arbitration organizations. Once established, such mechanisms are subject to regulation by the FTC. Among the basic responsibilities adopted by the merchants is the disclosure, clearly and conspicuously on the face of the warranty, of a statement of how consumers may submit a complaint to the dispute-resolution mechanism.

A key innovation in the Magnuson-Moss program is the nonbinding nature of arbitration, which is termed "advisory." The benefit of this provision is that dissatisfied parties can obtain broader judicial review of awards than they can under binding procedures. At the same time, however, the change does not mean that arbitration can be taken lightly by the parties, because the act provides that the courts will automatically adopt the arbitration awards as their own, except in cases where losing parties can provide persuasive grounds for other courses of action. Such an arrangement provides the benefits of both flexibility and finality.

Consumer advocates have found much to praise in the Magnuson-Moss law. By requiring the explicit disclosures on warranties, the statute promotes the causes of consumer education and consumer justice. The limit of forty days between initiation and completion of procedures ensures the speedy resolution of grievances. It places the cost on the shoulders of participating businesses and thus removes a fundamental obstacle from the path of the party less equipped to deal with it. Finally, by allowing public access to the records, the law protects and enhances the people's right to know.[30]

Some difficulties with the statute have arisen. Criticism, for example, has been voiced over the movement to written submissions in the arbitration in place of standard oral proceedings, which may place consumers at some disadvantage. The question has also been raised whether the statute provides sufficient incentive for the participation of businesses.[31] As a result, various tax breaks for participating firms have been discussed.[32] Despite such complications, the Magnuson-Moss legislation constitutes an important step toward improved justice for consumers, in which arbitration is a key ingredient.

Arbitration for Juveniles

With the growth of alternatives to traditional court proceedings in criminal cases, it was inevitable that arbitration would be applied to children who come before the juvenile court. The first such juvenile arbitration plan to be reported, the Community Arbitration Project, was established in 1976 in Anne Arundel County, Maryland. Originally funded by federal sources, this plan has won the "exemplary project" label of the National Institute of Law Enforcement and Criminal Justice for excellence.[33]

Juveniles charged with misdemeanors receive a citation rather than a summons from the police at the time of arrest or at home. No juvenile so charged is taken to the police station. The citation names the offense with which the juvenile is charged and notifies him of the date, seven days later, when he is to appear for an arbitration hearing. A copy of the citation also goes to the victim, if known; another, attached to the police report, is forwarded to the County Department of Juvenile Services, where the offense is checked against a list of those eligible for arbitration. If not eligible, the charges are either dropped (for insufficient evidence or lack of jurisdiction) or may be turned over to the state's attorney for formal prosecution or further investigation.

The arbitration hearing takes place in a courtroom-like setting. In attendance are the juvenile, parents, and, if he or she desires to be, the victim. The juvenile is informed of the right to counsel, who will be present at the hearing. The arbitrator, an attorney with juvenile-court experience, also informs the juvenile that if he prefers to deny the charges, the case can be heard in the regular court or be referred to the state's attorney for formal processing. If the juvenile and the parents agree to the informal hearing, the arbitrator reads aloud the police report of the incident, and the victim is given an opportunity to respond. Because the juvenile has agreed to participate in the proceedings up to this point, an admission of guilt is usually forthcoming.

The arbitrator explains to the youth the social as well as the legal implications of the act, stressing the harm done to the victim, because restitution to the person harmed is an integral part of whatever terms are to be imposed. For example, in a rock-throwing incident that resulted in a broken window that cost twenty-five dollars to replace, the juvenile was assigned to twenty hours of community service and ordered to pay restitution at the rate of two dollars a week for thirteen weeks. In this instance, the juvenile elected, from a range of choices, to perform as his community service landscape maintenance work at the public library. For the next ninety days the case remained open, pending satisfactory completion of the assignment, after which it was reviewed by the project staff and closed.

Prompt processing of cases within seven days after the charge has been filed helps to reduce the backlog of the court and at the same time holds the youth responsible while the incident is still fresh. By conducting the hearing in a courtroom setting, the seriousness of the charges is emphasized to the youthful defendant. Most important of all, the victim, normally excluded from any significant role in a court hearing, has an opportunity to confront directly the one who has offended and to have his comments solicited and considered, as well as having a voice in the final determination of what should be done with the offender.

Due-process rights of the defendants are safeguarded by the assurance of the right to counsel, through the strictly voluntary nature of the defendant's participation in the proceedings and by the right of the defendant at any point to request that the case be referred for formal processing. The requirement that arbitrators be trained attorneys ensures that the alleged offense under consideration meets the standard of legal sufficiency. All proceedings are confidential.

The opportunity provided for community service helps youths to accept responsiblity for their behavior and to make some redress for the harm they have done. In addition to community service and restitution to the victim, opportunities are provided for counseling, special educational and vocational training, and assignment to special programs such as motorcycle safety.

In the first two years of operation, the project received over forty-two hundred youth cases, nearly half of them adjusted informally. Less than 10 percent were referred to the state's attorney; 20 percent were denied for insufficient evidence and 20 percent closed with a warning. Of those committed to community service, 85 percent successfully completed their assignments within the prescribed ninety-day period; less than 5 percent were reported to have failed. "Most importantly," concludes the report, "CAP clients demonstrate significantly lower rates of repeat offenses than comparable youth who were processed traditionally—4.5% lower recidivism rate and 37% fewer re-arrests per client within one year after intake/arbitration."[34] Ninety percent of the costs of the program go for salaries of the eight staff members.

Further Applications of Arbitration

Prisons

Arbitration has been discussed and explored experimentally in a variety of other contexts. Among the most urgent is the area of inmate grievances, particularly in maximum-security correctional facilities. The past year alone has seen a tragic riot in New Mexico, which involved great loss of life, a minor incident in a prison in Indiana, and the preventive lockdown of a facility in Maine that was thought to be on the point of erupting. In view of the chronic overcrowding and substandard conditions in prisons across the country, similar incidents can be expected at any time. Against this background, the importance of internal dispute resolution channels should be readily apparent. Even without the constant danger of violence, there would be good reason to consider establishing new forms of dispute resolution for inmates because the regular courts are clogged to the point where they cannot always respond promptly or effectively to the needs, however pressing these might be.

Prison inmates themselves have done much to clog the courts in recent years, thereby exacerbating their own difficulties. As Leonard Orland has vividly recounted, in the turbulence of the late 1960s and the early 1970s, "prisoners developed an incredible legal sensitivity—a virtual obsession with 'the law' and with any real or potential violation of prisoners' rights."[35] The practical consequences on the already overburdened legal system can be imagined. Chief Justice Burger, in his efforts to improve judicial administration, has provided a brief case history that captures the prevailing situation. One prisoner, he relates, made the following demands upon the system: the primary attention of one district judge twice, that of three circuit judges on appeal, and numerous others indirectly, all in the interest of recovering seven packages of cigarettes that he alleged were taken improperly by a guard.

It is not surprising, therefore, that alternative means of resolving grievances have been spreading throughout correctional facilities. Mediation has been the preferred course, but arbitration has also been drawn upon to a significant extent. The first inmate grievance was formally submitted to arbitration in Concord, Massachusetts, in the spring of 1973. Since that time, other states have quickly followed, beginning with New York, Virginia, and Florida. Currently most states have passed legislation making it possible to mediate or arbitrate inmate grievances. The great virtue of arbitration in these settings is that it provides a quick and definitive resolution of problems when disputing parties have been unable to work out remedies on their own. This is particularly important in total institution contexts like prisons, where there are such harsh and enduring disparities of power that inmate groups have few resources to barter away by compromise.

Proponents of correctional arbitration point to tangible benefits. The resolution of grievances has led to important policy changes and clarifications, especially in situations where an arbitration award has "outlined the framework of a suggested new policy and recommended its adoption on a 'pilot' basis."[36] At the same time, research has indicated the ability of arbitration to divert cases from the courts. A recent arbitration initiative at Attica and Auburn, New York, for example, kept some 313 justifiable grievances out of the system, an average of nearly one each day. In the wake of such encouraging results, similar efforts will surely be forthcoming in the very near future.[37]

Medical Malpractice

Arbitration has proven to be a useful alternative to litigation when dealing with allegations of medical malpractice. In such contexts, two distinct but related techniques have been developed. The first is known as a review panel; it consists of a small group of physicians who listen to complaints and advise prospective defendants whether to settle or contest the matter in court. The second mechanism, a joint screening panel, includes lawyers in addition to physicians. In either case, when the preponderance of the evidence appears to be on the side of the patient, the panel agrees to make available expert witnesses, should the matter proceed to court. Consumers or patients are thus offered a double benefit: the relatively swift and inexpensive resolution of problems, plus the assistance of a powerful ally in subsequent litigation.[38]

The tangible benefits of medical-malpractice arbitration have been documented in recent research that compared two groups of southern California hospitals, one using arbitration procedures and the other employing traditional civil litigation. Over the course of five years, members of the Southern California Arbitration Project resolved malpractice claims 22 percent faster than their more litigious counterparts, while saving some 40 percent on total settlements and 20 percent on defense costs as compared with the baseline period of the five years preceding arbitration. The arbitration initiative also provided an unforeseen benefit: a slower rate of increase of malpractice claims than that experienced by the control group. Such results indicate that arbitration discourages frivolous or non-meritorious claims, perhaps as a by-product of eliminating emotional appeals to civil juries, ("juryatrics"), which have been known to produce astronomical awards.[39]

Landlord-Tenant Conflicts

A further recent example of how arbitration can be applied is in the area of landlord-tenant conflicts, a subject that is steadily gaining in significance due to the serious shortage of housing in the nation. The new procedures have been the logical outcome of the self-help remedies approved for tenants over the past decade by courts and legislatures. As the bargaining power of tenants has increased, especially through the permissible withholding of rent pending improvements in the dwelling, landlords have been more amenable to informal settlement.[40] That there is ample scope for such alternative methods of dispute resolution is evidenced by the brief history of neighborhood justice centers.

In Los Angeles, for example, 22 percent of cases in the first year of operation involved landlord-tenant complaints, and in Atlanta and Kansas City, Missouri, the figures were 17.5 percent and 11.5 percent, respectively.[41] Arbitration in such contexts could be provided through a clause in rental

agreements stipulating that disputes will be handled informally before proceeding to litigation.

Family Relations

Finally, arbitration is used in family relations, a context unsurpassed in the
informal resolution of conflict. The American Arbitration Association has
played a very important role in this development, reflected in its recent
publication of rules and procedures designed for family services in four
separate but closely related applications of informal dispute resolution:
conciliation, designed to assist couples in working out problems with a view
to their staying together; mediation, designed to assist separating parties in
arriving at the terms of an amicable settlement; reference to a referee for
binding arbitration of issues on which the parties cannot agree; and arbitration of disputes arising out of separation agreements.[42]

The new settlement techniques stand in sharp contrast to older adversarial procedures between the two attorneys for the estranged family
members, methods that did little to enhance communication between the
parties. On the contrary, they fostered a dependency upon professional
representatives, which tended to produce a low personal commitment to the
provisions of the final agreement. Where arbitration and mediation are
used, a very different, nonthreatening environment is created, which
facilitates communication on essential issues and gives the parties a more
direct stake in the outcome as complete participants.[43]

In such contexts, the presence of children has raised interesting and important questions, which may lead to modifications of traditional arbitration procedures. Ordinarily under the rules of arbitration, the interests of
an outside or third party are irrelevant, so much so that any award based on
the interests of an outside party could be declared improper and therefore
not binding by the courts. Children introduce a complication because of the
longstanding legal principle that disputes affecting a child must be decided
in that child's best interests. The courts have consistently cited this rule,
which in part explains their reluctance to give up *parens patriae* authority.
How then might the rules of arbitration be reconciled with the best interests
of children? There are at least several possibilities. (1) Prior to arbitration,
the parties could agree that an award should consider or even be based on
the best interests of children. (2) Statutes governing arbitration of family
matters could incorporate a similar provision. (3) Arbitrators could be given
legal authority to obtain professional opinions concerning the best interests of
children. Or (4) arbitrators could be allowed to speak with the affected
children in the course of settlement proceedings.[44] In this area, the move-

ment toward nonadversarial solutions may produce other important innovations.

A Concluding Note

The last decade has witnessed extensive experimentation with arbitration as an alternative means of dispute resolution. Although the process of arbitration has perhaps not demonstrated quite as broad an appeal as mediation, it has proven valuable in the handling of a diverse array of problems. In neighborhood and local community settings, the results have been mixed. The American Arbitration Association, which organized several experimental programs, now limits its involvement of the training of mediators and arbitrators. The vacuum created by the semiretirement of this eminent organization, however, has been quickly filled by others, prominent among them the federal government, which now advocates arbitration in the context of neighborhood justice centers.

As time goes on, the specific benefits of arbitration should become clearer. Current data suggest some tentative generalizations, which deserve to be tested in systematic research. Arbitration, it appears, may be the most desirable solution to problems in situations where the disputants exercise unequal power; the parties need a relatively quick and definitive resolution; the parties do not have a continuous or particularly close relationship; or processes of conciliation and mediation have not been successful. Research should try to pinpoint the characteristic limitations of the process, beginning perhaps with the types of disputes that people are reluctant to put before an arbitrator. Such investigations will help to obtain the maximum benefit from arbitration as further community initiatives are developed.

Two obstacles to the further application of arbitration procedures may be noted. The first is the understandable reluctance of the judicial and legal community to relinquish their involvement in, or control over, cases that go to arbitration instead of to criminal court. But with the criminal dockets congested with untried, continued, and otherwise unresolved cases, judges and lawyers should welcome a proven procedure for the expeditious and noncumbersome dispatch of many disputes in which the criminal content is not of major consequence.

A second source of opposition may spring from some who regard the extension of arbitration procedure—like other forms of community-dispute resolution—as an example of "creeping socialism." It is undeniable that while such community courts as the popular tribunals, comrade courts, or people's courts are found in postcapitalist regimes, they are also found in today's primitive societies. If a higher level of cooperative organization ever comes to this country, it will not be primarily through the conduit of community-court procedures but rather as the result of citizen demands that as they participate in the electoral process, they should also have a voice in other areas in which their destinies are involved. These may one day include not only the tribunal in which they are tried but other settings as well—their education, health services, housing and the places where they work.

The director of the Rochester 4-A Arbitration Center sums up the value of the arbitration procedure and the contribution it makes to community harmony in an age marked more frequently by strife than by amity:

> The 4-A program is designed to provide a forum in which a variety of systems of social regulation such as municipal law, ethnic traditions, conventional ethical beliefs, religious commitments, political persuasions, business practices, etc., intersect and present themselves as candidates for resolving the issue at hand. . . . The structure of the 4-A program makes a significant step towards enabling citizens to help other citizens jointly and freely address and resolve problems common to us all.[45]

Mediation

Mediation of interpersonal disputes is one of the most successful and popular community alternatives to the traditional court process. Known by the technical term *alternative dispute resolution*, mediation by community agencies offers benefits to all concerned: the disputants themselves (offender and victim), the community as a whole, and the criminal-justice system. For the parties whose conflict comes up for mediation, the process provides a level of respect for persons and a reduction in hostility and antagonism that generally is lacking in the formal tribunals. Those criminologists who argue that the victim bears some responsibility—even to the slightest degree—for the occurence of the criminal act against him, hold that the victim is therefore entitled to some participation—however slight—in the process of resolving the conflict.

Community mediation respects the other commitments of the disputants by enabling them to participate in the resolution of their problems. In contrast to the normal court schedule, mediation can take place at a convenient hour in the evening or over a weekend. As a result, the parties do not lose time or money from their jobs, so they are able to enter upon mediation without those frustrating and very real economic concerns.

Equally important, mediation removes disputants from the burdens of an adversary procedure that usually protracts and may even escalate the original conflict. The issue before the two parties, and their community mediators, is no longer one of simple guilt or innocence with respect to the specific isolated act; rather it becomes one of ascertaining the underlying problems, facing these forthrightly, and working out a conclusion satisfactory to both parties to the dispute. Unencumbered by legal rules of evidence and technical burdens of proof, the parties can speak with frankness, drawing on all relevant factors in the situation, including, most importantly, the underlying emotional aspects of their interrelationships. Mediation thus allows a degree of personal involvement unknown in the criminal court and leaves the parties with a sense of having directly shaped their own brand of justice. Together they have arrived at an appropriate solution instead of being the passive recipients of the results of a duel-like trial between defender and prosecutor. Because the disputants know from the start that the mediation process, if successful, can obviate a criminal record for the accused, fear of punishment is replaced by hope and the prospect of a fresh start.

Mediation represents a recognition of the seriousness of public concern over certain offenses, which helps to resolve conflict through conciliation and problem settlement. If measures are available in the community to resolve certain conflicts—between neighbors, among family members, between landlord and tenant, between school and pupil—such incidents are drained of their criminal content and recognized for what they are: disagreements or misunderstandings between individuals that arise from the fact of their living and interacting closely with one another.

Mediation not only allows but facilitates communication between disputants. The process makes possible the direct dealing with the conditions that gave rise to the dispute instead of concerning itself with determining who is right and who is wrong, the basic aim of the traditional court procedure. In reality, no party to a dispute is totally free of blame, as the age-old proverb tells us, "It takes two to quarrel." Alcoholism, for example, cannot be treated by a finding of guilt or innocence. The complexity of the roots of such a condition, or of marital and other family disputes, is more likely to be adequately handled by examination and exploration than by conviction in criminal court. In family disputes it is no help to either party to establish one as an angel and the other as the demon.

Mediation is best suited to dealing with people who have gripes against one another. Almost all of them have had some sort of prior relationship that will continue long after the instant dispute has been resolved. The criminal court is not structured to delve into the underlying causes of conflicts between such disputants, nor does its crowded calendar normally allow it the luxury of sufficient time in which to seek for resolution or compromise to alleviate the conditions that gave rise to the conflict before it for adjudication.

The benefits that mediation brings to the community are, perhaps, its most significant contribution. Conflicts can be mediated while they are still manageable, before they escalate into serious misdemeanors or felonies, with the consequent damage to both community and disputants. An unresolved feud between family members, neighbors, or friends, which could eventually lead to a serious incident, physical harm or death, can undermine a community's sense of wholeness and well-being. As mutual trust begins to break down and fear begins to spread, neighbor may tend to withdraw from involvement with neighbor, leading to further estrangement and hostility. Mediation works to restore a sense of community, to reestablish relations of trust, even to build up community spirit in new ways. It provides disputants with examples of direct experience of real concern and solid support by neighbors during times of trouble. People realize, some perhaps for the first time, that there are others nearby who care enough to help, who are willing to get personally involved. All who participate in mediation, particularly the mediators who represent the community, gain a better understanding of community problems and needs, a knowledge that often carries over to other local organizational efforts.

By reducing the time interval between complaint and resolution, mediation promotes efficiency in every branch of the criminal justice system. Police are liberated from the role of mediator in family disputes, which consumes a sizable portion of their time and often results in injury or even death as officers intervene to settle such quarrels. It has been estimated that one-fifth of all policemen killed, and two-fifths of those injured, are assaulted while intervening in family disputes. Prosecutors are enabled to focus on major cases; judges can concern themselves with reduced case loads. The crowding of jails is eased and the abuses of bail somewhat reduced. The significant savings that result may be passed along to taxpayers or transferred to other needed services. To the degree that mediation resolves conflict, it helps to prevent crime in that each case handled in this manner multiplies the initial benefits many times over.

Above all, community mediation provides a conception of justice as a living and concerned process. With punishment and stigmatization set aside, justice can connote a process of healing, of restitution and reconciliation, of meeting unmet needs. A high degree of satisfaction can be provided to both offending and injured parties, conveying a sense that their rights have been reaffirmed, their values upheld.

The resulting sense of forgiveness between the contesting parties adds a creative dimension that is rarely seen in the traditional practices of criminal justice. This creativity may well account for much of the enthusiasm expressed by those who are involved in the mediation process and explains the growing popularity of this approach. This capacity for reducing or overcoming alienation between disputants and between the offender and the community may account as well for the very low repeater rate of those whose disputes are settled through mediation. This approach is not only fresh and attractive, it can also be powerful and very effective. At the same time that it demonstrates the power of nonviolence, it points up the futility of violent responses to many of the problems of crime.

Mediation has been described as the art of changing people's positions, with the explicit aim of acceptance of a package put together by both sides, with the mediator as the listener, the suggester, the formulator of the final agreement to which both sides have contributed. The process starts with a statement of the extreme position held by each party to the dispute. Three elements make up the final agreement: clarification on the part of one contestant as to his desired objective, a parallel statement on the part of the other contestant, and finally, through a process of change and trading-off, the final solution.

This solution is incorporated in an agreement signed by both parties, and affirmed and witnessed by the mediator(s). The following agreements taken from the files of a court-mediation service are typical examples. The first case arose from antagonism between two neighboring sets of families and children in which both families agreed to:

1. Keep off the other's property.
2. Refrain from harassing members and friends of the other family by threats, abusive language, annoying phone calls, destruction of property.
3. Provide adult supervision (person over the age of 16) when parents will not be at home for a period lasting over one hour.
4. Investigate the use of family counseling as a preventive measure for dealing with family disputes.
5. If the above conditions are met, then the charges against Mr. K. will be dropped.

The second signed agreement provides sufficient detail to make possible the reconstruction of the events leading up to the original criminal complaint:

1. Mrs. P. agrees to keep her son, Bob, away from the U's property.
2. Bob agrees to keep away from the U's property and to refrain from uttering obscenities at the U's.
3. Mr. U. agrees not to make degrading remarks towards Bob; i.e. "animal."
4. Mr. U. agrees to call Mrs. P. before the police in the event that there are any future problems between him and Bob.
5. Both parties agree not to bring criminal complaints against each other if the terms of this agreement are honored.

A separation agreement by an unmarried couple sets out precisely how they shall divide property previously owned in common:

1. Alice P. agrees to let Edward C. take the following items out of their house at 10 No Name Street:

bicycle	suitcase
radio cassette	tools
end table	jacks
guitars	tire
amplifier	television
men's clothing	bar stools

2. Edward C. agrees to let Alice P. keep the dining room set, the bedroom set, the vacuum cleaner and all the dishes, pots, and pans.

Throughout the session the mediator maintains order, controls the flow of communication between the parties and the timing of events, and encourages the emergence of both factual evidence and the underlying emotions and unarticulated sources of discord.

The official complaint is not always the real issue at the heart of the dispute, so part of the mediator's role is to bring to light the source and nature of such basic issues. The mediation course helps to point out that neither party is completely in the right; it is not adversarial in approach or procedure. Its aim is not to assess blame or to prove guilt or innocence but to achieve consensus.

In action the process is challenging, rewarding, unpredictable, and at times uncontrollable. The final agreement is not an imposed verdict. Both sides bear an equal responsibility to make the agreement work, as they share the credit for having jointly forged it. Once the two parties have committed themselves to mediation, they have generated a certain momentum to complete the process. If it takes two to tango, it may be said that it also takes two to untangle, with the mediator helping to provide the tune—and the timing. The thrust of mediation is into the future; the past but serves to furnish up the means.

An Exemplary Project

One of the most important initiatives in mediation was the Night Prosecutor's Program in Columbus, Ohio, begun in November 1971 through the joint efforts of the city attorney and a professor of law from Capital University.[1] The program set out to handle minor criminal complaints by means of prearrest diversion. Disputants—complainant and the alleged offender—were brought together in a controlled setting to talk out their problems in the expectation that a settlement acceptable to both parties would be worked out without recourse to formal court procedures. This expectation has been confirmed by the decade of operation of the program, which has been cited by the Law Enforcement Assistance Administration as "an exemplary project" in citizen-dispute settlement, one worthy of replication throughout the country. The program focuses on criminal conduct involving interpersonal disputes in which there is a continuing relationship, such as disputes between families, neighbors, landlord-tenants, and employers-employees.

The program's location makes it rather unique: it operates out of police headquarters downtown because headquarters is open at all times, is accessible by public transportation, and the site facilitates rapid access to relevant information. The program's location further serves to remind that

the purpose of the program is *not* to remove the spectre of "the long arm of the law" from the process of dispute settlement. Rather, project founders believe that the no-nonsense atmosphere of the police station helps hearing officers by legitimizing their authority. . . . In addition, the proximity to the police, courts and jail remind the hearing participants that legal sanctions are a reality and that the project staff are a legitimate part of the criminal justice system.[2]

Within this setting, the program addresses several major goals: to dispense justice rapidly and fairly to citizens of the area involved in minor criminal conduct; to ease the burden on the criminal-justice system by reducing backlog in the courts; to provide working people with a public forum during nonworking hours; to remove the stigma of an arrest record; and to ease community and interpersonal tensions.[3] It deals with these types of cases: interpersonal, summons docket, and bad check. Hearings are scheduled at half-hour intervals because "it has been the experience of the program that most disputes can be resolved within this time or a decision can be reached as to whether a re-scheduling will be necessary."[4]

The Columbus project has deliberately kept its procedures simple. When a complainant appears at the city prosecutor's office to file a warrant, a clerk listens to the details and then decides whether the case can be referred to the Night Prosecutor's Program. Major criminal changes and cases in which a complainant appears to be in imminent danger are handled through the ordinary police and court procedures. To the fullest extent possible, all matters are diverted out of these ordinary channels to the night program. A few days after the complaint is taken by the clerk, an administrative hearing is scheduled, and the complaining party is told to appear with any relevant witnesses. At the same time a notice is sent to the accused, specifying the charges filed as well as the time and place of the scheduled hearing.

When the parties appear for the hearing, they undergo a process of direct confrontation and mediation. A volunteer law student who has received training in informal dispute resolution is in charge of the procedure, with sufficient authority and responsibility to keep the exchange reasonably orderly. Hearings begin with each disputant telling his side of the controversy, free of any interruption. The hearing officer asks a series of probing questions in an effort to clarify the underlying facts of the dispute. It is reported that a good deal of argument and emotion, which is kept within tolerable limits, is vented at this stage. The parties eventually either discover that they have arrived at agreement by themselves, or the hearing officer invites their suggestions for settling the matter. The hearing concludes with assent from both parties to abide by the terms of the agreement arrived at through the remedies proposed by each side. The agreement is then formalized by the ratifying signatures of both parties.

In the small proportion of cases where agreement cannot be reached, the matter is referred to the regular police and court channels, which otherwise would have dealt with the complaint. Resolution of some disputes re-

quires that the hearing officer be more than a skillful listener and con-
ciliator. Various unmet needs of the disputants may have surfaced that require attention. The hearing officer will then draw upon a list of available
social agencies and refer the parties to the appropriate service. If the hearing
officer considers that the conflict may flare up when the parties leave the
hearing room, a practice called prosecutor's probation is used, which functions as a special warning to one or both parties. Prosecutor's probation is a
written order to cease and desist from certain conduct for a period of sixty
days. It cautions both parties that recurrence of the forbidden behavior will
lead the prosecutor's office to authorize the filing of a criminal complaint.
Although this variation of probation has no binding legal effect, it has been
found to have real deterrent value.

In some instances, the mediation session reveals problems that have
contributed to the incident in dispute. The program addresses these related
needs through social-service referrals, including therapy and support groups
for problem drinkers and battered wives. As the program has expanded,
social-service capabilities have also increased. Recently the project staff
added a full-time mental-health counselor and several part-time social-work
students.

A number of features account for the program's general success. Participants have expressed satisfaction with the direct, personal, and speedy
process by which their disputes have been settled. Many have also received
restitution as a condition of their settlement. Thousands of cases have been
kept off the crowded court dockets. The program reports that less than 5
percent of the cases heard have resulted in the filing of a criminal affidavit
after mediation has failed. Figures from the program's first year show a
total of 3,626 complaints passed through the program, at a cost of $18,000.
Handled through ordinary justice channels, the cost would have been about
$725,000, an overall saving of nearly 90 percent. By 1976 the figure was
nearly 6,500 cases, and 1979 statistics reflect another sizable increase: 7,800
interpersonal cases and over 12,000 cases in the category of administrative
hearings. Such results make a very strong case for the long-term viability of
this model.

This program operates with very limited community participation. The
disputants themselves are members of the community, but the law students
who serve as hearing officers and the clerks are not necessarily drawn from
the same areas. They are paraprofessionals in training rather than
neighbors. Nor does the process of confrontation and mediation occur in a
community setting but rather within a police station, where the office of the
city prosecutor is located. Finally, the program was created and is maintained by the criminal-justice system, whereas a true community approach
would involve local initiative in program sponsorship, design, and operation.

A number of questions have been raised about this program. One commentator was troubled that the mediation sessions were too concerned with the allocation of blame. Another observer questioned the program's use of "the trimmings of authority."[5] Although the program is described as prearrest diversion, the staff consider some elements of judicial authority to be essential to the program's effectiveness. The document sent out to respondents is referred to as a subpoena, and respondents are told that they have been charged with the offenses listed. Mediation sessions of particularly difficult cases are taken up to the chief prosecutor's office at the police station where the American flag and shelves of legal volumes are thought to lend an air of dignity to the proceedings. The program seems to be aware of its lack of roots in the community and aims to compensate for that lack by emphasis on formality and authority. Despite these and other questions with regard to its procedures, the Night Prosecutor Program has proven to be one of the most influential pioneering mediation efforts and has given rise to similar schemes.

Dade County Citizen-Dispute-Settlement Program

Over the past few years, several programs closely resembling the Columbus design have been established in Florida. These citizen-dispute-settlement programs are located across the state, most visibly in Miami, Orlando, and Tampa Bay. The Miami center has received the most publicity and may be taken as representative.[6]

Since operations began in the summer of 1975, the dispute-settlement program has become well established and has experienced significant growth. Funding, originally provided from a federal source, has now been assumed by the county government. Over four thousand cases are referred annually, with 55 percent of them scheduled for mediation hearings. As in Columbus, the Miami project is quartered in a government building that houses the local court and district attorney's offices.

The Miami program differs from the Columbus model in that hearing officers are not law students but rather either social-science professionals or members of the bar. One-fifth of all referrals appear spontaneously as walk-ins, half of which concern family disputes. Such conflicts are regarded by the staff as particularly well suited to mediation. They typically involve repeated prior appearances in the criminal court, have a potential for violence, and are reluctantly dealt with by police and prosecutors.

The value of the program is further demonstrated by an evaluation of the first two years of operation. Interviews with some two hundred clients endorsed both the effectiveness of mediation and its diversionary benefits. More than one-third of respondents indicated that without the services of the center, they would have turned to the criminal court to resolve their difficulties.[7]

Community Dispute Center

This program is located in the Sugar Hill area of Harlem and is sponsored by the Institute for Mediation and Conflict Resolution of New York City, which also trains mediators for other dispute-resolution projects.[8] Referrals come primarily from police officers who, upon arrival at the scene of an incident, decide whether the case might be amenable to mediation. If mediation seems advisable, they give a referral slip to the complainants, instructing them to report to the center within seventy-two hours. When the complainants arrive at the center, they receive a description of the program. If they agree to submit the dispute to a procedure that combines mediation and arbitration, a letter is sent to respondents on police letterhead asking them to appear within seventy-two hours to answer the charges. Upon the agreement by both parties to submit to the process, a mediation-arbitration session is scheduled.

The program also handles a special type of referral, known as DAT cases. These are misdemeanor arrest cases that receive a desk appearance ticket (hence the initials) and are really delayed arraignment proceedings. Under a scoring system utilized in New York similar to that used for determining eligibility for release on bail, an arrested person who receives points (for being employed, living with a family, being a settled member of the community) may be released and ordered to appear within two weeks. The Community Dispute Center intervenes in this period. If the parties agree to participate in a successfully completed session, the complainant will withdraw the charge and the arrested person is spared a record.

The arbitration component is built into the program for two reasons. It ensures special protections for the parties involved, guaranteeing confidentiality of the proceedings, and it completely decriminalizes the original charges. It also ensures that the decisions of the dispute center are enforceable on both parties. Because 90 percent of all cases are settled by mediation, arbitration is seldom used by the Community Dispute Center, but it remains as a backup resource.

A frequent source of neighborhood dispute handled by the center is the problem of excessive noise. In these instances, mediators attempt to get both parties to agree to a schedule that specifies precisely when loud music may or may not be played. Other disputes are resolved in similar ways, with frequent examples of friends or family extending mutual apologies and agreeing not to harass one another further. Some agreements have resulted in the establishment of grievance mechanisms between tenants and building owners or superintendents. Agreements and awards frequently have included restitution or accord on the division of property between persons who are separating.

An unexpected benefit of the program has been its capacity to resolve cases that the criminal-justice system would not handle. For instance, there are a number of Hispanic persons in the community who are illegal immigrants and who would not turn to a court or other official agencies for resolution of disputes. When these persons bring their problems to the center, they are clearly demonstrating trust in the confidentiality and nonjudicial nature of the proceedings. Similar results follow gambling disputes, which are not ordinarily resolvable by court proceedings, because gambling is an illegal activity. But because the community recognizes gambling as a fact of life in the area, no objection is made to settlement by the center before gambling disputes magnify into serious criminal acts.

In its first two months of operation, 70 percent of the disputes brought before the center were successfully settled—50 percent by mediation, 10 percent by social-service referral, and 10 percent as a result of dropped charges. Of the remaining 30 percent, some 25 percent did not show up for mediation-arbitration after having been referred. The remaining 5 percent refused to participate in the process; one party, for example, insisted on divorce and refused reconciliation. The program is a splendid example of community participation. Over fifty volunteers are from the community, each prepared to assume role responsibility by undergoing fifty-five hours of training at the Institute for Mediation and Conflict Resolution.

One of the cases is an excellent example of how the program operates on the principle that restitution should involve the victim, the community and the offender. It involved a young girl who was apprehended in a department store where she took a shirt valued at thirteen dollars. She was wearing it when she left the store without paying for it. The store was compensated by having the stolen article returned; the community was reimbursed by requiring that the girl type for the mediation service at the court one afternoon a week after school. This time period was selected because this was the session during which the court heard shoplifting cases. One of the girl's jobs, in addition to typing, was to escort offenders from the court to the mediation session. Moreover the court found her a part-time job and as personal restitution on her own behalf, she was required to donate from her earnings fifty dollars to a local charitable institution of her choice.

A Model Program: The Dorchester Urban Court

When members of the Dorchester community undertook to remove from the bench a patently unfair and unjust judge, the momentum generated by that campaign, and the organization developed in the community to attain the victory, together with the confidence which that victory brought in its train, led to a unique and innovative program design to ensure continued community participation in the local administration of criminal justice.[9]

Since its establishment, the Dorchester Urban Court has won nationwide and even international recognition for the proven excellence of its threefold services. It began operation in November 1975 after a design developed by the Justice Resource Institute in Boston, a private research group devoted to court reform, and in close cooperation with the local Court Advisory Board, the Mayor's Office on Criminal Justice, the National Law Enforcement Assistance Administration, the county district attorney, and two police districts that serve the area.

The court offers three distinct services as an alternative to the criminal-justice system: services to victims, a disposition component, and a mediation component. In addition, one staff member is responsible for job development because unemployment is a basic cause of many of the disputes referred to the urban court for service.

Like the Columbus Night Prosecutor's Program, the Urban Court interprets the principle of justice as realizable through mediation and reconciliation. The program aims to resolve disputes between persons with an ongoing relationship by means of its four primary objectives: (1) to resolve potential criminal disputes in a manner that satisfies the parties that justice has been rendered and recurrence of future problems averted by addressing the basic issues of the dispute; (2) to enable community mediators to effect such resolution and thereafter to compare their results with other methods of informal resolution in the court and in the police station; (3) to determine the most effective models and intake points in achieving resolution of criminal disputes; and (4) to build community goodwill toward the court, the police, and the prosecutor's office. Together these objectives provide a unique opportunity for the community to play a constructive and vital role in the criminal-justice system in Dorchester.

The Mediation Process

Cases come into the court by referral from five sources: the clerk's office when a complaint is made; the district court prosecutor's office following screening interviews with victims; the bench following arraignment or preliminary hearing; the police; and community groups. The last two sources are purposely limited in the number of cases they may refer so that the program can fulfill its basic commitment of diverting cases from the criminal docket. Even with this limitation, community referrals and requests for assistance steadily increased as the Urban Court has gained community acceptance.

The mediation process progresses through four stages: setting the scene, defining the issues in dispute, processing the issues, and, finally, resolving them. In the first stage, the rules and procedure of the process are explained to the parties and succeeding stages define the parameters, hear the viewpoints of the opposing parties, and finally, a resolution agreeable to both parties is worked out, with the mediator acting as guide.

The program offers only mediation, not arbitration. If the disputing parties cannot reach a mediated settlement, the matter is referred back to the court—either to the clerk's office for a decision on whether a complaint should be issued or to the district attorney's office for processing through the normal court procedures.

The process begins when the clerk of the court, the district attorney, or the judge believe that mediation is an appropriate method for resolving a dispute. An Urban Court staff member explains the program to the complainant, and to the respondents if they are in court. If the disputing parties agree to mediation, they sign a voluntary agreement form. A time for the session is scheduled, usually within a week, and at the convenience of the disputing parties—weekdays, evenings, or Saturdays, if necessary. If the respondent does not appear at the time of the referral, a letter is sent requesting a call to the office within forty-eight hours. After the agreement to mediate has been signed by both parties, a panel of mediators is selected. Usually there are three mediators, but as they have become more experienced, only two have been used in many cases and some have begun to work alone. Mediation sessions seldom last longer than two hours. Repeat hearings may be held in complex cases. Seldom are more than two hearings required.

Urban Court Staff

Staff of the mediation component of the court consist of the director, a case coordinator, and one secretary. They do intakes on new referrals, provide necessary social-service referrals, and monitor the mediated settlements. All other staff members—almost fifty—are volunteers who have been recruited from the community. This is one of the strongest elements in the mediation program: that the people who sit in with the parties to a dispute know the community, make their homes—and frequently their living—there, and that they donate their time and services out of a sense of concern for their neighbors and their neighborhood. The initial campaign to enroll volunteers from the community was carried out by the court's advisory board through notices on bulletin boards, community publications, churches, advertisements in the local paper, and personal invitations to persons considered to be good potential mediators. The first response was sufficiently successful so that subsequent vacancies in the volunteer staff are met largely by referral from persons already enrolled in the work.

Initially eighteen community people were screened and selected for an intensive three-week training course. Two additional recruitment efforts produced fifty mediators. With few exceptions, mediators are residents of the immediate community and comprise a cross-section of men and women of a variety of ages and occupations. Mediators are available on an as-needed basis, some from eight to forty hours per month. They are paid a small fee per session, which provides for childcare, transportation, or meals; frees the project to make significant demands on its volunteers; and conveys to the community that their participation is appreciated.

Project and court personnel are convinced of the importance of volunteer citizen mediators. For nonpersonal cases using the arbitration model, staff concede that community involvement may not be as important. But for the Urban Court caseload, people from the community have a larger stake in the proceedings, so the project performs an important citizen education function, which helps to reduce the feeling of alienation from the court.

The initial training for community persons who volunteered consisted of a forty-hour program conducted by the New York Institute for Mediation and Conflict Resolution, which, like the American Arbitration Association, makes this service available to community organizations.

The sessions take place on two weekday evenings and all day Saturdays over a four-week period. The first meeting, an all-day session, introduces the trainees to the program goals and operation, followed by a discussion of the role of the mediator, the process, and the techniques. During the second session, the professional staff role-play a typical mediation session. This is followed by questions and comments from the audience on the following day, using videotape playbacks of the session. Specifics as to note taking, confidentiality, counseling, and hearing procedures are covered, leading to consideration of how the tentative and final agreements between the conflicting parties to a dispute were arrived at.

The trainees next participate in simulated dispute hearings, followed by a critique. Final sessions are devoted almost entirely to additional simulations, giving participants the opportunity to develop confidence in themselves as they develop their knowledge and skills. The final session recaps the entire experience and a review of the training materials, followed by a graduation ceremony during which an oath of confidentiality is administered by the clerk of the court, and certificates of appointment are presented. Subsequent training is done by supervisory personnel. Additional in-service training consists of a full day of training for all staff in reality therapy and case-management techniques, followed by a day of supervisory staff training. Periodic training sessions cover topics of special relevance to the project's caseload, supplemented by biweekly case reviews and monthly meetings of all staff members.

Mediation sessions are held at the storefront offices of the Urban Court, in a rundown block of the main street not far from the courthouse. This location provides an informal and relaxed neighborhood atmosphere.

Mediation Procedures

Parties to the dispute are asked to arrive at the offices at least fifteen minutes before the hearing begins in order to permit a staff member to learn the nature of the dispute. Very little background is given to the panel in order to avoid prejudgment. While the panelists discuss the format for the session among themselves, the staff member greets the disputants and endeavors to put them at ease. When the panel is ready to begin, both disputants are brought to the conference room by the staff member and introduced to the panel. The staff member leaves but remains available.

The session begins with one member of the panel outlining the mediation procedure in order to acquaint the parties with what they may expect and to initiate an atmosphere of trust, which is intended to prevail throughout the process. The fact that the conference does not take place in a criminal courtroom and that panel members are concerned community people, volunteers, who are prepared to listen and to help, serves to draw off some of the anxiety and distress that the parties to the dispute may feel. They are helped to perceive that the process is truly in the hands of the disputing parties and that if and when agreement emerges, it will be as a result of their attitude and their efforts.

The introduction is key, for it encourages disputants to relax and gives them an opportunity to ask questions and to establish rapport, thus laying the basis for trust, in a climate of neutrality and impartiality. They are told that the mediation hearing is not a court and that the panelists are not judges; rather the panel is there to listen to both parties and to assist them in resolving their conflict in a mutually satisfactory manner. The use of lawyers, or even their presence at the session, is regarded as partisan and therefore likely to be more obstructive than helpful in arriving at reconciliation, and is discouraged. The panel explains that if agreement is reached during a session, it will be one that the disputants themselves have shared in creating and feel they both can live with. The issue of confidentiality is explained; the notes taken by panel members will be destroyed before the disputants leave the session. Both disputants are encouraged to feel free to take notes.

The panel also explains that from time to time they may wish to confer among themselves or to speak in private with one or the other of the disputants

These individual caucuses usually occur two or more times during a mediation session, at which point one or both parties will be asked to leave the room.

After this introduction, each party to the dispute is invited to describe how they see the problem as fully as possible. Panel members may ask questions where appropriate in order to probe more deeply, in an effort to arrive at a complete understanding of each party's perception of the dispute and its underlying or aggravating circumstances. Emotions can run very high during this phase, but all parties are encouraged to speak openly. Once the basic facts have been aired to the satisfaction of all parties, both sides will be asked to leave the conference room while the panel members discuss the case among themselves. Panel members want to be certain that they agree on the character of the problem, and at the same time provide a short break for the parties who have been confronting one another.

When the panel has completed its deliberations, each of the parties is invited back to confer with the panel individually. Further questions are raised, and new information will often be proffered by a disputant at this stage. The panel at this point will encourage each party to set out the terms of settlement that each is seeking from the other, without making any suggestions of its own as to how this may be done. During this caucusing phase, the panel most fully mediates or "goes between" the parties, by communicating to each the terms that the other is seeking. Once each party has set forth its position, the panel can identify the areas of agreement and disagreement. This enables the panelists to convey from one party to another what each is asking, in positive, less-emotional fashion than might be possible if the two parties were in continuous confrontation with each other throughout the entire process. When the final agreement has been arrived at, the panel presents it in writing to both of the parties together. Each of them is free to request changes or additions. When both parties express satisfaction with the proposed agreement, they sign it, the panel members sign as witnesses, each party is given a copy, and the session ends. The agreement is not a legally binding document, but the panel encourages the disputants to get in touch with the program if they feel that the agreement is not working. The panel also informs the disputants that a staff member will be calling to monitor the agreement.

Disputants generally arrive tense, angry, and often frightened. After a couple of hours of the mediation process, they appear more comfortable and relaxed both with themselves and with their adversary. They have a sense of being heard; they have reached an agreement that can resolve an annoying or seemingly insoluble problem; they have helped to lay the groundwork for better relations in the future. Since the disputants themselves have hammered out and given consent to the terms of the resolution, the mediators know that it is a reasonable one and that it should have a good chance of success. A copy of the agreement goes to the district attorney and to the probation officer.

The procedure for officially closing the case depends on the source of the original referral. When a referral has come from the court clerk at the time of application for complaint, the mediation staff notifies the clerk in writing that the matter has been resolved and can be closed. If a referral has come from the bench or from the prosecutor's office, the parties who have successfully mediated their dispute must appear in court on the date of the continuance issued at the time of referral. At this point the case will either be dismissed or, as happens ordinarily, continued for three months and dismissed at that time provided that the agreement has not broken down.

Once the agreement has taken effect, Urban Court staff monitor its progress. Disputants are contacted two weeks after the initial mediation session and again in three months. They are asked whether the agreement is working, whether the parties continue to be satisfied with the mediation process, and whether any requested social services have been received. If the mediated agreement has begun to break down, additional efforts are made to settle the problem without further court action. Staff persons will contact uncooperative parties to remind them of their agreement and may call the parties in for a second mediation session. In some cases, the monitoring process involves more specific instructions, especially when an agreement includes an exchange of property. In these cases, resource coordinators will contact the parties to make certain that the exchange has taken place and may even help in the process if the parties prefer not to have further contact with one another.

Social-service referrals are available to the disputing parties and are offered at various stages of the process. A resource coordinator meets with each disputant prior to the mediation session to obtain their written agreement to submit the dispute to mediation. If either party requests assistance from the program at that time, the resource coordinator begins immediately to identify the needed resource. A complainant may request assistance in locating alternative housing, or employment. Services requested at this point are not always necessarily relevant to the dispute but are frequently part of the mediated agreement.

For example, a neighbor's larceny complaint against a youth was referred to the mediation program. The complaint was resolved by a mediated agreement after which the youth's mother requested that he be referred for counseling assistance and help with a reading difficulty, which was included as part of the final written agreement. The measures available for the resolution of disputes by mediation make possible a highly individualized set of disposition orders, some of which may have value as preventives of further violations.

Statistical results of the Urban Court mediation program confirm its effectiveness. An early evaluation of its operations showed that of 611 cases referred to mediation, close to two-thirds came from either the prosecutor's office or the bench and just under a third from the clerk's office. Of the cases referred, 70 percent went through the mediation process, and 75 percent of these were reported to have been resolved successfully.

This success rate was fairly constant across different types of disputes. Disputes between family members, between neighbors, and between friends were resolved in nearly 70 percent of the cases. Disputes between merchants and customers, between landlords and tenants, or within a school context were resolved at the slightly lower rate of about 60 percent. This difference may well reflect a variation in the degree of trust that characterizes these different sets of relationships. It is to be expected that bonds between family members, friends, and neighbors would be stronger than those between merchants and customers, landlords and tenants, or pupils, parents, and school personnel.

On the basis of its first two successful years of operation, the Urban Court mediation program was committed to handling some 350 referrals in the next year. About 85 percent of these were expected to experience the entire mediation process. Some 25 percent were expected to include social-service referrals, and another 20 percent were expected to involve some restitution or property exchange. This projected program was planned to operate with a staff of four paid staff who work with some 50 volunteer mediators drawn from the community. The volume of cases mediated runs between 500 and 600 annually.

The Dorchester Urban Court's mediation program early became a prototypical model for similar programs around the country. Its most noteworthy feature is the degree of community involvement and neighborhood volunteer participation that characterizes it. Locating the court in a storefront on a heavily trafficked street rather than in a criminal-court setting appears to be effective in helping to dissolve feelings of hostility and resentment that the disputants bring with them to the mediation experience. This approach is in contrast to the Night Prosecutor's Program, with its aura of and emphasis on judicial authority. The volunteer mediators, selected from the neighborhood and trained for their work, are truly community people, peers and neighbors of the people undergoing mediation. The program draws on other community resources when making its referrals, receives a sizable proportion of its referrals from community sources, and, most significantly perhaps, owes its origin largely to community initiative.

Some Typical Cases

Mediation sessions are closed to the public, but from time to time the personnel put on role-playing episodes based on cases drawn from Urban Court files, with staff impersonating the original cast. One such episode concerned a young woman who had been living with a young man under an arrangement whereby she paid the rent and he assumed responsibility for the food and utilities. When he failed to live up to his part of the bargain, the woman threw him out, but he kept his latch key. He came in freely to take away what he claimed was his property and frequently entered when the young woman was entertaining. He refused to give up the key or to stay away from her or from the apartment. In desperation she finally swore out a complaint against him for trespass, and the case was marked up for trial. The clerk of the court secured the agreement of both parties to turn the case over to the mediation board. Each side told its story in emotional detail, which revealed that the woman's older married sister had been a provocative element; she was overprotective of her sister and disliked the young man. As frequently happens in interpersonal disputes, third parties often serve to incite disputes between the conflicting principals. In the end, both sides agreed to resume their former pattern of life. The young man agreed to keep to his original bargain, and the older sister was persuaded to stay clear of the couple's apartment except when she was invited. The young couple signed a written agreement embodying the results of their mediated solution. The agreement was later submitted to the judge, and when he had assented, it became valid for a ninety-day period, after which the original criminal complaint would be cleared and the alleged trespasser spared a court record.

In this instance, the mediation board might be described as a domestic-relations tribunal of first instance, operating in preventive fashion and dealing with relations between a man and a woman who could be cited criminally under Massachusets law for lewd and lascivious cohabitation. It is one of the great advantages of such community procedures as this that they can take into account informal, irregular, and even legally forbidden relationships that the criminal court might find difficult to resolve, to say nothing of the unwillingness or hesitation of the parties to come into court and expose the details of their illicit relationships.

The wide gamut of the mediation service encompasses the old as well. An example taken from the files illustrates the constructive use of mediation to achieve both symbolic and actual restitution. An elderly woman returned to her home one afternoon to find her television set gone. The youth who had stolen it was apprehended and admitted that he had sold the set to a fence. Rather than face a fine or continuance under probation supervision, the defendant, in the presence of the mediation board and of the victim, sat down to work out a nonpunitive resolution of the case for submission to the judge for his approval. The woman began to describe her life and broke down in the course of telling the boy, "I live alone in public housing. I am a widow. I watch television all day. That is all I do. I watch sixteen hours a day. You have taken the heart of my life away." Confronted with the direct result and personal implications of his act, the youth agreed to accept a job in order to buy the widow a new set. In addition, he agreed that he would accompany her to the bank to cash her weekly check and also escort her to the market for her shopping. A postscript to the case reports that the woman invited the boy to have coffee with her, and she learned from him that his mother had died and that he lived in an uncongenial relationship with his father and brother. Thereafter these Saturday morning coffee hours became a weekly feature. The closing entry reports that the boy had volunteered to paint the woman's kitchen.

Many of the disputants in the mediation program are young men, as in the case of one charged with driving a car without authority and with malicious damage amounting to $700 to another car with which he collided while driving too rapidly around the corner when he spied a police car approaching. The insurance policy of neither the victim nor that of the owner of the stolen car would cover any of the loss to the victim.

When the mediation service arranged a meeting between him and the family that owned the car—neighbors who lived only a few blocks away—the victim was restrained with great difficulty from venting her anger in the face-to-face encounter. The youth was visibly shaken when he learned that the car that he had all but demolished was to have been the vehicle in which the entire family was to have gone on vacation the following day. The father of the family, who worked out of state, relied on his car to make his weekly visits to his wife and children. As the result of the incident, he was unable to use the car to commute to his job, was compelled to resort to bus travel in order to go to work, and could visit his family only once a month instead of weekly. The family was not only deprived of their vacation but had no funds to repair the damaged automobile. These detailed results of what he had done came out in the confrontation between the youth and the mother of the family. During the discussion the youth apologized and agreed to make restitution.

A job was found for him in a nearby restaurant, and over the course of the year, he made weekly installments to cover the entire damage that he had caused. The victim had never expected to recover damages, and after she had been reimbursed, it was reported that when she and the youth met on the street they reacted to one another in friendly manner without rancor or reference to the incident. One of the aggravating circumstances of this case was that only ten days before the damage to the car, the woman's house had been broken into (presumably by another party). This incident understandably exacerbated the situation and made the entire family angrier at the youth than might have otherwise been the case. As it was, the husband did not lose his job, the car was repaired, and the incident was settled amicably.

Another account of a successful mediation session was a neighborhood dispute between the heads of two families that was triggered by disputes between the children of the two families. In dispute were a mother against her next-door neighbor for his assault and battery on her son and a second complaint of threats. Present were the two contestants: the warring parents, the mother (Mrs. R) accompanied by her four children, and the neighbor (Mr. L), accompanied by his spouse.

Mrs. R began the session by relating a detailed account of a three-year history of problems between the two families, climaxing when Mr. L pushed young R into the bushes where he scratched his legs. Young R's brother was witness to this incident. The second incident involved slingshots in the hands of assorted neighborhood children, which ended in Mr. L's making threats against Mrs. R.

Mrs. R, the divorced mother of the four, described the difficulty of raising the children without a father. For his part, Mr. L described himself as coming from another country where children were better behaved than those who lived on his street, and he recounted a long history of harassment by them. Surprisingly young R admitted to having been a participant in that harassment. At one point, states the report, "Everyone in the room was talking, and although we learned a lot by this, it began to get loud and repetitious." The parties to the dispute left the room, and the panel caucused. This led to agreement that there were now sufficient facts to proceed to the next step: discovery of what each party was seeking and how much each might be willing to concede.

The panel recalled that Mrs. R, "nervous and very upset," described herself as a reformed alcoholic who was currently undergoing treatment. She disclaimed any wish to have Mr. L committed to jail and expressed some sympathy for the harassment that he had endured at the hands of the children. Yet she could no longer endure his chasing after and yelling at her children and making threats against her. She evinced an intention to try to keep her children away and if an incident occurred, to discipline them. She was adamant, however, that Mr. L admit that he had assaulted her son.

It was now Mr. L's turn to be heard alone, without his wife who had done most of the talking at the preliminary session. He conceded that he had a "short fuse" but refused to admit to the assault on his neighbor's son. For his part, he was ready to go to Mrs. R in the future instead of dealing directly with her children and in passing expressed some sympathy for her.

The panel caucused again and thereafter recalled Mrs. R. to recount to her Mr. L's expression of sympathy for her. Mrs. R, while holding out for Mr. L to admit his guilt, was apparently satisfied that at least the panel conceded his guilt in the matter. Additionally she did not want Mr. L to come running to her with each fresh grievance against her brood but would hear him out in any especially aggravating episode.

These understandings were now written up in a tentative agreement and, when read aloud to both parties, resulted in their assent to them. The children were present at this stage in the proceedings because they shared some part of the blame for the years-long disputes between the two families. The two disputant parties signed the agreement. Mrs. R and Mr. L shook hands, and both thanked the panel. The chairperson of the session ended her report: "Mr. L was still in his seat staring at the floor. Since he hadn't said anything, we were a little apprehensive. But finally he stood and shook Mrs. R's hand and said some kind words to her. Mrs. R's eyes filled with tears and I felt like applauding."

A file from the early days of the program tells of two boys, aged fourteen and fifteen, from adequate homes in a middle-class neighborhood who broke and entered a home not far from where they lived. They stole articles of value and destroyed and vandalized the content of the house in the amount of $600. Through excellent police action the two boys were apprehended, charged with breaking and entering and larceny, and turned over to the mediation session of the local court. They had not known that their victim was a blind man in his nineties, who was out at the time they broke in. The man lived alone and upon his return home was overwhelmed and utterly confused by what had happened to his living quarters. His guardian was informed and he, together with the victim and the two boys, were brought together at a mediation session. Confronted with their victim, whose age and condition had hitherto been unknown to them, the boys admitted their guilt, apologized for what they had done, described their action as a lark for excitement, and agreed to meet at the house that they had broken into. A member of the mediation staff took the boys to the house and served as intermediary. Inasmuch as an insurance policy owned by the occupant of the house would cover all but a small fraction of the loss, the boys agreed to contribute $50 apiece to replace the window through which they had entered and to help clear up and restore order in the home. The record indicates that they were not involved in any trouble with the police thereafter.

The pioneering example set by the Urban Court has resulted in the creation of programs patterned after it in eight other Massachusetts communities, all differing but slightly from the Dorchester model in the details of their operation.

Visitation Valley Community Board Program

This noteworthy program began operation in the summer of 1977 in the Sunnydale area of San Francisco. The idea of a community mediation panel had originated the previous fall through the active involvement of fifty area residents; it became a reality less than a year later with the receipt of $150,000 in initial grants from private foundations. (In fact, all of its funding to date has come from private organizations.) The project early received the support of important community institutions, including the San Francisco police department, the district attorney's office, the principals of several public schools, and churches, assisted by local foundations. Except for two paid staff members, volunteers take responsibility for the board program. Throughout the process, the community residents provided leadership, enrolled in mediation training, and thereafter volunteered to serve as panelists at the five-member board hearings. The program sees itself as unique because "it is the only program that is truly community based and not an outgrowth of a social service or court system. Not only will the community program accept referrals from schools, police and other agencies . . . but from any members of the community."[10]

A newspaper story on the board program has described its potential jurisdiction:

> The cases might involve a dispute between neighbors over a noisy or destructive offspring;
>
> Or a row over a dog accused of running loose, digging up lawns or barking too long and loud;
>
> Or constantly blaring radios or TVs, or too many loud parties in a neighborhood;
>
> To some San Francisco neighborhoods, such beefs have escalated from name-calling and fist-waving brawls into shootings and knifings.[11]

The board has set itself the following goals: to understand the factors that generated the initial case, be it criminal activity or a neighborhood dispute; to develop a community mechanism for constructive resolution of problems based on people's lives and real needs; and to demonstrate that communities can set their own standards and resolve individual and neighborhood problems without the intervention of the criminal-justice system. In order to achieve these goals, the board acts to bring all parties to a dispute together, without involving the criminal-justice system, in order to reach a solution agreeable to the parties concerned. Matters may come before the board by referral from the police, schools, citizens, or agencies in the community. Although the expectation is that parties to a dispute will accept the conditions finally agreed upon, initial appearance and participation in board proceedings are completely voluntary.

Neighborhood disputes, conflicts, and antagonisms as well as criminal cases are matters for the board's concern and action, to the end that once resolved, such matters will not have to come to criminal-court trial and disposition. The board acts neither as judge nor jury; it does not determine guilt or innocence; it seeks neither to blame nor to condone. Parties to a dispute who prefer to contest guilt or innocence are advised to seek redress within the criminal court.

The panel members are trained in mediation skills by the American Arbitration Association and the Community Relations Department of the U.S. Department of Justice. To date, panel members have included housewives, businesspersons, clergy, high-school students, and recent graduates. Training and supervision of the volunteers is done by the paid staff, who receive referrals, meet with the parties in dispute, and refer them to the panel for hearing. When the police respond to a call arising from a neighborhood dispute, they will determine whether the case should be referred to the community board and so recommend to the parties concerned. All police operating out of the Southeast Police Station give the parties involved the option of being called to trial or being referred to the board. To aid the board in its search for appropriate remedy or solution, referrals are also made to cooperating agencies in the community, such as family-counseling, alcohol, and drug-treatment programs, employment and training opportunities, and other resources. Figure 9-1 shows the board's procedure.

Of the cases dealt with by the board in its first year, more than half were by direct referral from the community, a quarter from the district attorney's office or from the police, and the rest from security guards at a neighborhood housing project or from the probation department. The following cases illustrate not only the board's procedure but the general run of neighborhood disruptions and annoyances.

One of the first cases brought to the board involved five teenaged girls, residents of a housing project in the area, two of whom had been involved in a quarrel that ended in throwing of cans, injuring one of the girls. The police were called to the school, and they and the school decided to refer the case to the community board for hearing. The board staff contacted the families of the five girls in the fracas and learned that their parents were concerned to resolve the problems since all of the girls had been close friends at one time.

Five days later, the girls, their parents, and some friends arrived for the evening meeting. The meeting opened with seventeen people present. After a lengthy and frequently emotional interchange of complaints and charges against one another, the girls agreed to cease fighting and not to engage in verbal or physical contact with one another for the next two weeks. They further consented to return at the end of that time for the panel to assess whether the agreement was holding. At the close of the session, the two girls, who had both been directly involved in the assault, spontaneously apologized to one another. One girl, a recent graduate of the school where the incident had taken place, asked for help of the staff in finding a job. A position was found for her at which she is currently working. All of the

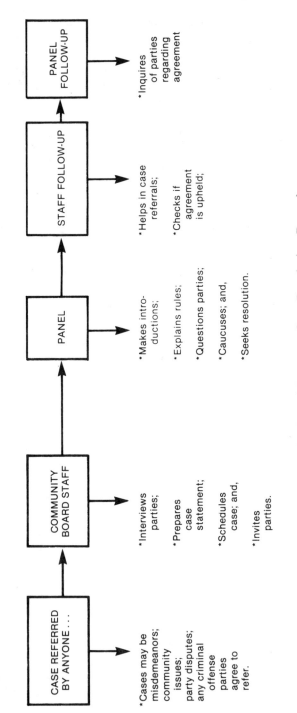

Figure 9-1. Community Board Program Case Resolution Procedure

individuals concerned returned to the follow-up panel hearing two weeks later to report that the resolution was working and suggesting an extension. The parents expressed appreciation, for after six months of fighting and recrimination among this group of girls, the panel had resolved their differences and made it possible for them to become friends again.

Another case referred to the board concerned a complaint by four people that one of their neighbors, an Asian, was operating a junkyard and automobile repair shop on the sidewalk and street near their houses. The neighbors had complained a score of times to the police, who, in response, had either ticketed or towed the vehicles. The repair man felt that his neighbors disliked him on ethnic grounds, and his reaction was to continue to operate his business despite harassment by boys on his street and the police actions against him.

A dozen neighbors appeared before the panel with a list of their complaints, which were matched by his complaints against them. In private caucuses between the board and with each of the parties, a resolution was arrived at. The repair man agreed to move his cars to an empty lot offered by one of his neighbors and to remove all but two of his vehicles from the street. He also agreed not to leave any cars on the sidewalk in the future but expressed concern that they were being vandalized by some local boys. One of his complainants offered to talk to each of the boys involved and let them know that the neighborhood would not allow any recurrence of that behavior. The case had been a source of sharp conflict and mutual resentment on the street for almost a year. Four days after the hearing, all but two of the cars were moved to the neighbor's lot, and the boys, who had been annoying the repair man, had been persuaded to desist from further vandalism.

In another case, the juvenile probation intake unit referred to the board a school burglary and vandalism charge against three boys, aged nine, ten, and twelve, who had no previous record. Twice they had broken into the school and stolen items from one of the classrooms. The principal of the school and the boys, with their parents, attended the two-hour meeting. The panel also met privately with the boys and then with the principal. In response to questions from the panel as to what their punishment should be, the boys volunteered to apologize to the principal, to the classroom teacher, and to the students while the class was in session. They also agreed to the panel's suggestion that they should pay off the cost of repairing broken windows by working with the janitor of the school at the rate of a dollar an hour, for a total of twenty-four dollars. The school principal was sufficiently pleased with the board procedure to offer that she would call the board prior to calling the police in future instances similar to this. The meeting concluded with the consensus that lack of adequate recreational facilities in the area was one of the reasons why children got into trouble and committed acts of vandalism. The panel agreed to refer the situation to the All Peoples Coalition, a local community organization, for action.

A charge of automobile theft was referred to the panel by the probation department of the juvenile court, which involved a fifteen-year-old minor who took part in joy-riding in a vehicle stolen by some older boys. The owner of the car was a former police officer currently serving in the navy shore police. He agreed to have the case heard by the panel because, he stated, in his experience probation departments and courts would neither impress the minor nor serve any other effective purpose.

The case was received on a Wednesday and heard the following Tuesday evening. Everyone involved in the incident was in attendance. The minor admitted that he had acted poorly; he apologized to the owner for his actions and to his mother for aggravating her. He agreed to get in touch with the others involved in order to return to the owner some of his stolen items, in particular, the automobile ownership certificate. He further agreed to contribute his share of restitution if the items could not be recovered.

Since the car owner was about to depart on naval duty for five weeks, the follow-up hearing was set for the time of his return, and the minor was allowed in the interim to secure the items or to pay his share of restitution to the owner. The owner was pleased with the process, both for its material results and for the manner in which the proceedings had been conducted. He thought that the boy had benefited more from this type of hearing than he would have from a traditional court proceeding.

The director of the program sums up the heart of the process in the term *community empowerment*, which has special significance now when polls report ever-higher levels of frustration and alienation from the traditional agencies of government, including its criminal-justice components.

In 1978, one year after the board began operations, Governor Brown of California sponsored legislation "aimed at moving numerous lawsuits out of courts and into arbitration and mediation." A key measure calls for the creation of several experimental neighborhood problem-solving centers to handle both civil and criminal disputes in the community.[12] Part of a large, comprehensive court-reform legislative proposal, the creation of such neighborhood centers is said to have been patterned after the Visitation Valley Community Board Program.

The proposal also drew upon the experience of the procedure introduced into the juvenile training schools of the state for resolving inmate complaints, which are processed through three levels: a committee composed equally of elected inmates and staff members, which attempts to mediate the issue; the institution administration, which decides the dispute if the first effort fails; and, finally, appeal of the decision to a tripartite panel consisting of one member chosen by the complainant, one by the administration, and a third outside arbitrator, a volunteer.[13]

Other Community Alternatives

We are impressed by the enormous proliferation in both numbers and variety of community alternatives to the adversary procedures and traditional modes of sentencing. One of the most recent of these is the opening of the Neighborhood Justice Center in Elizabeth, New Jersey, affiliated with a statewide agency. The new center is "not designed to replace courts [but] rather to help reduce the case loads of the courts and to provide immediate help for those who experience conflicts they cannot resolve themselves."[14] The procedures followed by the center differ little from other mediation programs we have described, but several distinctive features of the Elizabeth plan are worthy of note.

The descriptive brochure issued by the center appears in both Spanish and English and holds out the promise of evening and Saturday sessions, as well as workday times. In addition to inviting for mediation, landlord and tenant, juveniles, and consumer/merchant—the center specifies small claims involving money and personal property, as well as minor criminal matters. Counsel is not required at the hearings, but any party to a dispute may have a lawyer in attendance. The program clearly specifies as an important aspect of its mediation procedure that the "agreements made by the parties will not indicate guilt. Thus, an agreement cannot include fines, prison sentences or probation; however, an agreement may include payments for damages."

The Elizabeth program invites referrals from a variety of sources and at the same time issues a call for "objective third party helpers" to serve as volunteer mediators. Contributions are invited from the public to supplement funds received from the county Comprehensive Employment Training Act, private foundations, and business firms. The most striking feature of the plan is that it is only one of a series of such centers that are affiliated with an agency that will provide encouragement and assistance to a movement that has now evidently taken hold in the entire state.

Two recent developments of importance merit inclusion here. The first is a mediation program initiated by the Crime and Justice Foundation of Boston, in cooperation with the Massachusetts Bar Association, to provide mediation services to the Boston municipal court, the busiest trial court in the commonwealth.[15] In 1979 alone, sixty-seven thousand criminal and civil actions and other matters were entered at the court. A sampling of the court's criminal actions revealed a continuance rate of 69 percent and a default rate of 49 percent. The proposed mediation program is designed to help alleviate this tremendous volume and will focus initially on cases that ordinarily would reach prosecution.

The program will rely exclusively on volunteer lawyers to resolve disputes referred by the court. The foundation will administer the program and train the lawyer-mediators, and the bar association will recruit and coordinate lawyers who will agree to volunteer annually a total of more than two thousand pro bono hours of mediation services, the equivalent of approximately $45,000 at moderate legal billing rates. First announcements of the program resulted in the response of 67 lawyers for the fifty slots, a large percentage of them from the same language and ethnic backgrounds as their prospective clients. Most of their services will be used evenings and on Saturdays. Future plans of the foundation in the field of mediation include programs in public-housing projects, in public schools, and in status-offender hearings in juvenile courts.[16]

Recent also is the establishment of a novel application of the mediation philosophy and procedures in the criminal-justice system: prison disputes. The National Center for Correctional Mediation, newly organized, now offers its services without cost.[17] The need for other than court action in disputes arising in jails and prisons is indicated by the center's listing of seventy-five hundred legal petitions that were filed by inmates in 1975 for amelioration of conditions of their imprisonment. Excessive drain on the staff time of correctional departments and of penal institutions constitutes additional justification for the creation of this new center.

The descriptive brochure sets out the procedure for enlisting the center's services, which may be requested by correctional administrators, gubernatorial aides, state attorneys general, inmates, and prisoner-assistance and legal-aid groups.[18] Before involving itself in a correctional dispute, the center will evaluate the dispute, identify the key parties to it, and determine whether they are both sincere in their desire to mediate. This conflict-assessment phase can then be succeeded by an examination of the issues in dispute, as well as those that may be highly significant though not necessarily apparent on the surface. This issue-determination phase is followed by a series of formal and informal meetings between the mediator and each of the two sides. Thereafter mediation generally follows the normal process.

The special significance of this program is that it represents an extension of mediation from the court phase to the correctional phase of criminal justice. Its development will be followed with interest by persons concerned with the applicability of the mediation process to the resolution of a variety of conflict situations. The recent outbreak of brutal violence in the New Mexico State Prison starkly reminiscent of Attica a decade ago, provides urgent testimony to the need for program alternatives to the historic response of official violence to counter offender violence.

By early 1980, more than ninety mediation programs were reported to be operating in at least ten states. The interest generated by this community-based procedure for resolving conflicts between people is motivated by the support that has been forthcoming from a wide diversity of sources: governmental agencies, judges and lawyers, social agencies, and educational institutions. The extension of these mediation efforts may help to ease and reduce the kinds of tensions that arise between neighbors, friends, and family members. The media daily report the tragic frequency with which such misunderstandings end in serious injury or even death. The growth of the mediation process provides constructive recourse for the defusing of such conflicts—all the more intense by reason of the close bonds between the disputants—by making available an amicable resolution at the hands of concerned community people, redounding, in the end, to the benefit of the community at large.

10 Advisory Sentencing Panels

The benefits to be gained from citizen participation in sentencing and dispositions would reinforce the socializing effect of the criminal law upon many persons in the community. It should strengthen the forces tending to reduce crime and enhance community interest and participation in the administration of justice. At the same time, the primary values and interest that the community wants to see protected can be made clear in a variety of differing circumstances. Participation of citizens should thus foster the main purposes of sentencing and dispositions: the protection of the community by reinforcing fundamental values relating, for example, to privacy, property or inviolability of the person.[1]

Emile Durkheim has made the same claim for the value to be gained from the imposition of penalties for wrongdoing: that in punishing the law violator, society was reasserting the norms of behavior expected of all its members and was once again making clear to all, through the verdict and penalty imposed, that a harm done to one member of society would be considered a harm to the total body politic.[2] Today we see a lessened regard for the law and a consequent higher degree of lawlessness than prevailed in an earlier time. To what degree this may have been brought about by a diminution of respect for official authority, including the judiciary, is impossible to assess precisely. Certainly an increased crime rate is an index of the degree of social change occurring in society, plus citizen frustration with what they regard as mounting bureaucratic intrusion into their lives, and a sense of being increasingly locked out from any determining voice in the decisions that directly and profoundly affect their lives. Any observer of the sentencing session of a criminal court is bound to be struck with its swift, perfunctory nature and its impersonality as to the defendant, with little if any concern for the victim.

Nowhere is this feeling more widespread or keenly sensed than in the victimization felt by persons who are assaulted in their persons or robbed of their property. The role of such victims is limited to making a complaint or being called to give testimony in court. Their relationship to the person who has affronted them is, in the majority of instances, completely impersonal. They know nothing of him, his background, his motives for having committed the offense against them. Many victims hesitate to report offenses to the police. They know that if they file an insurance claim, they may well be penalized by an increase in their next premium, and as for what happens to the offender after he has been found guilty, they have even less voice, and interest, in that step of the process than they had in the determination of his guilt. One result of this system is a cynicism and alienation of ordinary citizens from the criminal-justice process, which contributes to the prevalent sense of malaise with regard to all government.

The notion that the victim should have any part in what happens to the person who harmed him is the very antithesis of the fruitlessness felt by most people who find themselves robbed, assaulted, or otherwise violated. After all, the indictment reads: "The State vs. the Offender"; in that process what power has the victim? How can he assert his rights or indicate his estimate of what should be done to the one who has harmed him? Any such feelings of impotence regarding the sentencing process are heightened by the power that has distinguished the judge from lesser mortals—his authority to condemn convicted offenders to penalties that will affect their property and their freedom. It is unthinkable for the ordinary citizen to conjure with the notion that he can play any part in such an awesome process, a process that is the prerogative reserved for and most prized by those who sit upon the bench.

The element of discretion that marks every stage in the criminal process—from arrest by a police officer, to the prosecutor's judgment whether to press charges, to the examining magistrate's decision whether to bind over the defendant for the grand jury—reaches its apogee when the judge who has presided at the trial that saw the offender convicted finally hands down the sentence. The authority granted earlier in the case to the officials who mandate these interim decisions is in no degree comparable to the discretionary power of the judge who commands the convicted defendant before him to rise and hear the imposition of his fate—on a scale ranging from a few dollars or days to life imprisonment or death.

The result of the broad sentencing powers allotted to the judiciary is that unequal, and even inequitable, sentences may be imposed on offenders who have violated the same law but each under such differing circumstances as may lead the judge to individualize his final decision with those circumstances in mind. Inequality of sentencing—by different judges at different times and in different places—is one of the most frequent sources of public discontent with the criminal-court process.

Watergate and its aftermath—the pardon of Nixon and the short prison terms served by his associates who were convicted—followed by such events as the commutation of the sentence of Patty Hearst, has documented to the public the inequities of sentencing and the readiness with which people of wealth or position receive lighter penalties of fine or imprisonment and shorter terms in prison than those who are less fortunate or who are members of minority groups. The uneven dispensation of justice, specifically the wide divergences in sentencing practices, has enormous impact within the penal institutions where sentences are served. Prison riots are frequently sparked by inmate feelings of outrage at the disparity of sentences no less than by capricious or discriminatory release policies by parole boards.

The popular stereotype of the judge sees his role as meting out punishment. It is expected that he will hand down a sentence that will serve to chastise the offender, condemn his criminal act, and provide a barometric reading of the prevailing degree of heinousness with which the particular offense is regarded and the public estimate of the degree of outrage that the particular convicted person's deed has aroused. Judges, with few exceptions, are remembered for their sentencing of particular defendants as much as for the manner in which they have conducted the trial itself.[3] A judge sitting alone determines guilt or innocence and sentences the guilty. In a jury trial his responsibility is to see that the trial is conducted fairly and thereafter to pass sentence.

A significant factor in the sentencing policies of judges is the degree to which they feel a sense of responsibility toward the community. This is especially true for judges who must stand for election. If a particular kind of crime becomes prevalent or particular kinds of individuals seem to be singled out for victimization, judges understandably are inclined to respond to community feelings and to reflect them in the sentences they impose.

Community reaction, therefore, has an influence on judicial actions. Yet except for a specific judge's sensitivity to community feelings, individual members of the community, least of all the victim, seldom have an opportunity to make a direct contribution to the decision-making process. But in recent years this concern has led to the creation of procedures designed to make possible the transmittal of community attitudes directly to the judge who does the sentencing.

Disposition Unit of the Urban Court

The Disposition Unit of the Urban Court of Dorchester, Massachusetts has been a pioneer in providing community participation in the sentencing process. Its establishment in November 1975 was the result of cooperation of a broad range of agencies and individuals. The fundamental goals of the disposition procedure are clearly set out in the initial proposal that led to its creation:

1. To provide the judge with recommendations for reasonable and effective dispositions in selected cases;
2. To do this in a manner that involves the Probation Department, thereby (a) promoting the institutionalization of the practice of providing the judge with relevant dispositional information and (b) enabling Probation to meet its recently articulated standards for presentence investigation and use of community resources;

3. To involve selected and carefully trained community people in the disposition process for the dual purposes of educating them to the difficulties inherent in the sentencing process and relying on their personal knowledge and associations to develop more dispositional resources, especially within the community itself. In fulfilling this latter function, the panelist's role as an advocate for the offender will be encouraged from the outset. Local social service agency personnel will also participate as panelists.
4. To test the hypothesis that a defendant will come to understand the human consequences of his deed and to accept a disposition as legitimate if he or she participates with community people and his or her victim in developing that sentence, and that this will contribute to his or her rehabilitation.[4]

The crucial ingredient in the disposition program is its resolve that defendants, by reason of their participation in the program, will come to an understanding of the personally harmful results their crime has wrought, that these will be personalized by confrontation with the victim, and that they will accept as fair and equitable both the legitimacy of the court and the justness of its sentence, all to the end that the experience will motivate a change in the direction of a law-abiding existence in the community.

In its day-to-day operations, the disposition unit involves professional staff, lay persons from the community (volunteers), the defendant, and, wherever possible, the victim. Its purpose is to develop a presentence assessment of the case, followed by a conference that includes these persons or their representatives. The ultimate goal is to arrive at a disposition that they can recommend for the purpose of sentencing a defendant who has already pleaded or been found guilty or on whom the judge has found sufficient facts for a guilty finding, which he may not choose to enter until he has seen the probation record. Where the facts of the case, together with the defendant's record, indicate that such a finding would not be in the best interests of the defendant and the community, the judge may decide to continue the case without a finding for three to four weeks. At this point, while the defendant is still in court, the matter is transferred to the disposition unit by the probation office. Cases may also come to the disposition unit by referral from the district attorney or from defense counsel.

A staff member escorts the defendant to the Urban Court offices for the intake interview, which includes an explanation of the disposition process. A date is set for the hearing, and appointments are made with an associate probation officer and the staff psychologist. After the initial interviews, the probation officer conducts an investigation of the defendant's family, employment, and schooling for incorporation into his report on the defendant.

The first meeting of the panel usually takes place a week later. Present are the probation officer, the psychologist, two panelists representing the community, the panel convener (a staff member), the defendant, and, in selected instances where he agrees, the victim or an advocate who appears in his behalf.[5] The agenda for this initial meeting varies with each case, but its purpose is the same in all instances: the development of a recommended sentence that will be acceptable to both victim and defendant, to be passed to the judge as an advisory opinion. The victim does not participate in the meeting until the probation report has been read and discussed, after which he is given an opportunity to present the options that he can agree to.

The role that the victim plays in the disposition proceedings is one of its most innovative and constructive elements. There is, perhaps, no more effective way of emphasing to an offender the direct results of his crime than by hearing it from the victim seated across the table. Initial contacts between the two are usually marked by hostility or indifference toward the offender on the part of the victims, who generally feel at this stage that their views do not matter. Once they are given an opportunity to participate in the hearing, however, and realize that they have a voice in what will happen to the defendant, victims often change their attitude and express interest in the process. Not infrequently they articulate their sense of relief, and even satisfaction, that they do have a role to play and that their remarks and suggestions have a bearing on the sentence that will be determined with their help. They are provided a chance to vent their resentment and anger; within the controlled setting of the hearing, this can be salutary to the end result. In the words of the unit director, "[Our] job is not to be comfortable or safe; on the contrary we are about exploring the tools and limits of primary interaction between real people. . . . Such [experimentation] requires very responsible and conscious direction. We are not promoting frivolous or chaotic events, but rather carefully developing a methodology of effective court/community-to-defendant communication."[6]

The role of the victim is the most delicate, fraught, as it must be, with all kinds of emotions. Realization of this uneasiness on the part of the victim is tellingly described by the Urban Court staff:

> Participation of the victim occurs in selected cases. The extent of that participation, and the question of whether the victim and defendant will be present at the same time, is handled on an experimental, case-by-case basis. In all cases, decisions regarding the involvement of the defendant and/or the victim will be made with extreme sensitivity to the issues of fear and revenge on the part of all concerned; in no case will a defendant or victim be coerced to participate.[7]

Considering the discomfiture of the victim when confronting the person who harmed him, it is a tribute to the sensitivenss of the staff of the unit that in 60 percent of the panel hearings, the victim or a representative of the victim is present at and participates in the hearings.

Not infrequently after such a confrontation, the offender says that had he known the victim before the incident, he might very well not have committed the act. And often the victim responds that simply coming to know his assailant after the fact does not constitute grounds for exempting him from paying the penalty for his original act. After such an interchange, the field is then clear for the two to work out a sentence to which they can both agree.

The initial hearing usually takes about two hours. The first hour is taken up with the report on the defendant, followed by a discussion with him; the second half of the meeting is devoted to a discussion by all members of the panel. At the end of the session, a preliminary sentence is ready for recommendation, including specific details of how restitution is to be made. The defendant may not be privy to the precise sentence recommendation at this point, but he is given an opportunity to state his preferences.

One week later the probation associate submits the plan that he has developed to a second meeting of the panel, together with the format in which it is to be submitted to the judge for approval. The convenor reduces this material to writing for presentation to the court.

The final sentence recommendation is the result of a range of options that the panel has reviewed and considered. It covers such elements as treatment (physical as well as psychological or psychiatric), support (home or school) employment, and training, as well as the elements of restitution and supervision on probation for whatever length of time the judge may order. Requiring the defendant to render some restitution to the community has both a punitive and a rehabilitative aspect: it compels the defendant to give up some of his liberty (his free time) while extending to him the opportunity to contribute to the community, to meet and work with caring and concerned neighbors.

The impact on an offender who experiences this process cannot be overstated. It is the opposite of the usual adversary process in a court where defendant and victim rival one another only in terms of conflicting testimony in an attempt to gain a victory: for the prosecution, a finding of guilt, for the defense, acquittal. In the confrontation process, by contrast, opposing parties face one another directly rather than through their respective surrogates. They can each speak freely without constricting rules of evidence, without contesting the truth or falseness of the charges, and with an opportunity for each to appraise and even come to an understanding of the other. The victim learns something about his assailant; the latter can neither evade nor escape facing up to the consequences of his action and the plight he has forced upon his victim.

Both parties to the dispute, together with the concerned and objective representatives of the community, now have the opportunity to design a constructive resolution of the conflict by agreeing upon the sentence that they will recommend to the judge as a result of their deliberations and joint agreement.

When this recommendation comes before the judge, the defendant is required to be present, as he would for sentencing in the ordinary trial process. In 90 percent of the cases, the judge accepts the recommendation of the advisory panel in whole or in part. This may require restitution to the victim in money, in kind, or in service; a stated number of hours of community service may be required; or the offender may be directed to comply with an order to enroll in some type of treatment or counseling program or to agree to go to work, if unemployed.

After his acceptance of the sentence, the defendant comes under the supervision of a probation officer of the Urban Court who helps him to carry out the terms of the court order, ensuring that restitution payments are made by the offender and facilitating compliance with the other specifics of the judge's decision.

The community panelists not only assist and participate in the disposition hearings but also assist the probation officers in the search for social-agency and employment resources. In some instances their relationship with the defendant continues beyond disposition, thus rendering an auxiliary service to the probation officer who has official supervision of the case. For compensation, they receive twelve dollars for each full session in which they participate. Although the manner of their recruitment follows the same pattern as that used for the recruitment of other community justice volunteers, their training for their work with the disposition unit is specialized. After they have been screened and accepted as volunteers in the project, they undergo a month of training, which takes place from 6 to 9 P.M. on weekday evenings, and all day on Saturdays, for a total of fifty hours.

The first training session is given over to orientation in the history and objectives of the program. The relationship between the unit and the court that it serves is set out, together with sufficient grounding in the legal language and procedures common to the process. Alternative options for disposition are discussed, and the issue of privacy is stressed. (Volunteers are required to sign an agreement that they will not divulge to anyone other than to an officer of the unit or of the court any information regarding the defendant that is contained in the probation report. They sign this agreement with the understanding that any breach of that confidentiality will make them liable to dismissal from their position with the unit, as well as subject to criminal prosecution.)

Succeeding training sessions cover a variety of topics: personal values and the role of the unit staff and panelists; skills of listening, attending, observing, and responding; probation theory and practice; court procedures; creative sentencing; and an overview of corrections as alternatives to sentences served in the community. Trainees attend court sessions, which are followed by discussion, questions, and a critique of court procedures. Mock sessions of the disposition process are held to give the trainees an opportunity to play the various roles of the participants in the actual sessions of the disposition unit. Lectures and group discussions help to round out the training courses. After completion of the course of training, panelists are expected to commit themselves to six to twelve months of service to the program.

Case Histories

One of the first cases that the unit dealt with involved the branch manager of a local bank (the complainant) and a machinist in a city institution (the defendant). The defendant had already admitted in court that he had cashed a check made out to a fellow employee, which he had found on payday in the corridor outside the paymaster's office. He had submitted a false identity card at the time the teller cashed this check. The camera positioned above the cage identified him. When he appeared in court, he had already been discharged from his job as a result of the incident, and he agreed to meet with the bank manager to arrive at a sentence that he could accept.

The hearing opened with the community representative (the case coordinator) at the head of the table. At his right sat the defendant with a representative of the probation department. When the bank manager entered, he was introduced to the defendant, who then described what had happened. With a degree of candor seldom seen in a courtroom, the defendant turned to the bank manager and said, "I figured you were covered by insurance, you are a big, wealthy bank, and I could find good use for that $130." "But it wasn't yours, Ed," the manager responded. "I know it wasn't," he countered, "but I didn't take it from anyone. I didn't pick anybody's pocket; I just found it and cashed it. I figured the city would give him another check, so he wouldn't lose anything, and the bank wouldn't either. Besides, you're a wealthy bank. What's $130 to you?" The coordinator then drew out from Ed his alcohol problem and his neglected diabetic condition, which accounted for his poor health and the number of lost days of work that resulted.

The bank manager introduced a surprise element when he turned to Ed and said, "You are right—we are covered for fraudulently cashed checks, so we stand to lose nothing by what you did. But someone was really hurt by what you did: the bank teller." "How come?" Ed asked. The manager described the system whereby his bank establishes a ceiling for the cashing of bad checks for the calendar year. Any teller who does not exceed that ceiling receives a bonus at Christmas; those who exceed it forfeit the bonus.

"In your case, Ed, when she cashed your check the teller exceeded her quota and she misses her bonus."

"I'm sorry about that," Ed says, quite spontaneously. "I didn't mean to hurt her—and I figured the bank could well afford it." "We can," the manager repeated, "but she can't." "If I make good on the $130 check will she get her bonus?" The manager assured him that she would.

The case moved swiftly to its resolution. Ed agreed to repay the bank as soon as he got a job, he pledged to enroll in a local Alcoholics Anonymous program, and an appointment was to be made for him at the local health clinic to get treatment for his diabetes. Because his mechanical skill was in demand, there would be little difficulty in finding him another job, and an appointment was made for him to meet with the employment counselor the next day. "Good luck, Ed," were the final words of the banker as he stood and shook hands with the check passer, who rose to thank him and wish him well.

The crimes charged against defendants who pass through the disposition process run the gamut of offenses; they include breaking and entering, possession of burglar tools, larceny, unarmed robbery, assault with a dangerous weapon, receiving stolen goods, and automobile theft. This list by no means exhausts the range of offenses with which the defendants who appear in disposition sessions are charged, but it does fairly reflect the range of criminal cases heard in the regular criminal session of any court of first instance.

Another case, a combination of petty larceny and assault, concerns a man who robbed a cab driver at knife point one summer evening. When the police arrived on the scene, the assailant was found giggling in the back seat of the cab, drunk. Charged with robbery and assault with a deadly weapon, he was brought to court and found guilty. Before the judge passed sentence, the defendant was referred to the community disposition panel, which spent three hours in discussion with him. The cab driver was invited to attend but had responded, "I never want to see that guy again. But I cannot believe that you are calling me. Didn't think anybody worried about the victim anymore. All I want is my fifteen bucks back." The disposition plan that the defendant helped to design, and to which he agreed, included two years in the county house of correction, suspended; participation in the local Alcoholics Anonymous program to help him with his alcohol problem; and his coaching basketball two Saturday mornings a month to boys at the local housing project playground.

Some cases involve much more substantial sums of money. One case recorded in the unit describes a trusted employee of a company for which he had worked for thirty years. At the age of sixty-one, in desperate need of funds to care for his very old mother in a nursing home, he began a series of thefts from the company, which stretched over four years. He filled and delivered orders to company customers, for which he was receiving a sizable discount from list price. The defendant was covered up by a confederate in the billing department of the company, with whom the defendant split the proceeds of his deception—about $80,000.

A conference and two hearings were held by the disposition unit on this case, attended by the president of the victimized company, a community victim-aide advocate, a probation associate, and the convener. The defendant, having admitted his guilt, described in detail the manner in which he had carried out the fraud. The victim then asked that a suspended sentence of imprisonment for one year be imposed "in order to impress upon the defendant the seriousness of his 'theft by deception' and in the hope of deterring other employees from stealing from the company." He also asked that the defendant be required to repay as much of the $13,000 as his assets permitted, this sum representing the difference between the total of the theft and the reimbursement to be made by the insurance company.

The defendant requested that his case be continued without a finding, in view of his age, his three decades of service to the company, and his lack of a prior criminal record. In their deliberations, the panel members, "after reviewing all the facts and keeping in mind the serious nature of the offense, were unanimous in regard to the recommended sentence, that the defendant be placed on probation for a year." They added that they "were cognizant of and sensitive to the severe mental anguish and embarrassment, loss of character and financial strain already suffered by the defendant and his family as a result of this incident . . . and were pleased to note that he voluntarily agreed to make restitution by forfeiture of a retirement profit sharing plan." This amount totaled $7,500, which was paid to the victim company. The defendant also agreed to meet on a weekly basis for a three-month period with the probation associate, who was helpful in placing him on a CETA job working with the elderly.

The disposition unit deals with juveniles as well as adults. In one case a fifteen-year-old boy, in the company of three friends was found in possession of liquor taken from a nearby store one night during a blizzard. The victim declined to attend the hearing but was represented by an advocate who reported that the victim, a widow, was angry at the defendant, that her husband had been killed in the liquor shop two years previously, that she had no insurance coverage and was anxious to recoup as much of her loss through restitution as possible, and that she wanted severe punishment imposed on the young defendant.

The defendant's prior record included three appearances in the juvenile court for larceny, breaking and entering, and use of a motor vehicle without authorization. All of these charges had been dismissed. His school report showed frequent absences. He failed to appear at the first hearing but did show up for the second. The panel's recommended disposition stipulated that the defendant meet with his associate probation officer weekly on a strict supervisory basis for three months and thereafter on a regular basis as specified by his officer; that he attend school regularly and not absent himself without a valid reason; that he cooperate with the job developer in finding employment and thereafter make restitution from his earnings up to one-half of the loss he had caused; that a worker from the local Youth Activities Commission supervise his evening activities; and that he be required to perform twenty-five hours of volunteer service in the community through the court clean-up campaign. The record of the case closes with a photostat of a letter from his school principal, dated one week after the disposition hearing, stating that there had been "marked improvement in his behavior, in his class work and his general attitude," to which some one had added a handwritten postscript: "You should frame this."

One of the unit's cases might have ended up in federal court on a criminal complaint had it not been disposed of informally, for it involved federal property, a mailbox. According to police testimony, a cab driver observed in the early morning hours and reported a mailbox being overturned, its contents spilled out on the sidewalk, and the mail thus removed, about to be destroyed. Placed under arrest and brought to court, the defendant freely admitted his guilt.

The victim—the postal authority—was not present at the hearing but was represented by a victim advocate. The social investigation revealed that the defendant had left school in the eleventh grade, had no fixed abode, and worked only intermittently. The representative of the victim claimed no restitution as a result of the incident. The defendant claimed that his irresponsible action was attributable to his having been drunk at the time and that this was an isolated incident, statements confirmed by his mother and brother. The panel reviewed with him the seriousness of his offense, pointing out that his conduct was unjustifiable and considered by the community to be intolerable. The defendant appeared remorseful and embarrassed and promised that he would not appear in court again. The panel "felt strongly that the defendant should benefit from the imposition of some structure in his life" and were hopeful that "his behavior problem would diminish or vanish provided his time was constructively occupied."

The panel agreed—with the concurrence of the victim's advocate and the defendant—that the case be continued for a year without a finding, during which time the defendant would report weekly to his associate probation officer for three months; that he would submit to an in-depth psychological evaluation at the court clinic and agree to receive ongoing counseling if this was deemed appropriate; that he would cooperate in finding a job; and that he would enroll in evening classes in his neighborhood with a view to obtaining his high-school equivalency diploma. He also pledged to take up fixed residence at his mother's home and to discontinue his associations with the peer group in the neighborhood in which the incident had taken place. The final stipulation served as a reminder to the defendant that he owed an obligation to the community by reason of his irresponsible act of vandalism, and by way of restitution he agreed to perform forty hours of community volunteer service through the court clean-up program in lieu of court costs.

These case histories illustrate the values which redound to the benefit of those involved in this procedure. The judge is assisted in the most difficult aspect of his job—arriving at the proper sentence. The victim is not only assuaged by being reimbursed for loss but has been presented an opportunity to try to understand why some people, at least his instant antagonist, engage in criminal acts. The offender has been freed to confess his guilt without the arduous process of standing trial, in addition to having to face up to and accept his culpability. No less important, he has cooperated in a process, which brings him into direct contact with the person he has wronged and has been aided in developing a perspective widely at variance with the one usually held—that of blaming someone else for his own dereliction.

From a psychological point of view, this confrontation constitutes one of the most salutary features of the sentencing advisory panel procedure. Although it is impossible to gauge the extent to which any offender's attitude is fundamentally changed by having experienced this kind of confrontation session, the success rate that the program has earned encourages all those who believe that the traditional punitive process has largely failed to rehabilitate offenders or to serve as a deterrent against further criminal acts.

An interesting postscript may be gleaned from a report on recent trends in sentencing in Finland. As in other Scandinavian countries, Finland has been reexamining its procedures:[8]

> The use of sentences is now motivated in Scandinavia by the view that they are necessary to emphasize public disapproval of an offense. The necessity to uphold the authority of the law is seen as not being allowed to operate in too much of a short-term manner. Thus, sentences should not be allowed to be raised or lowered every week according to current criminality levels in a particular area.
>
> Nor should a particularly sensational individual incident be allowed to suddenly raise sentences for other similar—or even totally unrelated offences.
>
> The behavior of the offender after the act is also seen as a factor to be taken into account when assessing the penalty. For example, the significance of remorse, admission of guilt, voluntarily turning oneself over to the police, scrupulously paying for any damages or apparent willingness to pay for those damages may often be taken into consideration by a judge in assessing a penalty.
>
> Similarly it is not unknown for recalcitrance, bad behaviour and deliberate lying during police examination, indifference to damage caused to the parties or attempts to escape after the crime to also affect the penalty.[9]

More specifically related to the thrust here is the statement, "Attempts are being made to replace punishments with arbitrated settlements where the offender and the victim attempt to reach a satisfactory solution. This measure is possible only in some offenses and even then it would presuppose the active support of the court serving as an arbitrator. *This would radically change the role of the courts* (italics added). This sentence is key to the process with which this chapter has been concerned: the reliance of the bench on community representatives to assist in the determination of sentences, in which process the victim no less than the offender plays a decisive, constructive part. The impersonality of the usual adversary proceeding is replaced by informal face-to-face sessions. When we consider the degree of anonymity or facelessnes with which many offenses today seem to be committed—brutal attacks on persons unknown to the assailant, vandalism against both personal and public property, the frequency with which the victim of a robbery or larceny is thereafter further assaulted or even murdered when no understandable motive in so doing is apparent—it is a welcome return to human confrontation to have both parties to a conflict work out together the compensation that the victim will receive from the offender, the contribution that the offender will make to the victim and to society as well.

Juvenile Juries

It is commonplace in any discussion of the factors conducive to juvenile delinquency to ascribe some degree of responsibility to the pressure of their peers on the young offender.[10] Adolescence is recognized as one of the most suggestible periods in the life span. In his theory of differential association, Sutherland, for example, stresses the learning process by which young people acquire both antisocial attitudes and values, and learn the means by which they commit offenses. In the light of the important influence exerted by youthful associates on one another, notably in gang behavior, a recent program in Denver, Colorado, provides an instrumentality by which students in junior and senior high school sit in judgment on their peers charged with offenses, determine their guilt, and impose sanctions.

The scheme grew out of a juvenile diversion program that the Office of the Denver District Attorney had initiated in 1974. The increasing number of offenses being committed by persons under age eighteen—55 percent of all crimes in September 1979—with a consequent rise in the number of serious, violent, and repeated juvenile offenses, pointed to the need for diversion from formal court hearing of as many lesser offenses as possible and the establishment of some workable procedure for their disposition.

The result was the creation in spring 1979 of the student jury program, in which a jury of six or seven teenagers decides the conditions under which appropriate cases submitted by the district attorney will be diverted. "The project is designed to ensure fairness both to the community and to the juvenile offender. Only juveniles who admit their involvement in an offense appear before the student jury—provided that the offender and the offender's parents opt for the Program." The role of the jury is limited to the determination of punishment or rehabilitation, in accordance with the guidelines of the program. Staffing and office space are provided by the district attorney's office. One condition or a combination of them may be imposed on the offender by the jury of his peers:

1. Restitution to the victim for any loss caused by the offender.
2. Reporting at reasonable, specified intervals to the Denver district attorney's juvenile diversion effort, in person, by telephone, and by letter.
3. Regular school attendance and participation in school activities.
4. Appropriate counseling.
5. Strict curfew hours.
6. Any other punitive or rehabilitative conditions deemed appropriate by the student jury.

Under this last provision, young offenders have been required to secure employment, write a letter of apology to a police officer, render unpaid community service (such as in a drug rehabilitation center) and enroll in a recreational program. In one instance the jury rebuked a parent for "being part of the problem of his son by belittling him." Once the defendant has accepted the conditions, he signs a contract, which, if not fulfilled, results in the case's being filed with the district attorney's office for hearing before the juvenile court. The young people who have served as jury members are between the ages of thirteen and seventeen. The jury meets four days a week to hear and dispose of cases. One advantage of the program is the speed with which cases are heard and decided; hearings take place within days instead of weeks, giving a sense of urgency to what is all too often a long drawn-out process of delays and continuances. Perhaps the most distinctive aspect of this program is that young, accused offenders may find it easier to accept from their peers than from their elders the realization that they are responsible for their actions.

A ripple effect of this pioneering experiment is reported from Brandon, Manitoba, Canada, which followed a recommendation by the provincial juvenile justice committee.[11] The Brandon plan is designed to provide the sentencing judge of the family court with a youthful perspective on each case. The defense and the crown have the right to challenge those selected for this advisory jury of youthful peers. In introducing the program, both judge and prosecutor pointed to its educational value for the young people who will be involved in it, and for its "serious attempt to involve the community more in its own problems." The attorney general added an interesting deterrent note: "The advice of an offender's peers will help the judge, but the major value is the exposure it will give students to the court system."

11 Community Service as an Alternative Sentence

> Many of the criminal justice system's difficulties stem from its reluctance to change old ways or . . . to try new ones. The increasing volume of crime in America establishes conclusively that many of the old ways are not good enough. Innovation and experimentation in all parts of the criminal justice system are clearly imperative.[1]

No description of community-justice programs would be complete without recognition of a growing trend to sentence convicted offenders to a term of service to—and in—the community in lieu of traditional fines, court costs, or imprisonment. This service may be performed as a condition of a dispute resolution through mediation or arbitration, or as a provision of a restitution agreement, which also carries some repayment to the victim for loss suffered as a result of a criminal act. It may also be a condition of a suspended sentence imposed by the criminal court or juvenile court after a finding of guilt or delinquency.

Judges are not alone in sensing a lack of sentencing alternatives, even though under the terms of probation concurrent with a suspended sentence a very wide range of individualized conditions can be imposed on the convicted offender for whom immediate imprisonment is not ordered. The requirement that an offender part with some of his liberty is an integral part of imprisonment. By specifying that some of this free time be devoted to service to the community, several advantages immediately accrue. The offender is given an opportunity to make repayment to society for the harm he has done it or one of its members; the community benefits from services that it would either have to pay for or do without; and time spent by the offender at a community-service job leaves him fewer hours to get involved in further criminal activity. When used in connection with restitution to the victim, service to the community rounds out the package, bespeaking a totality of reparations, in the area of sentencing at the same time that "it gives an offender an opportunity to contribute in some form in the community, and thereby gain status and approval for his actions."[2]

Deploring what he termed "the extravagance of imprisonment," Milton Rector, president of the National Council on Crime and Delinquency, has called for "creative sentencing," using this argument:

> Judges and probation officers dealing with white middle- and upper-income offenders from good families very often exercise considerable

ingenuity in locating or creating alternatives to imprisonment. They may not have the time to serve similarly as advocates for all low-income non-dangerous offenders from bad families that come before them, but with a little effort they can recruit volunteer advocates from the community. The involvement of such volunteers would enhance community support for a wide variety of alternative sentences. Communities and volunteers can devise, manage, and operate a variety of noninstitutional sanctions for all nondangerous offenders—and can do so at a cost far lower than the amount of interest now due for amortizing the construction outlay of $50,000 per cell and the annual operating expense of $10,000 per prisoner (whose theft averages about $300).

No public outrage was expressed when a heart specialist who had stolen over $200,000 was sentenced to perform free surgery for indigent children. Nor did the heavens fall when a Phoenix physician, convicted on a drug charge, was sentenced to serve as Tombstone's town doctor as a condition of probation, and when a Phoenix youth convicted of armed robbery was placed on probation for five years during which he was required to complete two years of college work. Creative use of probation can find unlimited alternatives for the unskilled as well as the skilled, for nonwhite as well as white offenders.[3]

As in so many other areas of contemporary life, in the area of sentencing, time and money are almost completely interchangeable commodities. It is not only the bandit who demands "your money or your life"—the two are in daily practice the most readily available sanctions from which a judge can select his final sentence. To persons who are well off financially, even a heavy fine may constitute little significant deprivation. But for the large majority of indigent offenders, the leveling of a fine may impose a burden; for the unemployed, it is an impossibility. Yet rich and poor alike share one asset in common; they all have twenty-four hours available to them every day.

Periodic Detention, New Zealand

This innovative program, among the earliest of the community-service sentencing programs, was established in accordance with the principle that persons who steal or destroy the property of others should be required to make good the losses they cause and also contribute of their own labor to the community. This same principle had led to the West German practice of "requiring vandals as part of their punishment, to work in their leisure time on projects of value to the community." This precedent, together with the Danish practice of weekend imprisonment, gave impetus to the adoption in New Zealand of the periodic detention scheme,

> designed to place an offender under a form of control which does not remove him from the community and yet is more coercive or supervisory

than probation. The crux of the scheme is control of a significant and substantial part of an offender's leisure time.

The scheme was first enacted in 1962 for the young offender between 15 and 21 years of age, and the adult was included in 1966. A young offender reports at a center early on a Friday evening and resides there until about noon on the following Sunday. In addition he reports to the center on an evening during the week and stays there for two or three hours. The adult offender reports for the day on a Saturday. All offenders under this scheme are expected to work on a Saturday, preferably on projects of benefit to the local community. For instance, offenders have worked at such places as an intellectually handicapped children's home, and at old people's homes. There is a counseling and educational program for offenders in the evenings. The center is directed by a warden who is assisted by his wife, and the warden is responsible to the local head of the probation service.

Persons who have been convicted of an indictable offense or have failed to pay a fine previously imposed by court order are eligible for this type of sentence. Periodic detention can run as long as a year for offenses ranging from disorderly conduct to burglary.

Court Referral Programs

In the last three years of its existence, this program in Alameda County, California, has placed thirteen thousand offenders in a variety of community slots.[5] Since the inception of the program, judges have made use of these assignments to local voluntary and public agencies either as supplement or alternative to traditional sentencing.

Female traffic offenders were the first beneficiaries of the program because of the finding that many of them were unable to pay money fines and a term in jail created disruption or hardship to the family. As the program developed, men and misdemeanants were referred and, at a later stage, selected felons and juvenile offenders. Most of the participants in the program are persons convicted under traffic and parking ordinances; a third are offenses under the criminal code. Of this group, close to one-half had committed offenses against public order, malicious mischief, or minor thefts. An increasing number of persons in the program—about 20 percent—are under probation supervision by the courts.

The program regards itself as an "aspect of a community service volunteer program" and not as part of the criminal-justice system. This is a reflection of the decriminalizing stance that the program takes, as well as of the fact that it plays no part in the decisions regarding sentencing, which are the sole responsibility of the court. Prospective participants are referred by the court to the program after the court, in consultation with the defendant, has agreed on a community work sentence, as well as the number of hours to be served. Participation in the prorgram is voluntary on the part of the offender, who is made aware that the service he will be expected to perform is in lieu of a fine or term in jail, which he may prefer. Willingness and ability to perform some service are among the criteria for admission to the program. All referrals from the court are interviewed, screened, and then matched by interest and talent with the needs of the agency where the service is to be performed. Of all persons who have been interviewed, work placements were arranged for 98 percent. Approximately 10 percent of these were later referred back to the court when they failed to appear. Exactly half of the community service assignments were for forty hours or less, a quarter for forty-one to eighty, and a final quarter eighty-one hours or more.

Maintenance and clerical work engage more than half of all participants in the program, who range in age from fourteen to seventy years. Skilled and unskilled tasks include maintenance work, animal care, janitorial and security work, carpentry and general repairs. Clerical tasks include typing, filing, addressing, and collating. The beneficiaries of their services range widely: free clinics, rest and convalescent homes, libraries, the Red Cross, counseling and rehabilitative services, legal, housing, and employment agencies, parks, churches, and branches of local government. Ten percent of the participants in this community-service program are reported to have continued on as volunteers after their allotted term of service has been completed. In 1976-1977, some six hundred different agencies benefited from the services of court-referred volunteers, over 80 percent of whom completed their court-assigned terms of service, for a total of 400,000 hours since the program began. This total should be contrasted with the program's budget of $145,000 as part of the county probation department with eight full-time and five part-time staff.

The number of referrals has increased each year that the program has been in operation, indicating a growing confidence on the part of the judges in the program, even though it does not include significant numbers of juveniles or felons. For offenders in these two groups, it may be felt that a larger measure of supervision may be necessary than is available through a program whose main objective is the provision of opportunities for community service. The steady rise in the number of referrals from the court to the program, as well as the growth in the number of community agencies served, "is clear evidence of the program's success in stimulating judicial interest in the concept of symbolic restitution and involving the community in the criminal justice process."

The success of the Alameda County pioneering efforts in community service has resulted in the spread of the idea to close to fifty other communities throughout the state, and the organization of the Association of Court Referral Programs, which holds monthly meetings, distributes a bulletin monthly and acts as an informational and promotional voice for all of the California court-referral programs. The Orange County program has distinguished itself by its attention to evaluation of program results. After the first sixteen months of operation, the evaluation report concluded that the program in that county "has been of value to the courts as a sentencing alternative, to the agencies as an additional source of numerous volunteers, and to the many offenders who benefit from serving as a volunteer in their community rather than paying a fine or being put in jail."

In Solano County, California, the local court referral program does not aim to involve the offender and his victim in any relationship in order to give the former an opportunity to make restitution, in the belief that most victims prefer not to have any dealings with them. Instead this program provides convicted offenders, including felons, with the chance to devote up to a thousand hours to community service, the longest period reported by any of these programs. In three years, 625 persons convicted of offenses as serious as child molesting, manslaughter, rape, and burglary have participated in community-service work in assignmments as diverse as assisting teachers in the classroom, driving retarded children to school, and helping to renovate a summer camp. Of those who completed their court-assigned service, 42 percent are reported to have devoted more hours than was required under the terms of the program. An additional 14 percent were offered permanent jobs with the agencies where they had volunteered.

California is not alone in using community service in lieu of traditional sentences of fine or imprisonment. For example, the county that includes Portland, Oregon, since 1972 has conducted a program that offers misdemeanants the opportunity to perform unpaid volunteer service for a nonprofit agency. This alternative offers "the court a sentencing mechanism for distinguishing between the lawbreaker and the criminal while providing much needed and appreciated help to the community [which] repays the community for the expense it incurred as a result of the wrongdoing."

The Portland plan differs from that of California in that it is an integral part of the court and is administered by a full-time court staff member. The astonishingly low annual budget, $18,000, is borne by the court. As of October 1977, this program was handling 180 referrals a month, whose services were placed at the disposal of over 150 community agencies, including day-care centers, youth clubs, alcohol- and drug-rehabilitation programs, charitable organizations, animal shelters and zoos, and recycling programs. A taxi driver provided needy persons with forty hours worth of free transportation to medical facilities; a carpenter built a ramp for the handicapped; other volunteers made repairs to the homes of senior citizens. Five years after its founding, the program had made possible the contribution of close to a quarter of a million person-hours by over eighty-five hundred persons charged with misdemeanors.

The program serves as a pretrial diversionary tool in some instances, but its primary function is to provide alternative means of sentencing. The court allows offenders to choose the kind of work and the agency where it is to be performed, with some exceptions. A drug violator, for example, might be assigned to a drug-counseling program and a vandal to remove graffiti inscribed by others on walls. By allowing the defendant to select his choice of service, conflicts with employment and daily personal commitments are kept low. The minimum sentence is twenty-four hours; the maximum eighty, in accordance with the general lines of the following schedule: first offense, petty theft, twenty-four to forty hours; minor in possession of liquor, twenty-four hours; possession of less than an ounce of marijuana, twenty-four hours; and driving while drunk, forty hours. There has been a drastic reduction in court cases as a result of the program, which now handles more persons than does the court probation service. The judge reports that 80 percent of program participants complete their agreed-upon work assignments; the remaining cases receive traditional sentences.

A parallel program, which is also court directed, is found in Winona County, Minnesota. This program, like that in Oregon, is court funded. The judge who initiated it allows offenders who come before him to suggest their own alternative sentence. When approved by the court, this becomes a contract, which the program monitors in order to ensure compliance with it. The project reports a significantly lower rate of recidivism among its clients than with other types of sentence.

Implementation of a program of restitution through community service does not necessarily require an elaborate organization or a staff specially trained in the implementation of a program. More important is the conviction on the part of someone—in the following instance, the judge—that the fundamental aims of justice can be served by combining the needs of many youths who come before the court: the need for a job, the opportunity to render some form of worthwhile service, and a chance to perceive themselves as something other than failures. Erik Erikson has said that most delinquents are convinced that they can never accomplish anything of value and hence tend to regard themselves as worthless.

These three needs are admirably served and combined in a program that was conducted for four months in Woburn, Massachusetts, during the late fall. The judge of the local juvenile court assigned twelve youths to clean up a town lake. Debris—cans, bottles, and old tires—lay four feet deep in some places. Few residents of the town had seen the water in more than twenty years because it was screened by high marsh grass. Youths who accepted the challenge of cleaning up the more than two miles of shoreline had been charged with a variety of offenses—shoplifting, breaking and entering, car theft, and armed robbery. One of them had a record of ten offenses of breaking and entering and one assault and battery. All participants in the clean-up project came from low-income families, many of them single-parent. Their probation reports indicated failure at school and lack of a consistent work history. Some of them had served time in secure holding facilities. They were enrolled in CETA, which provided them with $110 a week, $5 of which they paid as restitution to the local boys' club, a favorite charity of the judge who heard their cases.

"Eight months into the program there has not been one dropout" reports the state commissioner of Youth Services who later established a statewide program of restitution for juveniles:

> I couldn't quite believe what I was hearing, so I visited the area one cold December day.
>
> "Bobby, what do you like about the program?" "The money," he responded. "That can't be. You've been in every program DYS has. You've busted out of all of them. We've even gotten you jobs with good wages. You've been earning money before."
>
> Bobby pauses a minute and turns toward the lake. "See them beaches over there? Nobody swimmed there since anybody can remember. We uncovered those beaches. I got kids in my project. Know what? They'll be swimmin' there this summer."
>
> It should be noted that there existed added incentives. The neighbors [abutters] got so excited about their emerging and long-forgotten vista over the pond, that they vied with each other to see who would give coffee and donuts to the kids each morning. The mayor visited twice. Townspeople stopped by all the time to thank the kids for their effort. Here is paying back, but here also is a delinquent kid who has been at the bottom of the heap earning money, helping a victim and performing a very positive community service.[6]

When one considers how many scenic areas of our country, to say nothing of the roadsides, city streets and parks, could benefit from the services of young offenders who might otherwise find themselves locked up, it is heartening to be able to report a similar project, also in Massachusetts. Under the Earn-It program, the judge who created that program assigned a total of forty-five juveniles, five of them girls, from his district court to reclaim one of the islands in Boston Harbor, Peddocks, abandoned for almost thirty years since it was used as a military installation in the two world wars. The overgrown foliage and vegetation had made the roadways impassable and concealed many of the buildings: a church, a gymnasium, headquarters, a fire station, and others. The youths were ferried out to the island from the mainland nearby to unveil the buildings, clear the brush, picnic areas, fireplaces, and camping grounds, and ready the island to be used as a picnic and recreational area for Boston residents. The youngest in the group was fifteen, the oldest eighteen; most were sixteen. Their pay from CETA provided them with pocket money. Only one of the forty-five assigned to the project did not remain with it until the end. All the others repaid their victims in full. For most of those involved in the project, it was their first job experience. Screened before being assigned by the probation department, some had violent behavior on their prior records; others were suffering from alcoholism or drug abuse. Because of these backgrounds, they were considered to be too big a risk to be placed in private employment, but here they were under constant supervision by skilled and trained counselors who worked alongside of them. For those considered deserving of it, work recommendations were provided in order to help the youths obtain future employment.[7]

An evaluation of the results of the Earn-It program, now four years old, reports that 60 percent of the youth enrolled in it complete their restitution payments from the proceeds of their community work; another 30 percent do so after some prodding by project personnel, leaving a failure rate of only 10 percent. The project is no less successful from a monetary viewpoint. The $35,000 repaid as restitution in 1975 has swelled to $150,000 in 1979. During these four years, twelve hundred offenders have benefited from this unique program of repayment to victims and service to the community.[8]

Bronx Community Service Project

The aim of this pilot project is to make available the community-service sentencing option on a limited basis to defendants whose cases would otherwise be dismissed or discharged, or for whom probation would be a more appropriate sentence in order that they "not be drawn into the net of a new sanction."[9]

The project initially accepts each weekday one defendant who has pleaded guilty to a misdemeanor, where the court has conditioned discharge on the satisfactory completion of two weeks of full-time participation in a community-service project (five days per week, seven hours per day). After a substantial period of testing, the project hopes to be able to provide evening and weekend community service and to impose sentences longer and shorter than the seventy hours proposed in the initial phase. The project will supervise no more than ten participants in any one day during the first nine to twelve months and will identify prospective participants who are "paper eligible"—that is, defendants charged with property crime (misdemeanors, or felonies if screening indicates that grand jury presentation is unlikely), who have at least one prior conviction, and who have a verified Bronx address.

If both prosecution and defense attorneys in a paper-eligible case express interest in a community-service disposition, a member of the project staff immediately interviews the defendant and determines acceptability because of drug, alcohol, or emotional problems. In order to eliminate favoritism or bias in the selection of candidates for the limited number of available slots, the staff will enter the court list at a different point each day and will offer participation to only two out of every three eligible defendants. When both defense and prosecution attorneys have indicated an interest in disposition of the case by conditional discharge to community service and the staff can offer the opportunity to the defendant, plea negotiations will be complete.

The relevant statute permits the court to require performance of community-service work as a part of a conditional discharge only "where the defendant has consented to the amount and conditions of such service."[10] The defendant must understand and accept the terms of this sentence and the possibility of return to court for resentencing if those terms are violated. An agreement embodying the terms would then be executed by the defendant and by a project representative.

A sentence to community service would be followed immediately by an orientation interview, and the offender (now a project participant) would proceed, with a staff member, to the site where he is to begin work on the next weekday. There he would be introduced to the site supervisor, to volunteers from the community who work there (not under sentence), and to other project participants on that site.

The initial sites offer a variety of tasks associated with the rehabilitation of abandoned buildings and the production and distribution of topsoil for converting vacant lots into gardens. (Other sites are under development, particularly for bad-weather days.) The new participant is shown how his work benefits the community and how to reach the site. He is provided with the necessary fare, appropriate work clothes and tools, and three dollars daily for lunch, to be eaten on site.

Members of the project staff plan to seek ways to make each participant's participation a rewarding and interesting experience. For those participants with personal or family problems, project staff offer assistance, but rehabilitative treatment and services are not pressed upon participants.

Although project staff attempt to assist participants in meeting the conditions and although there is some flexibility afforded, it is anticipated that failures will occur. In the event that a participant is to be terminated for violation of the conditions of the sentence, the project staff will arrange voluntary appearance at court for hearing and resentencing, which the district attorney's office will expedite. If a violation is established, the new sentence should be neither more nor less than it would have been initially. It can be expected, therefore, that some defendants who agree to a term of community service will end up sentenced to jail, to probation, or to a fine.

Community Service in a Federal Court

At least one federal district court—that of Memphis, Tennessee—operates a program of community service for convicted offenders placed on probation.[11] The chief judge who inaugurated the program did so for what he envisaged as a number of advantages that such a program would bring. First, it would require the probationer to work without pay for a good cause, which would have a therapeutic effect by providing an opportunity for concrete and constructive restitution. It would further require a regular work schedule. Second, the community would receive valuable services that it might not otherwise have been afforded. Third, the supervisor of the community agency would supplement the supervision of the probation officer. And finally, persons who accepted community assignments might otherwise not have been placed on probation, with consequent incarceration for them and increased costs to the government.

For all of these reasons, the chief judge believed that barring any legal or constitutional objections, the program should go forward. Assured by federal counsel that such a plan would constitute no denial of "substantive or procedural due process, no involuntary servitude, and no violation of the minimum wage laws," the judge proceeded to put his plan into operation.

The first step was the preparation of a list of community agencies that might be willing to accept the services of probationers. The one possible stumbling block was the question of workmen's compensation liability for the unpaid community-service workers, but this was more than offset by the benefits that the agency would receive in the way of service to them at no other cost.

The program called for a report from the employing agency to the court at the end of the first month of work. If this was satisfactory, the agency was not expected to file additional reports unless the work or conduct of the probationer fell below acceptable levels. A warning from the judge would follow any unsatisfactory work performance, with the possible penalty of revocation of probation and the imposition of a sentence of imprisonment.

For those who did well consistently, there was available the possibility of having probation terminated prior to the expiration of their term. The judge reports that "a very high percentage" of probationers in his court were required to perform unpaid community service. Only those who are physically incapable or who currently hold more than one job and do not have any spare hours available are exempted. All others are required to donate eight hours of work each week for the entire period of their probation. This may be modified in some instances to only the first year of a two-year sentence of probation. Agencies that have accepted probationers from the court include boys' clubs, the public library, a hospital, the Salvation Army, the local and national park service, a Head Start program, a house for runaways, and the veterans' hospital. In several instances probationers have been hired by the agency for which they had originally worked without pay. In the first year, fifty-three probationers were assigned to the program. "We have had to revoke probation and impose incarceration for poor work performance in only two cases," reports the judge.

Community Service in Great Britain

Britain's scheme for providing community service by offenders originated with a recommendation by the Advisory Council on the Penal System in its 1970 report to the Home Office.[12] The council sought alternatives to the rising prison population through the adoption of new forms of noncustodial penalties. The basic proposal urged that the courts be given the power to order convicted offenders to perform a specified number of hours of work for the community in their spare time and that probation and after-care services should be responsible for administering the arrangements. The recommendation was accepted and later embodied in the Criminal Justice Act of 1972, which introduced the community service order as an alternative to a prison sentence, in certain cases of fine, default, or violation or a probation order, which might otherwise result in revocation of probation followed by commitment to imprisonment.

Before deciding to allow an offender to work out his sentence in the community, the court must first determine that the offender is seventeen or over; he or she has been convicted of an offense for which a sentence of imprisonment can be imposed; the offender gives consent; the offender lives in an area where arrangements exist for community service to be rendered; and the court has considered the report by a probation officer on the offender and is satisfied that he is prepared to work. If these conditions are met, the court then determines how many hours of service to impose—not fewer than 40 or more than 240—to be completed within twelve consecutive months. When more than one offense is involved, the court may make separate work orders and specify whether they are to be concurrent or consecutive. In the latter event the total hours to be worked must not exceed 240. Before imposing the order, the court informs the offender of his obligation to report to the administering officer before changing his residence. He is warned that failure to comply will constitute a breach of the order and that he may be returned to the court.

Provisions for dealing with violators of work orders closely follow the usual practice whereby the probation officer decides to initiate proceedings. Each offender has to appear before the court, and the judge may impose a fine up to £50 and leave the work order standing or he may revoke the work order and try the offender for the original offense.[13]

The probation service is responsible for organizing the work program in each community, beginning with appointment of a community service committee to oversee the plan and of an organizer called the relevant officer, who is responsible for planning and staffing. After the community plan has been approved by the home secretary, the organizer's main functions are to obtain work placements; to match and allocate offenders to their tasks; to provide close liaison with the court, probation services, and the work-providing agencies; and to take appropriate action against uncooperative offenders and those who violate the terms of their court order. The court has no determination over the precise task that the offender is to perform under the work order that it imposes.

Experimental community-service schemes began in five areas—Durham, Inner London, Nottinghamshire, Lancashire, and Shropshire—early in 1970 and were closely monitored by the Home Office Research Unit. The unit concluded on the basis of the first year's work that the scheme was working well and urged that it be extended.[14]

A valuable feature of the community-service program is that it entails the kind of work that is usually done by volunteers and is unpaid. A wide range of agencies have cooperated in providing a variety of tasks within two broad categories: those of a practical sort that do not involve relationships with individuals and those that involve contact with the beneficiaries of the offender's services. Some projects have been organized by the probation service; other offenders have worked singly or in groups for local voluntary bodies, often alongside and supervised by volunteers. Organizers seek to find for offenders the kind of tasks that suit them personally and are flexible in finding other assignments where the first placement may not have been successful.

Community-service work has included painting and decorating houses and flats for the elderly and handicapped; taking part in archeological excavations; repairing toys for needy children; building playgrounds; demolition of buildings and site clearance; and helping in conservation projects. Personal tasks have included coaching handicapped children in swimming and visiting and helping the elderly and hospital patients. The pilot areas reported cases where offenders had worked well and with enthusiasm, particularly when involved in helping people whom they saw as worse off than themselves.[15] Tradespersons are given an opportunity to place their skills at the service of particular groups of beneficiaries: an electrician may wire a home for battered wives; a cab driver may provide transportation for old-age residents; a hairdresser may give a number of hours at a hospital or home for convalescents. Many of them, probably for the first time in their lives, are finding that they can be of use to others and be accepted for what they can give.

One offender assigned to hospital work is now employed there as a full-time nursing aide. Another young man completed his one hundred hours of service within two and one-half weeks working with young children to construct a playground in London. Some offenders in Nottingham assigned to work with a family-service agency have stayed on as volunteers or as part-time supervisors with the probation service. An offender in Merseyside was accompanied by his wife, thus doubling the contribution made by his services to a charitable organization. Both man and wife are continuing to work as volunteers for the same organization. A young woman completed her forty-hour work order during Christmas by helping in a hostel for needy adults.

In the three years since the home secretary's order permitting the expansion of the community-service work program in August 1974, it is reported to be in full operation in thirty-three probation offices in England and Wales. "The latest position is that financial provision is being made for the extension of the scheme to the whole of England and Wales and I have no doubt that this will be accomplished."[16]

In the first year of the adoption of the community-service plan nationally, some five thousand court orders were imposed. The annual intake rate in Nottinghamshire alone has quadrupled and is reported to be still increasing: "With national extension still not fully completed, and many local schemes still in infancy, it does not seem fanciful to assume a rate of 15,000 a year before long." This optimistic projection of the program into the future is supported by this conclusion:

> The community service order is unique among sentences in that it deprives the offender of his leisure but puts him in the position of helping others instead of being an object of help. More time will be needed to show what the long term effects are on those who take part in it, in particular upon their reconviction rates. But as a method of treating offenders, the initial experience is encouraging and suggests that it is a very useful innovation. In the expansion phase, the probation service is putting much effort into setting up well-based local schemes which, it is hoped, will command the confidence of the courts and enable the community service order to be widely accepted as an important and worthwhile addition to the variety of non-custodial sentences available to offenders.[17]

The report goes on to say that although the original plan did not have scope for the extremely violent, for drug addicts, for alcoholics, or for the mentally ill, experience has shown that persons even in those categories have successfully completed work in the community when they and their task have been carefully matched, and they have been given adequate supervision. "It seems desirable, therefore, that a person before the court who is considered for enrollment in a community work program should not be excluded on the *a priori* basis of the offense which is alleged to have been committed."

This program is reminiscent in many ways of the early days of the halfway house movement in the United States when offenders such as arsonists, drug addicts, persons convicted of violent assaults, and homosexuals were not considered fit subjects for residential treatment in the community. But over the years, these restrictions have eased. The experience of the halfway house movement has clearly demonstrated that circumstances other than those of the offense that brought the offender into conflict with the law are more likely to be indicative of the kind of persons who are candidates for community treatment. "Relatively few cases end in violation or re-sentencing, which is all the more remarkable in that one-half of the community service sentences are given in cases which would otherwise draw jail time." (The economic significance of this may be seen in the average per-capita weekly cost of the community service scheme of £8, as against the average weekly cost of imprisonment of £45.)

Alternatives to probation or institutionalization are also available to juvenile offenders, who are given an opportunity to do volunteer work in institutions aimed at "utilizing all kinds of young people . . . in service to the community, and in developing in-depth understanding of community problems by volunteers. This service, modeled partially on the U.S. Vista program, has been in existence since 1962 and is funded by a foundation and in part by the Department of Education and Science. Disadvantaged young offenders are offered community service as a sentencing alternative to probation and also as a means of rehabilitation by giving them the opportunity to get involved in the rewarding experience of helping others. Assignments have included "taking blind kids on tandem bike rides, shaving old men in old people's homes, giving 'keep fit' classes in mental hospitals, working in shelters for the down-and-out."

A community-service program in Gwent, Wales, will accept any offender recommended by court probation, despite a less than good prior work record. Because of the high unemployment rate prevailing in that community, half of the persons subject to community-service orders had been unemployed for some years; rejection of such persons would have cut the program in half. The results of this forward-looking approach have proven its worth. Although persons subject to community-service orders are reported to have found the first few days of work to be difficult, "after they have established a routine, many respond dramatically. They regain confidence in their ability to work regularly and have actually found full-time employment during or after completion of their orders." The result has been that many persons have been accepted for vocational training by the Department of Employment; the completion of their community-service order is accepted as an indication of their potential for the acquisition of skills and their aiblity to hold steady jobs.[18]

Other Examples

Several instances of community-service sentences, personally experienced by students in our classes in criminology, have been described to us. The first is of a young woman, who as a fourteen-year-old student at a private girls' day school in a middle-class suburb, made a Saturday morning practice of meeting several of her schoolmates at the nearby shopping mall to engage in shoplifting. The object was to shoplift something from one of the stores in the mall to show off to their classmates on the following Monday. This scheme required that the portion of the sales tag usually removed by the cashier was to be left on the stolen article in order to prove that it had not been paid for. One morning, with a friend, she entered a shop and stole a lipstick, eye makeup, a black bra, and a bikini. Apprehended as she left the store, she was turned over to the police who recognized her and took her home instead of to the police station. But instead of dismissing the incident with some punishment of his own, her father insisted that the girl be made to appear before the juvenile court.

The judge, with the agreement of both father and daughter, continued the case subject to the girl's spending every Saturday for the remainder of the school year working in a detention home for girls who had not been as fortunate as she. She completed her term of service, the case was dismissed, and the record sealed. Years later she described her satisfaction at having made amends and attested to the lessons learned from her work in the detention home and to the deterrent effect upon her of the total experience.

Another incident was reported by a first-year law student. In an undergraduate course she had learned about community-justice alternatives to traditional court proceedings and had participated in a mock mediation session, which had evidently impressed her deeply. During the Christmas vacation of her first year at law school, while visiting her aunt, she reported that her cousin, also home on visit, ran down and killed a fifteen-year-old boy on Christmas night, while under the influence of alcohol. The young man had some history of problems with drinking, moved in a circle of artists and writers, and though he had no prior criminal record, impressed the court as a somewhat unstable person. The sentence that the judge might have imposed was five to ten years. But both his family and his counsel feared for the effect of a prison sentence on a person of his temperament. His cousin, recalling her experience with mediation and community service, persuaded the defense counsel, and ultimately the judge, that a sentence to community service would be highly preferable. The young man agreed. The case was continued. The defendant pledged to enroll in an alcohol treatment center and to continue psychiatric treatment, which he had begun shortly before the incident, and committed himself to volunteer two thousand hours—twenty hours a week for the next two years—in the pediatric clinic of a local hospital. Those concerned believed that he could help a large number of other children in pain by his efforts. A recent letter reports that he has initiated a popular arts and crafts program in the children's ward.

The most thorough and informative study made to date of the community-service programs throughout the country indicates that they are most effective when used as alternatives to incarceration rather than as substitutes for fines. In Solano County, California, for example, the 131 offenders sentenced to community service in lieu of fines worked off a total of $7,767 in fines. However, if community services had not been an available option for these offenders, most of the fines would have been dismissed for non-payment. By contrast, the 103 offenders sentenced to community services instead of incarceration would have had to serve a cumulative 980 days in jail. Their community-service work saved the county $15,550 in jail costs, as well as providing hundreds of hours of useful work. From across the country come reports of the extent of this form of alternative sentence:

> Community service in lieu of incarceration is also quite effective when measured against standards other than cost. In Pima County, Arizona, 129 participants, almost all young men convicted of felonies, provided 5,000 hours of service valued at $35,000 over an 18 months period. Only 2.3% of the participants failed to complete the required number of hours.

> Georgia has ten residential centers which combine the concepts of restitution and community service. Approximately 85% of the participants have been convicted of felonies. A recent evaluation showed that victims received $1,587,770 in restitution payments from offenders in these centers. About 90% of the offenders were employed while in the program. In a year's time following release from the centers, 70% of the ex-offenders were still employed, and only 11% had been reimprisoned. The cost of operating these centers was only $1,560 per inmate per year, much less than the cost of imprisonment which can be as great as $26,000 per prisoner per year.

> One surprising aspect of the spread of community service programs is that is has occurred almost completely as a result of local initiatives with little statewide or national encouragement. However, states are beginning to get more involved in pushing community service as a sanction. Maryland has recently passed a law which explicitly authorized community service sentences and facilitates the establishment of new community service programs. Under the new law, any offender who has not been convicted of a violent offense will be eligible.

> The Harris study notes several possible dangers of community service. For example, restitution sentences are used most often for white, middle class, first offenders, and thus do not affect the class of people most often imprisoned. Another danger is in assigning too many hours of community service for minor offenses (2000 hours for shoplifting was one such sentence meted out recently in California). To the extent that community service is used to burden persons convicted of minor offenses with hundreds of hours of unpaid labor, it only serves to escalate penalties and reinforce our over-punitive, over-incarcerative criminal justice system.[19]

Postscript

Incidents recently reported from two cities, four hundred miles apart, and in successive months are graphically illustrative of the extent to which the idea of community service in lieu of punishment seems to be taking hold in some jurisdictions.

The first recounts a sentence imposed by a judge in the East Boston, Massachusetts district court on four young defendants who had been charged with involvement a month previously in a demonstration. This area, among others in the city, has been plagued by outbreaks of racial violence following upon a federal court order to integrate the public schools of Boston. The defendants, ranging in age from sixteen to twenty-six, pleaded not guilty to charges of disorderly conduct arising from the violence with which they had attempted to prevent school buses from delivering pupils to the local high school.

The judge allowed them the opportunity to agree to perform seventy-five hours of public service in the community, which they accepted. In imposing this alternative, the judge stated that the evidence warranted a finding of guilt. If the work were done satisfactorily and the youths stayed out of trouble, their cases would be continued for a year, at the end of which the charges would be dismissed. Should their work not be performed satisfactorily, fines or a jail sentence could be imposed. The defendants were represented by counsel at each step in the proceedings and assented to the disposition suggested by the judge.

The incidence of school violence against both teachers and students increasingly plagues our public-school systems. School vandalism, estimated to cost the nation $600 million annually, is a closely related outlet for the feelings of frustration that a large proportion of school children seem to harbor.[20] Community service provides an opportunity for constructive use of free time and represents a saving to the community.[21]

The second account involved "the 19-year-old driver of a pick-up truck that had crashed, killing ten teen-agers in Maryland's worst traffic accident in a decade." Despite the outrage expressed by the parents of the dead teenagers and by the community at large, the judge imposed a three-year suspended sentence for the ten counts of manslaughter by automobile. In doing so, he is reported to have relied heavily on the presentence report of his probation officer that described the defendant as a "passive, dependent person with depressive features" and recommended against a prison sentence.

The order of the court specified $400 in fines, the assignment of the defendant to a program of psychotherapy, drug and alcohol rehabilitation, and volunteer community service for the duration of the probation term, to be performed in a nearby institution for disturbed children. Although some parents expressed rage at the sentence, other parents did not view it as excessive leniency on the part of the judge. "Jail would not accomplish anything," said one. "It's not going to bring anyone back." Said the mother of a fourteen-year-old daughter killed in the crash, "I think it's far better for a person to be rehabilitated than to [spend time] in jail."[22]

Less than two months after disposing of this serious homicide case through community service the same judge had before him a defendant who had been caught in a football betting raid. He was offered the choice between paying a fine of $500 to the court or donating that amount to a local charity. In commenting on the alternative sentence, the judge stated, "It works well in cases in which the defendant doesn't perceive himself to be a criminal. He's an ordinary citizen, holds an honest job, has no criminal record—he just happened to do something that's illegal, and he doesn't try to lie his way out of it. He says, 'You're right, I did it, I'm sorry.' And that's it. I find that in many of these cases it makes the defendant feel better about himself and about the way our system of justice works if he can come out of the experience with a positive feeling rather than a negative feeling." Citing the gratifying results of his program—only 11 failures out of 375 community-service sentences—the judge concluded, "I don't want to get revenge against a person who made one foolish mistake, I want to help him and help the community—if it's the kind of case in which that kind of procedure will work."[23]

Such sentiments are a reflection of a movement in some parts of the world, notably Scandinavia, to place more emphasis on the circumstances of the crime and its consequences (including the possible consequences for the offender) than on the sole question of guilt or innocence. The Council of Europe has stated the idea in a different way:

> The definition of crime should be confined to acts genuinely disturbing to the life of society. Such acts as shop-lifting and issuing worthless cheques should not be seen as real crime, while such things as pollution and the invasion of privacy should be. They stressed the relativity of the very concept of offence, which varies according to place, time, and the status of the person concerned, and suggested that the moralistic attitude toward crime be replaced by an objective consideration of the interests of society.[24]

How the criminal-justice system determines the sentences to be imposed on offenders is forever in process, swinging back and forth between emphasis on the act and on the actor, in its assessment of what to do with the guilty offender. The first juvenile court law in Cook County Illinois in 1899 embodied a new doctrine: children, because of their immaturity, were not to be punished but given "aid and encouragement and guidance." Their delinquent acts were to be seen as symptomatic of their basic "need and condition" rather than as grounds for the determination of their guilt or the penalty to be imposed on them.

This doctrine has seen lean and full years. Today it is particularly difficult to maintain in the face of pressures being exerted from many quarters to try children thirteen years and older in adult criminal courts, and, if found guilty, to sentence those as young as sixteen or seventeen years to adult penitentiaries. The small percentage of truly violent young offenders who require intensive care and custody have thus unwittingly brought down on all juveniles a measure of repression that has been most forcefully expressed by a former president of the United States that if children commit adult crimes they should be treated like adult criminals.

Vengeance dies hard. Every human being seems to be equipped with some measure of it. Its value as a necessary means of self-defense cannot be discounted, but the degree of vengeance to be imposed varies with time and place. At the moment it seems to override other considerations: the criminal act is all and the criminal actor must pay the price. That the United States imposes longer and harsher sentences than any other Western nation seems to have little effect on our mounting crime rate[25] to which the official response is increasingly, more prisons, longer terms, the discontinuance of good time, and the abolition of parole.

Alternative sentencing is designed to substitute service to the community for deprivation of liberty and help to counter today's repressive penal philosophy. That such alternatives to the prevailing hard line in criminal justice are not without their adherents may be seen in the recent creation of the National Institute for Sentencing Alternatives, which has come into being as the result of the national interest generated by the Earn-It program. The overwhelming volume of requests for information with regard to the program that the Quincy court received led to the joint endeavor between the court and the Center for Public Service at Brandeis University in Waltham, Massachusetts. Based at the university and funded by a private foundation, the institute plans to conduct a series of workshops on the use of restitution and community-service orders in the sentencing of juvenile and adult offenders. The workshops to begin in early 1981 are designed to assist judges, probation officers, and administrators from related agencies in developing programs that will make possible the broader use of these sentencing alternatives. Workshops will include such topics as the philosophical and legal bases for restitution and community-service sentencing; a survey of models for programs addressing different intervention strategies for both juvenile and adult offender; methods for dealing with community resistance to sentencing alternatives and tactics for building local support; involvement of the private sector and practical program planning and development, including strategies, support services, program evaluation, insurance and worker's compensation, and management structures.[26]

One of the most notable features of this development is its blending of court and university in a program of national promotion for two innovative thrusts in community justice, restitution and community service. Here is a further example of the close links between the various ways in which justice can be brought to the community outside the courtroom yet encouraged and fostered by the court itself.

Finally, and from the most unexpected source—prominent Watergate defendants who served terms in federal penal institutions—come unsolicited endorsements of community service as an alternative to imprisonment. Wrote Jeb Magruder from Allenwood, "Prison for black or white does not accomplish much beyond punishment. Certainly those who would not be a threat to the community would benefit society to a much greater extent if their sentences followed the pattern of long terms of supervised community service." In an article in a University of Arizona newspaper, former presidential aide John Ehrlichman advocated "use of the talents of skilled and unskilled federal prisoners in public service jobs, instead of the waste of imprisonment." To which Charles Colson, in a letter to John Mitchell and H.R. Haldeman on the occasion of their imprisonment, added the hope that "someday soon . . . we will reserve prison for violent criminals, about 20% of the population, who are dangerous to society; and the other 80% will be punished in ways constructive for themselves and others."[27]

**Part IV
Community Courts**

12 Informal Tribunals in the United States

Around the globe are found a fascinating array of informal tribunals that administer popular justice and resolve disputes. Some combine socialist ideology and indigenous culture, and some derive from local tradition in contrast to the procedures of the central government. Many variations are found, but certain common features emerge, especially the resort to other than the adversarial process, the inclusion of a different dramatis personae from that of the courts as we know them, together with a use of language and lay notions of evidence in contrast to the strictly legalistic or formal. Some of these courts carry forward historic customs from a distant past. Their philosophies, structures, and procedures are nonetheless highly relevant to notions of community justice today.

The models described in this part are evidence of the deeply ingrained sense of justice found in all peoples, despite broad differences in the methods whereby justice is sought. There are some common essentials in community arrangements for the resolution of the kinds of interpersonal conflicts that take place daily in every society in the world. However much individual courts may differ from one another, the issues in dispute before them spring from two basic sources: offenses involving property and those involving the person. The aims of all of these courts are also basically identical: to determine the extent of the affront or injury done to the victim, to assess the blame, to identify the offender, and to extract—in property, or loss of liberty or sacrifice of life, in shame or pain—a penalty that represents some kind of quid pro quo. The courts are at the same time anachronistic and forward looking; some hark back to ancient times, while inherent in many are attitudes and forms that are highly advanced by today's standards.

Most of these courts are found in countries that did not inherit the tradition of early feudal development through which much of Western Europe passed when duels and tourneys between contestants or their agents sought to resolve disputes through superior force, speed, or skill at arms. Today's adversary process between defense counsel striving to prevail as against the plaintiff's surrogate, the prosecutor, looks rather to force of mind, to eloquence, and legal competence. In the process, the plight of the victim, the wisest sentence for the defendant, and the best interests of society are all too frequently lost sight of.

197

An Indian Tribal Court

Under U.S. law, Indian tribes are allowed to retain a portion of their original sovereignty and to enjoy powers of self-government in certain areas.[1] This is particularly true of the Pueblo tribes of the Southwest who acquired their lands at the end of the Mexican-American War, together with the transfer, unimpaired, of the rights and grants conferred on them by the king of Spain. The federal government and the several states in which the Pueblos live retain and exercise jurisdiction with regard to thirteen types of crime. With these exceptions the Pueblos have jurisdiction over their own disputes and enforce their own norms in their own tribal community courts.

Pueblo culture influences the enforcement through the courts of a strong ethic of community responsibility, which in turn flows from the tribal weltanschauung. This perspective has been described by a Pueblo anthropologist:

> The dominant integrating factor of Grande Pueblo culture is the view of the universe as an orderly phenomenon. People or things are not merely "good" or "bad." "Evil" is a disturbance in the equilibrium that exists between man and the universe, while "good" is a positive frame of mind or action that maintains harmonious balance.

> To keep man and universe in harmonious balance, all must work together and with "good" thoughts. Unanimous effort of body and mind is not only a key value, *but it is also enforced*. . . . The cacique [the priest-chief] and the War Captains exert strict control over the activities of village members and see that all physically able members participate in a rigid calendric series of ceremonies. Among the members of a village there is a serious concern over a neighbor's behavior and a perpetual watch is maintained over his or her activities. Any action, whether physical or verbal, which is construed by Pueblo authorities to be contrary to group concerns and unanimous will of the village is promptly and severely punished.[2]

The Pueblos of Sia and Santa Ana, New Mexico, annually elect a number of at-large officers: a governor, lieutenant governor, four governor's assistants; a war captain, and four or six assistants; and the sexton responsible for the church and his lieutenant. The governor and the war captain are pivotal figures; the former, as governor, the highest official, bears the ultimate responsibility for the administration of justice; the war captain has final responsibility for trying cases of witchcraft and violations of religious law. Court procedures and administration appear to be guided by two basic principles: a case should be settled with the minimum of persons necessary and quarrels should be avoided because they "poison the mind and interfere with the good thoughts necessary to maintain harmony in the world."[3]

Minor complaints are generally taken to one of the governor's assistants rather than to the governor. For such offenses as petty theft, damage done by wandering animals, or a minor automobile accident, the lieutenant governor tries to get the accused to pay satisfactory damages. If reparation is made, the case is closed. If the accused refuses to pay and the plaintiff insists on damages, the case is taken to the governor.

The governor will make his own inquiries and on the basis of his findings may simply hand down a decision, which is binding. If the alleged offense involves substantial damages, the governor will generally convene a council of from two to four of the leading men of the village, plus himself. The council then makes its own inquiry and hands down a decision. If a defendant convicted by the council fails to pay the fine or damages imposed on him, the governor, after consultation with other village officers, may convene the full tribal council. Cases involving adultery or illegitimacy are especially likely to be brought before the full council since they are deemed to be criminal matters involving failure on the part of the accused to conform to important ceremonial requirements.

The full council generally convenes in the governor's house or in the house of the war captain for cases of witchcraft and violation of certain religious duties. A very serious demeanor and a sense of decorum is maintained by all those present. Because emotions can run very high and often lead to angry speeches, only one person at a time may speak. The presiding officer opens the proceedings with a statement of the case, including the position that he and his staff have already taken, if it is a criminal case. The governor or war captain thus acts as public prosecutor and magistrate in a process of judicial review of earlier judgments. Litigants may be advised by kinsmen or members of their medicine society, who are generally invited as a matter of courtesy. Confession and admission of guilt on the part of the defendant are pressed for with great intensity. In one case of desertion, for example, the defendant was harangued for a full six hours until he finally agreed to reconciliation with his wife.[4]

Pueblo courts thus provide an illustration of the advantages inherent in the community court process. They have exclusive jurisdiction and adjudicatory capacity, yet they also perform in the manner of community moots. The authority of the court is accepted by the tribal members whom they serve, and their verdicts are accepted as just for the very fact that they are designed and staffed by community members. Justice is swift, direct, and personal and emphasizes the restoration of harmony and reintegration of offenders into the community rather than punishment. Although the court process may seem to some to be overly authoritarian, this attitude derives from the Pueblos' distinctive view of the world, as well as from the unanimity with which that view is held among them. Given the far smaller degree of consensus prevailing in American communities in such fundamental matters as these, authoritarianism is not likely to be a problem in the forseeable future.[5]

A Mexican-American Community Court

In the eastern, largely Mexican-American, section of San Jose, California, an alternative small-claims court has been operating since early 1977.[6] Although this body does not display all of the features of community courts described by Danzig and Fisher, it does provide an interesting example of a community court in practice. Known as the neighborhood court, it was established as a specific response to the widely felt concern that the regular small claims court in the city was being underutilized. To some extent community residents feared and distrusted it because of the formality and impersonality of the court proceedings, which resulted in a widespread feeling that litigants could not freely or adequately represent themselves in court.

In response to the initiative of the Santa Clara Bar Association, a Citizens Advisory Committee was established to select a neighborhood site for the proposed alternative court. The eleven-member committee of local people included the director of the Housing Service Center, the executive director of the apartment owners' association, the area supervisor of a finance company, the executive of the Mexican-American Service Agency, and other persons experienced in small-claims court procedures. A former president of the Santa Clara Bar Association chaired the committee, whose mandate was made official when it was formally appointed by the judge of the small-claims division of the municipal court.

The neighborhood court involves lawyers as mediators and arbitrators, for two reasons. Minor disputes are as likely to involve rules of law as are disputes about large sums, and the parties are equally entitled to have them resolved in accordance with the law. Furthermore, lawyers can advise the parties as to a likely judicial decision, so that solutions that may be contrary to legal principles are ruled out early. Participating lawyers, selected from nominees by the Santa Clara Bar Association, are appointed by the municipal court. They are required to have had at least five years of experience, including some service as temporary small-claims court judges. Lawyers also volunteer for administrative and public-relations duties.

Residents in the area served by the court may file claims two evenings a week from 5 to 9 P.M. upon payment of a small fee. Cases are restricted to the maximum statutory limit of $750. Bilingual law students, trained as clerks for the proceedings, greet people as they arrive to set a tone of informality from the outset and to assist with basic information about the process. When a claim has been entered, the complaining party pays an additional fee for notification to the accused by certified mail. The order to appear in neighborhood court is identical to that issued by the regular court. Hearings are scheduled for the early evening on alternate Tuesdays.

Disputants arriving for the hearing go to a private room where they are met by a volunteer lawyer, who will serve as mediator. The lawyer briefly describes the purpose of the hearing and then invites the complainant and the defendant to state their cases. The mediator examines any documents or other evidence provided by the parties, making sure that each party sees the other's evidence. With this explanatory process completed, the mediator begins to probe for some common ground on which a settlement might be based. Once this has been identified, the mediator proposes a settlement. If both parties accept the proposal, it is summed up in a judgment, as in other small-claims courts. If the proposed settlement is rejected by either party, the mediator recommends that the case proceed to arbitration.

If both parties are agreeable, the matter is generally heard the same evening by another lawyer acting as arbitrator, with fairly broad options for settlement available. If the evidence is complex or unclear or if feelings between the parties run high, the arbitrator may take the case under consideration until a later date. If such an extension seems unnecessary, the arbitrator may announce a decision on the spot, although it does not become binding for five days after the hearing, thereby providing an opportunity for the disputants to secure a de novo trial in the regular small-claims court if they so desire. Since a decision of the neighborhood court is not binding unless both disputants agree to it without appeal, the procedure of the court is equivalent to a pretrial hearing subject to the review and approval of a judge of the municipal court.[7] When the parties accept the arbitration award, it is made a formal judgment and becomes part of the court record.

Funding and administration of the court are assumed by the Santa Clara Bar Association. Contributions have come from foundation grants, as well as from the bar association itself. Expenses are minimal; they include salaries for the two law students who serve as court clerks and for security personnel, and public information material. Space is contributed by a neighborhood recreation center.

The program may be criticized as falling short of the ideal of a community court because of its reliance on the bar association for its design, funding, and staffing instead of on the people in the community which it serves. Nevertheless the program has an advantage over many other arbitration, restitution, and mediation projects in that the cases that come before it arise directly from the parties in dispute rather than by referral from the bench, police, or prosecutor. The court also responds directly to local community needs, in that it provides speedy, personalized resolution of everyday disputes involving relatively small sums of money. Results from the first six months of the program seem to indicate a growing community awareness and acceptance of the court, which in that period received a total of 164 inquiries, resulting in 60 actual filings. "Of all sixty cases filed in the first six months of operation, forty were completed at the mediation stage (this figure includes defaults, dismissals, and transfers); nine went on to arbitration; and eleven were continued or reset for a later date. The average time for mediation was about forty-five minutes, double that spent on the average arbitration hearing."[8] It is anticipated that many more of the 45,000 residents of the area served by the court will take advantage of its facilities in the near future.

Community Courts in Chinatowns

Chinese communities have a long, established history of settling their own disputes.[9] This developed in the early years of their immigration to this country because they were denied standing in the courts and because Chinese-Americans continued to experience discrimination long after they were officially permitted access to the regular courts. Another strong impetus toward the formation of community courts derives from a long tradition of distrust of courts in general and a reliance on the close social networks of the Chinese village for dispute resolution. As a result of this background and of the historic cultural emphasis on compromise, together with the language barrier, strong and effective community courts developed early in Chinatowns from the Pacific to the Atlantic.

To understand the operation of these courts, certain features of the social structure of Chinatowns should be noted, especially the network of associations organized around fundamental social ties. These associations are based on family, religion, business, dialect, education, and other bonds. The largest and most important association is the Chinese Consolidated Benevolent Association, whose voting members come from almost all the other organizations in Chinatown, except trade. Each of these individual associations has a procedure for settling disputes among its members; the benevolent association serves as the final arbiter.

Two persons involved in a dispute will generally attempt to settle it within an association to which they both belong. This is often a family association, whose membership includes all persons with the same Chinese-character last name. A minor dispute might well be handled by the association's president and secretary over tea with the conflicting parties, while more serious cases would be heard at the association office. When this level of mediation is still unsuccessful, the matter passes to the benevolent association.

The benevolent association hears disputes of all sorts except criminal cases. Several conditions must be met before a case will be handled: the parties must have paid their annual dues and any outstanding debts to the association for the previous three years, and they must give evidence of a willingness to compromise and to appear voluntarily. The settlement process begins with a meeting of the association's top officers with the contesting parties. The complainant states the nature of his complaint, to which the accused is asked to rejoin. In serious or more complex cases, witnesses may give testimony. On the basis of all the evidence adduced, as well as the results of private investigation, the issues become clarified to the point where terms satisfactory to both complainant and accused begin to emerge. The presiding officer is ready to propose a tentative decision, accompanied by pleas to the honor of each of the disputants. In the great majority of cases, these advisory decisions are accepted; in only a small fraction does one of the parties request some slight modification. Appeals are said to be extremely rare.[10]

When accord is reached, a brief celebration generally follows. If one side is found to have been clearly in the wrong, his apology is frequently forthcoming over a cup of tea. If the honor of either side has been a major item of contention, a dinner or party follows, expenses of which are either borne by the party at fault or shared if both are to blame.

Although decisions of the Chinatown community courts are not legally binding, they have long been effective in resolving conflicts because of the tight fabric of social life in Chinese communities, which has historically subjected disputants to a range of informal pressures toward compromise and compliance. The decisions of dispute resolution sessions are not only publicized in community media but are spread by word of mouth. Any person who defaults on an agreement is exposed to criticism from all sides, especially since the backsliding reflects badly on the associations to which the person belongs. Continued refusal to abide by an agreement may result in loss of face and social isolation, which may also be accompanied by stiff economic sanctions such as denial of employment opportunities. The following case, briefly summarized, illustrates both the kind of issues that come before Chinatown courts and the approach and procedure employed to resolve them amicably, without recourse to more formal tribunals.

The association of shirt pressers once threatened a strike unless workers received a 10 percent wage increase. Mindful of a strike several years earlier that had lasted two days, during which many shirts were ruined by mildew and customers were lost, the owners and workers met several times, but without arriving at a settlement. The benevolent association was invited to mediate, and a date was set for the following day. The association then announced a special board meeting in the Chinese newspapers and talked to both parties in order to discover the reasons for the wage demand and how a compromise might be reached.

Approximately one hundred persons attended the meeting, at which only the association's board members and representatives were allowed to speak. Both sides were given an opportunity to present their side of the case, after which negotiations went on from early evening until twelve o'clock, in a friendly atmosphere. When the disputants failed to reach agreement, the board members proposed an arbitrary decision that the pressers would receive five cents per shirt while the employer's association and the laundrymen's association would split the cost of the increased wages. At midnight the dispute was resolved and the strike averted.[11]

The procedure of the Chinatown courts illustrates the responsive, informal, and personalized justice that community courts can provide. Yet it would be unrealistic to suggest that its procedures could be duplicated in American communities. The strength of the Chinatown courts derives from centuries of informal dispute resolution guided by an acceptance of the duty to compromise. Chinese mediators and arbitrators are held in high respect within their community, which can rarely be equaled elsewhere, and Chinatown courts form an integral part of an extensive enforcement network that takes in a large portion of the Chinese community. In their traditional form, Chinatown courts exemplify the exclusive jurisdiction advocated by Fisher, as well as the institutional linkages proposed by Danzig, and in this sense probably surpass the expectations of either author. The blueprint for community dispute resolution that they offer is as distinctive as it is impossible to replicate in other communities.

Jewish Conciliation Board of New York City

Since ancient times, Jewish communities have had local forums for the resolution of minor disputes.[12] Known as Beth Din or rabbinical courts, these centers have appeared in Jewish settlements of every size in every part of the world. They flourished throughout Europe in the Middle Ages, usually with the sanction of the Christian authorities. Such bodies can be traced through the biblical era and have, in fact, played a role in some famous events in the Scriptures. When the elders leveled their accusations against Susannah, for example, they brought her before a court of this type. Daniel provides another good illustration, for his decisions, which so wisely joined holiness and earthy common sense, capture the style that continues to distinguish Beth Din from other community bodies performing similar functions.

This blend of the worldly and otherworldly, sacred and secular, "of the principles of the American law and the other different but equally complex principles of the Jewish rabbinical tradition," can be found today in the Jewish Conciliation Board of New York City, a community dispute-resolution center that has been operating for some sixty years.[13] Since 1920, when Louis Richman, a lawyer, and Samuel Buckler, a rabbi, combined forces to found the center, community mediators have used religious tradition and Anglo-American legal principles to resolve thousands of interpersonal grievances. This unlikely normative mix provides the board with remarkable flexibility, which produces justice with a strong situational flavor. Close to a thousand cases are brought to the board every year, although only a small percentage of them ever come to trial.

The board has had several purposes from its earliest days. First has been the objective of handling matters that might be incomprehensible to those not of the Jewish faith. The need for such a service was made clear in the early decades of the twentieth century when large numbers of Jewish immigrants came to the United States, many of them from small, homogeneous Eastern European communities and villages. When they began to go to American courts with complaints of violation of Sabbath laws or burial customs, disputes involving ritual and protocol, and grievances founded on the obligations of children, Jewish-Americans found that the secular legal system was unable to help them. The categories of disputes remain largely unchanged over the years: marital disputes, business disputes, disputes between members and their lodges, clubs, and societies, conflicts between family members, friends and neighbors, and between religious officials.

Other purposes have included the recognition and protection of distinctive Jewish traditions and customs, understandable objectives in the light of the persecutions that they have suffered in this century. The board makes it possible for those with conflicts to resolve them relatively quickly and with little expense. There is no fee charged for the mediation service, and the center discourages the appearance of private lawyers. Cases are typically disposed of within a couple of months from the time the complaint is filed.

A final purpose of the board sets it sharply apart from the formal system of criminal and civil justice. From the start, it has tried to go beyond the demands of simple justice and to seek to make peace among the disputants. This emphasis is made explicit in the very name of the center, where "conciliation" is the key word. The volunteer judges often make this purpose a central point in their stated decisions. In the words of one, "Our religious tradition teaches us that it doesn't matter who is right or wrong. There should be a sense of compassion and forgiveness."[14] "What characterizes many of their most interesting decisions is a paradoxical mixture of pragmatism with idealism, toughness with compassion, strict adherence to law and logic with a romantic conviction that truth can only be found if law and logic are transcended."[15]

Cases that come before the board begin with the appearance of a complainant in the office of the board's executive secretary. The secretary receives complaints and engages in a preliminary, informal screening by discouraging litigants whose allegations appear to lack substance. For matters that seem to merit a hearing, the secretary prepares a written report, which is entered in a permanent file. She will then contact the person named in the complaint and schedule the case to be heard at the next open session of the board.

When the parties appear to resolve the matter, they are asked to sign an arbitration agreement. A form similar to that used in labor-management disputes is presented to them, which stipulates that they will abide by the decision of the board. This procedure is for purposes of possible future enforcement in a loose sense, since it is rarely invoked in practice. The signed agreement puts teeth into the board's decisions, because the courts recognize the conciliation center as a legal arbitration agency and will confirm its decisions.

The disputants then proceed to the room used for mediation. They meet a panel of three volunteer judges, whose composition is designed to represent the diversity of the community. The first is a rabbi, whose presence lends prestige to the court and whose knowledge of the Torah and the Talmud provides the basis for many decisions. Next is a lawyer, a valuable aide both in the questioning of witnesses and in the evaluation of evidence, who helps to ensure that the proceedings will not unwittingly violate some legal regulation. Finally, there is a representative member of the community (referred to as the businessman) who brings to the proceedings the benefit of practical experience. Volunteer panels serve for a few weeks at a time; individual volunteers may sit a few times each year.

The judges are provided with a brief summary of the complaint, which they examine prior to the opening of the session. When the case is called, each disputant tells his side of the story. Judges may interrupt at any point in this testimony in order to get additional information on particular points or to resolve discrepancies. Witnesses may be called by either side, and physical evidence may be adduced. The entire process is informal and often somewhat disorderly, since the disputants may interrupt one another with objections and accusations and also because most people have only a very vague notion of what constitutes evidence or proof in any way approaching its legal significance.

When all relevant testimony has been heard, the judges ask the litigants to leave the room while they deliberate. At this point, they exchange their impressions of the disputants and the conflict and discuss possible bases for a solution. Special attention is given to the exact wording of the decision and to the manner of its presentation, for these details will bear strongly on the success or failure of the conciliation process. Intuition is of the utmost importance here; precedent is never a consideration. There is an unspoken sense that the decision will more likely be accepted if delivered by the rabbi or perhaps by the businessman. Compromise is generally emphasized, and a generous dose of flattery may be included to soothe everyone's feelings. This distinctive combination is well illustrated in the following case.[16]

The court succeeds in bringing off another such impossible triumph in the case of Mr. Berenfeld, who was once a cantor in a synagogue but is now old, poor, and unable to sing. Twenty-eight years earlier, when the congregation was short of money, they persuaded Berenfeld to take a drastic cut in salary; in return they promised to give him $1000 as soon as the synagogue was sold to the city. Berenfeld moved to another synagogue, the whole matter was forgotten. Only one trace of it remained—the congregation had put the promise in writing.

Now, twenty-eight years later, the city has finally bought the synagogue in order to build an express highway. Suddenly, to the astonishment of the officers, old Berenfeld appears with his contract and demands his $1000. They refuse to give it to him, and so he has brought them to court. . . .

"For twenty-eight years this whole thing has been buried," says Bloch, the president of the synagogue.

"This contract was made, however," says the judge.

"Yes, but without the intent that it should carry over for twenty-eight years. Since that time we've built a new building and amalgamated with another synagogue. We don't even have the same name anymore."

"The new synagogue takes over the obligation."

"If it's legitimate."

"Why not legitimate? You made a contract."

"Twenty-eight years ago!"

"You can't let the date interfere," says the judge. "You made this in good faith. You made a contract."

"I didn't make it," Bloch cries, "I wasn't president then! I wasn't even *in* the congregation!"

"Let us not get excited," says the rabbi-judge soothingly. . . . Bloch gets a sudden bright idea. "He left the synagogue a few years later. When his employment ended, this contract was voided."

The lawyer-judge frowns at the contract for about half a minute, then says, "There is no doubt in my mind that this contract is valid."

Bloch is desperate by now. "What about a compromise? Two months ago I offered him $150 to forget the whole thing. Suppose I raise that to $300?"

"Excuse me," says the rabbi, "but $1000 is what it says in the contract."

So old Berenfeld gets his $1000, and the judges have proved to their own satisfaction what hard-boiled characters they are.

Neighborhood Justice Centers

From a number of sources and the experiments in community justice that have been conducted for some years in widely scattered areas of the country has evolved an effort by the federal government to formulate a coherent national policy on the resolution of minor disputes.[17] The Dispute Resolution Act of 1980 seeks to "provide financial assistance for the development and maintenance of effective, fair, inexpensive, and expeditious mechanisms for the resolution of minor disputes."[18]

The origin of the term *neighborhood justice center* may be traced to the Pound Conference on the Causes of Popular Dissatisfaction with the Administration of Justice held in 1976. At the conclusion of the meetings, American Bar Association president Lawrence Walsh appointed a follow-up task force headed by Judge Griffin Bell, which advocated the development of community centers designed to "make available a variety of methods of processing disputes, including arbitration, mediation, referral to small claims courts as well as referral to courts of general jurisdiction."[19] The neighborhood justice centers were to allow for many variations in design of the dispute-resolution process to provide for mediation, arbitration, fact finding, malpractice claims, and an ombudsman.[20]

The neighborhood center is distinguished by its establishment as "a government agency with close ties to the courts," possessing greater adjudicatory powers than the community moots (mediation panels) proposed by Danzig but lesser powers than the alternative community courts advocated by Fisher.[21]

Attorney General Bell in announcing the formation of the neighborhood justice centers stated, "This is one of our efforts to make justice faster, fairer and more accessible to the people for many types of disputes. . . . It costs too much and takes too long to go to court. . . . The Centers will provide an avenue to provide justice for many persons now shut out of the legal system. They will also help relieve overburdened courts." He called the formation "a major step in an effort to help provide new or improved forums where citizens can obtain redress for any legitimate grievance."[22]

These proposed centers followed one year after a bill was proposed by Governor Jerry Brown of California to establish neighborhood centers in his state for resolving both civil and criminal disputes outside the traditional courtroom. At the time of their launching, the U.S. Department of Justice introduced the proposal in this way:

> Throughout the United States persons with grievances involving relatively small amounts of money or consisting of altercations with neighbors or relatives often are unable to find a satisfactory forum where they can seek redress. For disputes of relatively minor dimensions, the traditional legal procedures of the courts are generally slow and costly.
>
> Moreover, the adversary process is not always the best mechanism for resolving such disputes. Many of the more informal mechanisms for resolution of these grievances, such as the justice of the peace, the responsive ward committeeman or precinct captain, the policeman on the beat, have faded from the American scene. Furthermore, many people are unaware of the formal mechanisms that have been created such as small claims courts, and of other small dispute resolution services that may be available, such as consumer protection offices or family counselling services.[23]

The neighborhood center justice program was devised by the Department of Justice to meet the conditions it described in order to give "national leadership by designing, testing, and promoting the widespread adoption of new and improved mechanisms to provide more just and efficient resolution of disputes arising in the course of daily life."[24] It was hoped that the three pilot experimental centers, for which $625,000 was initially appropriated, would develop as models to be replicated in other parts of the country. Among the services offered were mediation and arbitration through a panel of members drawn from the community and trained in these procedures for those disputes in which both parties agree to participate.

The proposed location for the centers was to be in a municipal or public building or agency other than the police station and physically separate from those other agencies in order for it to achieve its own identity. Such a location was to provide services at minimum cost, to be consistent with the conception of the center as an extension of local government in the community and to endow it "with an aura of seriousness and authority." By locating the center away from a police station, the center would be able to handle matters beyond the jurisdiction of the police, at the same time recognizing the reluctance that some people may have to enter a station for any purpose.

To date, each center has had a small staff, recruited from the community being served. The director's duties include supervision of staff members and volunteers; paraprofessionals have the responsibility for meeting with complainants, arranging mediation sessions, making referrals, and conducting follow-up work. The day-to-day work of mediation is conducted by volunteers who are paid a small fee on a per-case basis. One of the most important features of the newly created centers is a board consisting of representatives of the community and the local government. Additional members are drawn from schools and colleges, the local bar, and legal aid offices. The board has responsibility for the operation of the center, for the determination of policies, and for seeking community support and cooperation. It seeks endorsement for the aims of the center from local merchants and landlords and from other business and community groups, as well as from local government officials, including the judiciary. It strives to reach agreement with local merchants and landlords for securing their participation in mediation for specific types of complaints, such as shoplifting and tenant-landlord disputes. These activities, the obligation of the center board, aid in acceptance of the program by the local community that it serves.

In the first six months of operation, the three pilot centers in Atlanta, Los Angeles, and Kansas City, Missouri, handled 1,577 cases, with an 86 percent success rate in the cases that went to hearings.[25] Thereafter an evaluation developed jointly by two offices of the U.S. Department of Justice over a fifteen-month period found that the centers were working well. They had demonstrated an ability to handle large caseloads (nearly 4,000 in the fifteen-month interval) representing a broad variety of disputes.

The great majority of clients expressed satisfaction with the process (nearly 90 percent in Atlanta), and the agreements arrived at were found to have held up after six months. The evaluation reported that interpersonal disputes were being handled more efficiently by the centers than in the courts, and that court personnel held a positive view of these neighborhood alternatives.[26]

The recommendation of the evaluation team that neighborhood justice centers deserved further support came very close to realization with the passage of the Dispute Resolution Act in February 1980. The legislation authorized the establishment of a dispute-resolution program in the Department of Justice under the supervision of the attorney general, to include an advisory board and a resource center. The board was to formulate policy and the center was to gather information, approve and fund research, and provide financial support. Some $45 million was to be appropriated over a five-year period. Regrettably, a delay in funding the program and the resignation of Attorney General Bell, who had been its strongest advocate, has prevented this admirable federal pilot project from expanding beyond its short-term experimental stage.

Our most recent state, Hawaii announced the opening of two neighborhood justice centers in November 1979 to receive disputes from throughout the island of Oahu.[27] Traditionally the Hawaiian method of dispute resolution was accomplished through discussion in the family, or extended family, setting, known as Ho'o Pono Pono. The success so far achieved is reported to have encouraged the initiators to extend the three basic services to other communities in the islands: holding mediation hearings, serving as training center, and providing research assistance. The service operates out of the university, using mostly students as staff. A broad range of trained community people such as teachers and attorneys serve as mediators. The membership of the mediation panel aims to reflect the ethnic, racial, and sexual characteristics of the parties involved in the dispute.

13 Examples from the Socialist World

Soviet Comrades' Courts

The comrades' courts of the Soviet Union may be taken as the prototype of community courts in other socialist countries.[1] Their cultural basis is grounded in the Marxist-Leninist view of the future in which human beings would no longer exploit or dominate one another in a just social order, which would ultimately be stateless as well as classless. For these ends to be attained, people would have to assume the functions previously performed by the state, among them the administration of justice. Today's comrades' courts can be regarded in ideological terms as an initial step and an integral part of building toward that future order.

The Soviet comrades' courts date back to the immediate postrevolutionary period, specifically to Lenin's decree of November 14, 1919, "On Workers' Disciplinary Comrades' Courts." The order established three-person tribunals in local trade unions, composed of representatives of management, the trade unions, and the collective at the enterprise. The initial intent appears to have been to deal with violations of labor discipline that interfered with productivity. In time additional legislation expanded the jurisdiction of the courts to include offenses committed by administrative and technical personnel, as well as incidents of personal misconduct.

The original philosophy behind the establishment of the comrades' courts is seen in an instruction issued in 1921 for the guidance of the courts: "If a worker who has committed a theft, instead of being imprisoned, is forced to go on working at his own factory under the responsibility of the other workers, the arrangement for him to remain among all those honest people—who will wait to see if [he] will steal again, if he will, once again put the factory to shame or if he will become a really conscientious comrade—will have a much stronger and more desirable effect than his investigation and trial. The working community will be able to rehabilitate weak and irresponsible comrades."[2]

Within the first decade thereafter, the courts had expanded to most areas of Soviet life, including factories, trade cooperatives, rural areas, and housing complexes. Two lines of policy were apparent in the operation of these courts from their earliest days: the application of stringent measures against serious offenders and the exertion of social influence on chance or accidental violators of the law. By 1938, forty-five thousand comrades' courts were said to be functioning within the Russian republic alone. With the outbreak of World War II, the comrades' courts virtually ceased to exist for a variety of reasons: lack of uniform legislation, the pressures of war, and state policy reducing direct citizen participation in state administration. The courts were revived in July 1951 upon enactment of a statute recreating them at enterprises and establishments, although their activity was now linked to labor discipline, violation of safety rules, and related offenses. The death of Stalin in 1953 led to the further resurgence of the courts in response to demands for a return to popular participation in the administration of a system of decentralized justice.

Additional impetus for the expansion of the comrades' courts was provided by Premier Khrushchev, who urged the expansion of their role to a wide variety of cases involving morals charges as well as the disregard of common standards of social behavior. In a sense the courts would perform a crime-preventive function by helping to create a climate of social morality. The model statute, enacted in 1963, was widely adopted throughout the country and served for all of the member republics of the Soviet Union. By the end of that year, nearly two hundred thousand courts were hearing some four million cases per year.[3]

With the fall of Khrushchev in 1964, the emphasis on popular justice began to be replaced by a concern for socialist legality and a call for increased professionalism and stricter due-process safeguards. This arose from alleged abuses such as incompetence and the infringement of citizen rights. By 1970 the official government newspaper was calling for stricter supervision of the courts by a variety of state agencies, and recent years have been marked by the relative decline of the courts although it is safe to assume that they will continue to function as popular tribunals of justice.[4]

Under the 1963 statute, the courts enjoyed a broad jurisdiction not only over such acts as violations of labor discipline, failure to observe industrial safety rules and the unauthorized personal use of state property, but also over petty theft, hooliganism, drunk and disorderly conduct, abusive language, minor property disputes, obtaining stolen property, and failure to aid a sick person.[5] Such statutory phrases as "other unworthy conduct in public places" and "high-handed acts" exemplify the extensive and open-ended nature of the courts' jurisdiction. The single limitation upon the comrades' courts is that they may not hear cases in which official court verdicts have already been delivered. Here is at least one parallel with the traditional common-law protection against double jeopardy.

The composition of the courts specifies that its membership shall be drawn from the collective that the court is to serve, that they should be persons who have demonstrated maturity, who enjoy prestige in the collective, and who have the requisite educational and political background. Members serve for two years in one of three capacities: chairperson, vice-chairperson, or secretary.

The 1963 legislation does not set out in detail the procedures to be followed by the courts. Theoretically the procedure is to be without formalism. Hearings are to be held after working hours, at a well-publicized time, and in a place readily accessible. Cases may be brought by public organizations, state agencies, cooperative bodies, or the courts themselves and are expected to be heard within two weeks after the case has been filed. Charges of speculation and "hooliganism" must be handled within one week. Courts are directed to verify material and documentary evidence prior to a hearing when this seems desirable but are not required to observe any other prehearing practices.

Hearings must be held publicly before at least three members of the court. At the opening session, the chairperson describes the alleged offense and the harm it is said to have caused. All those in attendance at the open session are free to make statements concerning the case, as well as to question the accused and all witnesses. In some cases attempts by the accused to justify his behavior may be greeted with reproaches. When all present have had a chance to express themselves, a member of the court summarizes the testimony. Then the court comments on and criticizes the evidence introduced and the various points of view expressed, and finally makes its decision.

The decisions of the comrades' courts are not strict judicial acts; rather they represent the application of moral or legal norms by citizens of the community with regard to specific acts. Many disputes between members of living or working groups are handled informally at what we may term the precourt level—that is, before they have escalated to the point where they require adjudication by a formal court body, however lay its composition. For example, a dispute between tenants over the sharing of a common facility such as a bathroom or kitchen may be mediated by members of a committee from the housing project. A divorce complaint or other serious dispute will be the subject of long discussion and study sessions, which may include officials of the street committee, members of residents committees, as well as friends and the spouses themselves. Representatives from the work place of husband and wife may also be present to testify.

More serious charges are heard at the court level, where a variety of dispositions may be imposed: a fine, a recommended demotion or dismissal or transfer to a lesser job, an order that restitution be made. If the court determines that criminal prosecution is called for or that another court should hear a complex civil dispute, it will certify the case to the appropriate agency. Although such decisions are final, some appellate procedures have evolved whereby the courts may rehear a case on their own motion or reconsider their decisions at the request of a trade union or of the executive committee of a local soviet. When the final decision has been reached, the court continues to monitor the conduct of "convicted" persons to see whether they adhere to the standard of conduct specified by the court. When an instance of serious noncompliance with the court's decision occurs, the matter can be referred up to the official judiciary for review and subsequent enforcement.[6]

Although the courts and their lay personnel theoretically are independent of the formal state apparatus, they have been subjected to varying degrees of guidance and control throughout their history. In addition to the pressures already mentioned, several sorts of assistance have ensured that the operation of the courts conforms to current government policy, such as consultations with judges from the regular people's courts or assistance from councils of lay assessors of the people's courts. Regional councils review the work of their constituent courts, publicize examples of outstanding decisions, and conduct seminars on relevant statutes, much like the sentencing seminars conducted for judges in the United States and in Great Britain.

Constant commentary by the press is an important influence on both the procedures and the decisions of the comrades' courts. Some courts have been held up as an example to the nation, while others have been criticized for the slowness of their proceedings, for exceeding their competence, or even for failing to hold hearings.

The Soviet comrades' courts have a dual character; they are instruments of both control and change. They serve the prevailing state policy at the same time that by reason of their decisions and their proximity to the everyday life of the Soviet citizen-worker, they inevitably have some degree of influence upon that policy.

As with other political, economic, and social institutions in noncapitalist countries, it is important to view these courts objectively and not solely by comparison with the institutions to which we may be accustomed but rather historically and in comparison with the institutions that they have replaced—in this instance, the courts of czarist Russia. From the prerevolutionary past, the comrades' courts of today have inherited the Continental inquisitorial system rather than the adversary procedures that derive in Anglo-Saxon jurisprudence from the common law.[7]

East German Social Courts

Two types of social organ have developed in the German Democratic Republic to handle simple disputes, minor violations of law, and conduct deemed antisocial.[8] The jurisdiction of Disputes Commissions established in 1953 to settle labor disputes in factories was expanded ten years later to include offenses "against socialist ethics," minor disputes under civil law, and minor violations of criminal law by workers. Arbitration commissions were also set up in the mid-1960s in urban areas, villages, production cooperatives, and private factories to hear matters similar to those coming before the dispute commissions (with the exception of labor disputes) and in addition, complaints against citizens charged with failure to engage in socially useful work. With the adoption of a new constitution in 1968, these two commissions were converted into social courts, and their jurisdiction expanded to include violations of community morals, failure to help persons in danger, and violations of administrative responsibilities. They simultaneously lost jurisdiction over offenses against socialist ethics on the grounds that these were not violations of legal norms. (One is reminded here of the trend in the United States to decriminalize so-called victimless crimes: alcoholism, drug addiction, vagrancy, and sex offenses.)

The social courts operate upon the request of workers, factory directors, public prosecutors, and labor groups. There is no uniform procedure for the informal hearings, which are held after working hours and are open to the public. Such factors as subject matter, type and seriousness of alleged offenses, and their special circumstances determine the approach to be taken in specific cases. All persons present at the hearings have the right to contribute their views on the facts, the character of the parties involved, their estimate of possible causes of the offense, and proposed remedies.

The East German commissions have certain of the characteristics of a formal court in that they are required to keep written records of applications for hearings, of the proceedings, and of the decisions adopted. Decisions, comparable to formal court verdicts, are binding. Like the formal courts, the social court must adhere to detailed procedural requirements, which may differ depending upon the area of their jurisdiction (whether urban areas, state factories, production coooperatives, villages, or private factories). Elaborate guidelines set forth the details of jurisdiction, remedies, and appeals.[9]

In cases involving violations of law or ethics, the commissions seek to discover and eliminate the causes and conditions leading to the offense. Commission members often focus on the situation and personality of the accused and search for an understanding of the underlying patterns of behavior that may be related to specific incidents. In the full conduct of their inquiries, the social courts can delve into virtually any aspect of an individual's life that may be considered to be connected with the person's social reeducation, and extend their concern to other abuses associated with the offense in question.

The remedies available to the commissions emphasize private reformation rather than public punishment or social pressure. For minor offenses the social courts may reprimand offenders, order them to repair damages, require compensation in money or in labor, levy fines, or stipulate an apology to the offended persons. They may also adopt noncoercive measures directed at reeducating the parties, such as recommending attendance at school or other educational measures in order to reduce the likelihood of a recurrence of offenses.

Cuba's Popular Tribunal

The idea of the popular tribunal is said to have begun at a meeting of Premier Fidel Castro with a graduating class of law students in 1962 at which he contrasted the basic concepts of the prerevolutionary judicial system with a system in which there would be true participation of the people in the administration of justice.[10] Castro recalled that they had begun to experiment with such ideas in the rebel army in the Sierra Maestra mountains where soldiers were selected to be judges by their peers. A number of the law school students, impressed with the significance of the idea, went to a small village to begin the first popular tribunal on an experimental basis.

Two years later the popular tribunals began in accordance with the principles of socialist legality—that is, the system of laws and legal institutions that has been established to secure for all citizens entitlement to "the basic necessities for full human development (food, health care, housing, education, etc.)" and the concomitant "collective right and obligation to protect their socio-economic system and goals."[11] Three main assumptions undergird the Cuban legal system:

1. Crime is caused by the individual's inability to acquire the basic socio-economic necessities. Criminal behavior can only be reduced when these necessities are satisfied on an equal, non-competitive basis.
2. People acquire an understanding of, and respect for, law when they participate in its formulation and administration.
3. The rehabilitation of offenders is more important than mere capture or punitive isolation.[12]

Details of the procedures for enlisting citizen participation in the formulation of the laws, the provision of the policing services, and the penal programs of Cuba today are beyond the scope of this chapter. Of these it may be said that their initial and principal purpose has been to encourage the citizenry to accept the laws of a new and rapidly changing society by making the courts familiar, popularly accepted institutions to be run by and for their citizens. At the same time, the tribunals aim to introduce a revolutionary perspective in that disputes are to be interpreted and resolved in accordance with political theory and socialist principles. Each of the popular tribunals is designed to serve a district of about thirty square blocks, for a total of one thousand tribunals for the entire island with its approximately nine million inhabitants. Courtrooms are located on main thoroughfares in former residences distinguished from those on either side of them only by a modest identifying sign. All proceedings are open to the public, decorum is maintained throughout the proceedings, and the taking of pictures within the court is prohibited.

The tribunals hear a broad range of cases under the general heading of antisocial conduct and without formal distinction between civil and criminal wrongs. In terms of American law, the jurisdiction of these popular courts would include torts, for small amounts; misdemeanors; violations of health and sanitary codes; juvenile delinquency; and personal quarrels. The tribunals do not try felonies, tort claims involving large sums of money, contractual disputes, traffic violations, or counterrevolutionary activities.

The category antisocial conduct comprises two broad classes of offenses. The first and more serious is "delicts," which are comparable to misdemeanors, misconduct thought to affect the fundamental interests of society. Delicts include threats against the person, physical assaults resulting in minor injuries, defamations, and minor libel offenses. The important category of delicts against the popular economy includes altering prices, hoarding, selling excessive amounts of scarce goods to family or friends, illegal exports, violation of rationing regulations, false weights or measures, and clandestine business. This last results in large numbers of black market cases during periods of scarcity.[13]

The sentence imposed on a chronic drunkard who disturbs the neighborhood may be that he not enter any of the local bars for a year. He may be forbidden to drink alcohol until he has demonstrated the capacity to refuse drinks voluntarily or to drink in moderation.

The second category of antisocial conduct deals with contraventions, less-severe offenses not considered to affect the fundamental interests of society but which involve violations of custom and proper decorum.[14] These offenses include indecent exposure, using obscene language in public, dealing in pornography, swimming in the nude, and voyeurism.

The popular tribunals employ a variety of sanctions, all of them intended to be mild and rehabilitative in nature. The most common and mildest, public admonition, is the delivery of a lecture by the president of the court, either in the courtroom or in the accused's work place. There is always at least a small audience, and the lecture is intended to educate the community with regard to the law and social responsibility. When educational improvement is ordered by the court, the intent is generally to bring the accused's educational level up to sixth-grade standards. More severe sanctions deprive accused persons of the specific rights that they are found to have abused. Offenders may be banished from places where they have caused trouble or may be ordered to other specific places as an alternative to complete deprivation of liberty. In some cases, offenders are ordered by the popular tribunals to relocate in another neighborhood, or they may choose to do so on their own request.

The most severe sanction available to the courts is deprivation of liberty. When the court decides upon this penalty, there is the option of imposing or suspending the order of internment. If internment is not required, offenders may be required to perform specific work in order to repay damage that they have done. They remain at liberty except during the hours of their compensatory labor. When internment is required, offenders are forced to live and work elsewhere, generally in agricultural enterprises, for periods of up to six months.

When a case comes before the popular tribunal, the procedure is inquisitorial rather than adversarial, Napoleonic rather than common law. Litigants and defendants are not required to be represented by counsel, but either party may request a lawyer. The defendant has the right to defend himself or to choose a lawyer. A lawyer, however, may not seek to defend a client's innocence when he knows him to be guilty. He may still defend the case, but the emphasis he will place will be on the defendant's conduct and potential for change or self-correction. Defendants are guaranteed certain other rights, such as the right to modify any earlier statements given the court, but these are not so detailed or so numerous as in adversary procedures guided by due process. The judicial proceeding consists mostly of questions to the complaining and accused parties, as well as to witnesses and other persons whose information is considered relevant. After the panel of judges has finished the questioning, they retire to deliberate and return with a verdict.

Trials generally take place within a couple of weeks of the original complaint. Accused persons have the right to appeal the verdict as well as the sentence but not on the grounds of procedural error. Appeal of severity of a sanction is considered by the same three judges who presided at the original trial. Such procedures may be initiated by either the parties themselves or by the appellate lawyer-judges acting "in the name of justice."

An interesting feature of the Cuban popular tribunals is the large attendance of spectators, which is deliberately encouraged. Because they function in neighborhood settings, the social courts are readily accessible to all. Audiences have been known to display exceptional interest in trials, responding to the questioning and the verdicts with exclamations reminiscent of those heard at sporting events. Spontaneous witnesses have even emerged from the audience to provide information at critical moments. As a result, these tribunals present a combination of dispute resolution, social instruction, and revolutionary theater.

The key participants in the social-justice drama, in addition to the contesting parties, are the judges and justice-lawyers. Judges are lay persons whose only legal backgrond is a three-week training course and the practical education that they receive on the bench. They are elected by the several thousand residents of the judicial district in which they live and so are indistinguishable from other persons in the courtroom in terms of their social or occupational characteristics. Nominations are submitted by the local Communist party officials and members of the neighborhood Committees for the Defense of the Revolution. After their short training course, their names are submitted to the community for ratification by secret ballot. They serve indefinite terms, for as long as they themselves and their constituents are mutually satisfied. While serving on the bench, they are paid whatever salary they would receive in their work place or occupation.

The justice-lawyers, or assessors, serve on courts of appeal and also participate in the training and selection of the popular judges. After the elected candidates have completed their studies, the justice-lawyers supervise their first few months in court by attending sessions to give advice and to correct serious errors, as well as by joining the judges in their deliberations. The assessors also administer the popular tribunal system, report regularly to the Ministry of Justice in Havana on the performance of their districts, and receive and implement the latest instructions on policy.[15]

Many of the same procedures were used in Allende's Chile between his election in 1971 and his death in the military coup of 1973 that overthrew his administration. Known as neighborhood courts, these community-led tribunals resembled their Cuban counterparts, both in the local community lay personnel who administered their procedure and in the types of cases that they heard and resolved: property offenses, instances of black market operations in times of economic scarcity, familial and intraneighborhood disputes, violations of the sanitary code, and complaints of drunkenness.

That these neighborhood courts were established by the residents of the *compartamentos* or "clusters of squatters" settlements in and around the large Chilean cities is evidence of the display of community concern for community problems among the most deprived and depressed inhabitants of those areas. These tribunals "were able to provide an additional forum which made residents more aware of the societal sources of their problems, and of the necessity for them to take control of the processes which might alleviate them."[16]

This is the essence of the community-court movement. The fact that the experiment has, for the time, ended in Chile with the overthrow of the government under which it was establshed does not negate the value of the community approach to the resolution of disputes. It indicates, rather, the promise that this approach holds as an alternative to traditional forms of justice.

Mediation Committees of the People's Republic of China

No other nation has more fully and systematically developed the concept and practice of community justice than the People's Republic of China.[17] Interpersonal disputes and minor infractions of law reach the formal courts only as a last resort, when all efforts to handle such matters informally in the community have failed. Large numbers of people are directly involved in informal dispute settlement and the public disapproval of deviant acts. Their services are available to virtually everyone, at any time, and without cost.

In China a petty thief may in the first instance simply receive some private "persuasion education" or criticism from his small group. But if he fails to reform, he may be censured by a meeting of the entire neighborhood convened by the resident's committee. An especially recalcitrant offender may be stigmatized as a bad element and given one of several possible forms of compulsory labor by the public security apparatus.

So strong is the commitment to this community approach that it promises to remain an integral feature of Chinese society for the foreseeable future. To appreciate the pervasiveness of popular justice in China, it is necessary to understand the sociocultural context in which it has emerged and flourished, together with traditional Chinese culture, and the dynamics of the contemporary revolutionary era.

Confucian philosophy spoke of a harmonious universe characterized by cooperation among all beings, with government as the promoter and preserver of the natural harmony among humans. This ideal could not be achieved through any system of positive law with its abstract definitions and clumsy deterrent measures but rather came about through the living out of interpersonal ethical and moral principles (li), including the great virtue of yielding (jang), which prevented disruption of the harmonious order through compromise, the generally valued way of resolving disputes.

Historically the social system functioned to promote informal dispute resolution in conformity with this ancient ideal.[18] Mediators were plentiful, for as in other rural village-centered societies, people were caught up in a broad network of close personal ties, and they could easily turn to kinfolk, friends, neighbors, members of guild groups, and local leaders or respected persons for assistance whenever conflict broke out. There was a premium on maintaining good relations with others whom one would continue to see daily. This extended family was always available, in contrast to the central imperial government, which was distant and unapproachable. Due to the great gulf between the common folk and the official apparatus staffed by the elite, persons who took their troubles to the authorities, without the guarantees of individual rights taken for granted in the West, risked and often received a most arbitrary response. Recourse to the local magistrates and their clerks became known as "a great foolishness," cautioned against in a variety of popular sayings. Certain groups, such as the guilds, explicitly forbade their members to go to the authorities until all community remedies had been tried. Acting together, Chinese social and cultural factors made informal dispute resolution the long-standing rule and litigation the exception. Face-to-face resolutions of differences have always been preferred to court decisions and trials, and this attitude has carried over into present-day China.

This approach has been continued and even extended under the leadership of the Chinese Communist party, but for a very different set of reasons. Among these is expediency; the revolutionaries did not have the extensive resources of the deposed Nationalist government and so had to rely more on unofficial methods and nonprofessionals. Resort to mediation by the Communist leadership had also been firmly rooted in Marxist-Leninist theory as developed by Mao, which consistently emphasized direct popular government and sponsored official campaigns attacking bureaucratic structure and attitudes. The ideology of building socialism, especially in its Maoist form, stresses the value of "resolving contradictions among the people," which means settling conflicts and dealing with deviant behavior through mediation and conciliation among the litigants in civil disputes and in criminal cases, through criticism, self-criticism, and efforts to reeducate the offender.

As the official ideology has become accepted throughout the nation, the informal, direct, popular approach to disputes and minor legal infractions has been consciously integrated into the national life-style during the past three decades. The pervasiveness of community-dispute resolution flows from the "mass line" that aims to implement all official policy through the efforts of the great majority of the population rather than through the efforts of the government acting alone.

Although the new leadership has retained and extended informal administration of justice procedures, it has also significantly altered their character. In contrast to the traditional emphasis, mediation and informal dispute resolution are seen as instruments of the class struggle and of the unending campaign to build a new socialist order. Traditional techniques have been politicized so that solutions to disputes and responses to minor acts of deviance are expected to be both politically and ideologically correct, as well as direct and informal. This necessitates constant study of Marxist-Leninist theory, as well as of the latest political directives. "Most serious" offenses—murder, rape, robbery, aggravated assault, and embezzlement of public funds—are referred to the courts, where they are handled in more formal fashion.

Current community-court structures date from 1954, when provisional rules were enacted for the formation of a nationwide organization of People's Mediation Committees. The new bodies were charged with three tasks: to make timely settlement of civil disputes, to strengthen the education of the people on patriotism and observance of the law, and to create unity among the people to heighten their efforts for production and national construction. Mediation committees were to be established in each area or street in the cities and in every district in the country. The elected assessors, three to eleven in number, politically upright persons with close ties to the people, were to be elected to two-year terms in the district where they live. They were to mediate cases only when the parties had voluntarily agreed to the process, and were not to prevent them from going to the formal courts if they so desired. Cases were to be registered, and terms of agreements were to be issued to the disputants when this seemed necessary.

Community justice operates today primarily at what the Chinese call the basic level of local organization. Small groups, the most fundamental component of popular government in China, are made up of representatives from fifteen to forty households.[19] Residents' committees are the next level of political organization. They draw their membership from activist members of small groups and exercise responsibility in such diverse areas as public health, propaganda, culture, women's work, and welfare. The next layer above the residents' committees is the local people's mediation committees. Staffed by activists from the small groups and residents' committees, party cadres (party members and others who hold paid administrative posts in government), and members of such groups as the Women's Association, the committees operate at the small-district level. Parallel structures of popular justice and dispute resolution are built into work organizations, labor unions, rural communes, and formal organizations of all sorts. Together they handle the bulk of everyday disputes and minor infractions in contemporary China. The strength of the leadership's commitment to this community approach to conflict resolution, in contrast to the adversary, litigious process as we know it, is dramatically highlighted by the statistics of the legal profession: three or four law schools operate in this nation of almost one billion people. The law department of Peking University annually graduates only a few hundred lawyers. A student of the Chinese legal system estimates that there are approximately ten thousand lawyers in China today.

By contrast, the number of lawyers in the United States exceeds 500,000, with one-fifth that number of students annually enrolled in the law schools of this country.[20] The number of lawyers in the United States has more than doubled from one for every 1,100 Americans in 1900 to one for every 530 today. The last decade saw a 14 percent increase in the total legal profession compared to a population growth of only 6 percent. Of every 125 adult males in the United States, one is lawyer. In San Francisco the ratio is even higher; one of every 100 residents in that city is a member of the bar. The 1,312 judges, commissioners, and referees in the state of California alone constitute "a far larger judicial system than exists in any *nation* [author's emphasis] in the world."[21]

Complementing the very small number of professionals in the justice system of China are the lay groups of volunteers or members of small groups, in addition to over a million lay mediators. A county of China with over half a million population employs no more than 300 police, who are assisted by several thousand neighborhood volunteers. With such a force of vigilant and cooperative people in their communities, it is no wonder that the country as a whole reports a very low crime rate, due also, if only in part, to the low level of mobility in the population, 80 percent of whom live in village communities. (In contrast, in the United States one person in five moves every year.) It may be difficult for Americans, accustomed to a court system that excludes from the process persons who may have personal knowledge of the defendant or the circumstances of the offense (except as witnesses), to appreciate that in China such persons are regarded as sources of information to the court in reaching its decision or in assessing sanctions. Because the community courts are staffed by neighbors, disputants are neighbors, and in all likelihood all the parties to a dispute have known each other for many years.

Information on popular justice and dispute resolution in China today is largely limited to a description of the community mediation bodies and an estimate of their pervasiveness. Their jurisdiction is quite broad and flexible and makes little reference to published legal codes, reports of court decisions, or the law journals common in the West. Community groups rely not on precedent as our courts do but on current resolutions, instructions, and policies of the party, as well as on Marxist theory, to determine whether an offense has been committed or how a specific dispute is to be resolved within the community setting.

14 A Miscellany of Community-Court Models

Lay Judges and Mixed Tribunals

The administration of justice has become highly professionalized. At the same time, the direct involvement of lay persons who have, historically, always played a part, however small, has received renewed emphasis with the recent development of community-justice programs. The idea that only those persons who were trained in the law should determine guilt and pass sentence comes to us from ancient times. The Romans, who "bequeathed to Europe the concept of a judge as a trained, specialized professional," nevertheless themselves relied on lay persons to render judgment, so much so that "when professional judges began to emerge in the late classical period, the lawyers of that era preferred to ignore them."[1]

The role of lay persons in the administration of justice has become an issue of some controversy, particularly in the United States. The traditional forms of citizen involvement—the jury and the justice of the peace—are being questioned. The jury has come under scrutiny primarily because of its role in increasing the already long delays in civil trials. The grand jury has been criticized as an instrument of oppression, because of its use in fishing expeditions, unfocused searches more for the purpose of inquiry into unpopular political views and activities than for indictment for alleged violations of the criminal code. Some jurisdictions have considered abolishing jury trials for certain offenses, and others have adopted the use of smaller juries, especially six-member panels.

The justice of the peace has been attacked on constitutional grounds, with plaintiffs arguing that it violates constitutional guarantees of due process. This complex debate, developed over the course of the past decade, has come to a head in a series of court cases. The constitutional question was first raised in 1969 in *Melikan* v. *Avent*, but a three-judge federal court unanimously ruled that the argument was "unique and of no merit."[2] In *Argersinger* v. *Hamlin* (1972), the argument was extended to include the charge that accused persons were being deprived of their constitutional rights because lay justices of the peace could not comprehend, and therefore should not rule on, complex legal issues. Although rejected at the time, this reasoning was accepted shortly afterward in the landmark case, *Gordon* v. *Justice Court of Yuba City*. The judges in that 1974 California case were particularly impressed with the plaintiff's argument because the possibility of a jail sentence was involved. Their decision has given rise to a new round of debate, with some states accepting the California Supreme Court's position and others continuing to see no problems with the role of justice of the peace as it operates in their jurisdictions. The controversy has come to include the related issue of the right to a trial de novo. Some states believe that this right compensates for any problems with the justice of the peace, while others see it as an unrelated consideration.[3]

The justice of the peace, dating from colonial times, has been gradually declining in importance for a variety of other reasons. The office became subject to abuse early because of the practice of payment by fees, in which a JP received full payment from a plaintiff only when a guilty verdict favorable to the plaintiff was returned against the defendant. The situation became so notorious that it was popularly said that "JP" really stood for "judgment for the plaintiff."[4] The practice was finally overturned by the U.S. Supreme Court in 1927. Since then, most states have moved to restrict the justice of the peace or the justice courts. Many of their previously extensive powers have been revoked, and much of their criminal jurisdiction has been taken away. In addition, as the country has continued to become urbanized, the justice courts have been progressively supplanted by new systems of municipal and district courts and today are found largely in rural areas.[5] The importance of the justice of the peace has further decreased with the nationwide movement toward unification of state court systems. Whatever role these lay justices may play in the future will be largely exercised within unified state judiciaries.[6] These developments have resulted in increasing interest in the use of lay persons in the administration of justice in other countries, which readily provide a variety of models for possible adaptation in America.

In Great Britain, the cultural context closest to the United States, lay persons recently have found a new and expanded role in the administration of justice. Although the institution of the justice of the peace has become nearly obsolete there, a system of magistrates' courts has risen to replace it, to the extent that, according to recent figures, some 96 percent of all criminal cases pass through these courts for settlement.[7] The services of the persons who currently donate their time as magistrates help to reduce substantially the caseload of the higher courts and result in speedier justice. "Because British magistrates are selected by the community, live in the community, and work in the community dispensing justice, they are better able to weigh the effects of both the offense and the punishment on the individual and the community."[8]

British lay magistrates are appointed in behalf of the queen by the lord lieutenant of the county from lists submitted by the local board of senior magistrates. Candidates for appointment must be persons of "clean record and good standing" who are also representative of a cross-section of their community. Any man or woman may apply who is over twenty-one years of age. Applicants are required to be sponsored by two people in their community who have known them for some years. The best possible sponsor is a magistrate who is currently serving. Once appointed they may hold the office for life, receiving in the course of their service no remuneration except for their actual expense of transportation and travel.

As preparation for their work, they are required to complete a training program, which covers court procedures, rules of evidence, appellate review of decisions, sentencing, and general issues of punishment and treatment. Further, magistrates are required to visit at least one prison and one juvenile or adult detention center during the first year of their appointment. They are authorized to hear all indictable offenses, including motoring violations; excepted are very serious crimes, separation, and custody of children after divorce. The magistrates' courts sit five days a week in banks of three. Each magistrate is committed to serving thirty-two days a year. Some specialize in the licensing of pubs and hotels, others in juvenile cases.

The responsibility of magistrates is to determine whether there is sufficient evidence for the case before them to be held for a jury trial, which may be waived by a defendant who opts for trial in the magistrate's court. Cases deemed to be within their competence are tried before them, beginning with the reading of the complaint by the clerk of the court. Clerks are the legal and procedural guides for the magistrates; they are required to hold a degree in law and to have had at least five years of experience as solicitors before they may be appointed.

Less serious cases, though indictable, can be heard by the magistrates, if the amount of money involved does not exceed £500. Most cases are heard within a month of the filing of the complaint; rarely, it is said, does a case go unheard for as long as three months. A presentence report by a probation officer must precede any sentencing order. Thereafter the magistrates may impose sentences of a fine up to £1,000 and of imprisonment up to six months, shortly to be raised to nine to twelve months. They may also commit to Borstal (youth training schools), jail, or prison. Such sentences may be two or three in number, usually concurrent, only rarely consecutive. Magistrates' courts are also authorized to commit persons to prison for nonpayment of fines or damages, although this is seldom resorted to. Convicted offenders may be ordered to make restitution to victims or assigned to community service in such places as parks, schools, and public institutions.[9] Any disposition of the court may be appealed, though it is reported that less than 5 percent of all defendants whose cases are decided by magistrates take advantage of this right.

While seemingly firmly established and accepted by the citizenry, the magistrates' courts have been the subject of keen debate. Supporters point to the flexibility provided by the system, as well as to the speed with which

criminal matters are heard and dispatched. Critics argue for more profes-
sionalization in the courts and cite magistrates for what they perceive as
harsh, lenient, or inconsistent decisions. They also question whether lay
magistrates are releasing too few persons on bail and are extending too little
in the way of legal aid.[10]

In many parts of Europe, another form of lay participation in the administration of justice has become widespread: mixed tribunals, in which lay
judges decide cases along with their professional counterparts. The spread of
the mixed tribunals has accompanied the decline of the jury.[11] And where
juries do operate, they are subject to restrictions. For instance, "Austria has
an eight-man jury operating under severe restrictive controls by a three-man
professional tribunal. The ten-man Norwegian jury is similarly
constrained."[12] West Germany has had no jury since 1924. Before that, juries
were strictly limited; they were of the French type, which decided "specified
questions of fact put to them by the presiding judge rather than the general
question as to whether the defendant was guilty of the crime charged."[13]
Other examples of mixed courts are the Swiss *éechevinages*, the Swedish
namnd, Yugoslav district and provincial courts, and Vietnamese courts.[14]

A similar plan is operative in Poland, except that there the lay judges do
not participate in appellate review. Lay justices hear approximately one-
half of all criminal trials, for a total of close to 250,000 cases per year.[15] All
capital cases must come before the mixed tribunals; the only matters that do
not are petty offenses and those cases considered to be of overwhelming
legal or factual complexity. Lay judges, who are involved in deciding all
questions of fact and law as well as the issue of guilt or innocence, sit an
average of twelve days per year.

Although these mixed tribunals are widespread in Poland, they have been
the subject of considerable controversy. A study by the legal branch of the
Academy of Sciences during a three-year period found that members of the
legal profession had serious reservations about the performance of lay justices. Although the lay members were felt to enhance the independence of the
courts (since the professional judges could always plead that they had been
outvoted), the study concluded that citizen judges tended to be more lenient
on issues of guilt as well as on sentencing.[16] The regard paid by lay judges to
matters of law and official criminal policy came into question with the finding that "lay judges seem to be guided more by the personal circumstances of
the defendant and his subjective fault than by the nature of his act." Also
"they do not seem to feel that stealing social property should be punished
more severely than stealing of personal property; rather they favor the opposite view."[17]

Another example of the mixed tribunal combining both lay and professional judges is found in the labor courts established in Israel in 1969. These
courts serve to provide a judicial body with expertise in the area of labor law
and labor relations; decide employer-employee disputes much more quickly

than could be done in the regular courts; enable claimants of limited means to enforce their rights; and prevent strikes that might be detrimental to the nation.[18] The labor courts are part of the official judicial system of Israel; their professional judges are subject to the same regulations and enjoy the same privileges of independence and life tenure as do judges in other tribunals. Each court has two public representatives (one for employers and another for employees), who are appointed after consultation with employer organizations and trade unions, respectively.

Labor courts are more than administrative bodies, as evidenced by the broad powers to provide any relief that might be granted by a regular district court, while the national labor court may grant any relief that might be provided by the supreme court. The labor courts, in fact, do not even have to follow the precedents of the Supreme Court, as in the landmark case of *Engineers' Union* v. *Civil Service Commissioner*, when the national labor court ruled that any labor court is empowered to issue an injunction against the government, thus treating it like any other employer.[19]

These alternatives provide an interesting contrast to the role of the lay citizen and the extent of citizen power in the Anglo-American jury. The jury is a group of six or twelve lay persons selected at random from lists of citizens who are convened for the purpose of a particular trial. They are entrusted with far-reaching powers of decision. Their verdicts are delivered in one or two words arrived at after secret deliberations, without having to share their reasons with anyone. When their civic duty has been discharged, they are disbanded and allowed to go home. "The jury thus represents a deep commitment to the use of laymen in the administration of justice."[20]

Currently in West Germany, most criminal matters come before mixed tribunals. Exceptions are petty offenses, which are tried by a single professional judge, and serious political crimes. Inasmuch as a two-thirds majority is necessary for an unfavorable verdict, lay judges have control over the fate of defendants in the courts where they sit. A summary of the composition and jurisdiction of various courts follows.[21]

Courts	Composition	Jurisdiction
Trial Courts		
Amstrichter	1 professional judge	Petty misdemeanors
Schoffengericht	1 professional judge 2 lay judges	Other misdemeanors
Erweites Schoffengericht	2 professional judges 2 lay judges	Felonies not involving imprisonment or for which punishment is less than three years.
Grosse Strafkammer	3 professional judges 2 lay judges	Other felonies, and minor political offenses

Schwurgericht	3 professional judges 6 lay judges	Serious felonies involving the actual or intended death of a victim
Oberlandsgericht	5 professional judges	Serious political offenses
Appellate courts		
Kleine Strafkammer	1 professional judge 2 lay judges	Review of facts and law from *Amstrichter*
Grosse Strafkammer	3 professional judges 2 lay judges	Review of facts and law from *Schoffengericht*
Oberlandsgericht	3 professional judges	Errors of law from *Amstrichter*, and decisions of *Kleine* and *Grosse Strafkammer*
Bundsgerichthof	5 professional judges	Errors of law from *Grosse Strafkammer, Schwurgericht* and *Oberlandsgericht*

Community Courts in the Philippines

A most informal, even picturesque, community-court procedure is found among the Yakan people of the Philippines, a nation of some sixty thousand persons, who share the island of Basilan with Christian Filipinos.[22] The principles underlying their community courts are a blend of local culture and Islam, for the Yakan are professed Moslems. An outside observer would have difficulty recognizing their community courts as legal forums because there is virtually nothing about them to suggest a judicial atmosphere. As one observer has reported, Yakan community courts are unique, specifically in the distinctive talking behavior that occurs within them.

Yakan speech behavior is a complex composite of four basic types: discussion, conference, negotiation, and litigation. Discussion speech topics can include any subject of interest; its purpose is simply to talk, and the roles of the various talkers are relatively undifferentiated. When conference speech is taking place, topics consist of specific issues. The purpose is to reach some decision on the issues, with speaker roles still largely informal. At the negotiation stage, the topics are disgreements, and the purpose of talk is to arrive at a settlement, with the roles differentiated into clearly opposing sides. Finally, with litigation, the topic is the dispute. The end purpose is a ruling, and the roles played at this stage resemble the structured roles found in other court proceedings.

Disputes formally arise when an identified party is charged with an offense and refutes the charge. The burden of making the charge, determining the identity of the offender, and accepting responsibility for an accusation, rests upon the victim. Once the charge has been made public, the accused may counter in several ways. He may deny the validity of the accuser's interpretation of his behavior, such as illegitimate sexual advances. Or the accused may deny that the alleged act in question qualifies as an offense; he may deny responsibility on the grounds that someone else actually committed the act or that it had resulted from unjustified provocation.

After a charge has been leveled and has been countered in one of these ways, the case may go to a community court. For the actual trial to take place, a neutral site must be selected, one that will not require anyone to play the host, which would necessitate the provision of food. The site finally selected is often the porch of the house of one of the judges. Here proceedings take place without the typical court trappings. Dress is informal, and participants are free to smoke and to chew betel.

The choice of site for a trial depends also upon determining the appropriate jurisdiction, contingent upon the social distance between the accused and accuser and the seriousness of the charge. When both contending parties belong to the same local district, one or more district leaders may hear the case. If the disputing parties come from different districts, the court must include representatives from both. When the matter becomes serious because each side has many active supporters, the case will go to the highest court in the community-court system, which includes those at the district, commmunity, and tribal level. District courts handle relatively trivial conflicts among local persons, such as fights among young men. The community-level courts, which meet about once a week, hear the great majority of cases. The tribal-level court convenes for very serious cases, in the yard of the tribal chief.[23]

Selection of judges is governed by criteria of competence and social position. To be eligible, a person must be a district leader with the knowledge and ability to act as judge and with enough political influence to make his rulings effective. Various elements of leadership qualify a person to be a judge: influence and prestige acquired through economic success, religious learning, speaking ability, having made a pilgrimage to Mecca, or election to office in the Philippine political system.

Rules for the conduct of court sessions include unlimited speaking time for any person present, so long as its content is relevant to the dispute. Any person may speak without being called upon, or judges may call on them. Violence and overt expressions of anger must be avoided, although allowances are made for people to say unkind things about one another. Each party of disputants has the right to confer in private, at will.

Once the trial has begun, the procedure follows a standard sequence:

1. Presentation of the case by the person to whom the complaint was originally made.

2. Taking of testimony from each side and from witnesses.
3. Arguments from each side.
4. Private conference of the judges.
5. Presentation of a ruling.
6. Further arguments.
7. Private conferences by each side.
8. Expression of acceptance or rejection of the court's ruling by each side.
9. Final decision for disposition of the case.
10. Acceptance by both sides of the decision.
11. Ritual handshake of peace between the disputants.[24]

Rulings generally involve three sorts of acts: payment of fines, listening to an admonition from the court, and performing a prayer of reconciliation. Fines, in turn, have three components: compensation for the offense itself, an amount to cleanse any sin against God associated with the offense, and a payment to the court. When fines are levied, the court must explain in detail how the amount was determined and relate it to standard fines for the offense, as well as to the case at hand. Admonitions given as lectures at the conclusion of the trial are intended to make both sides realize their share of responsibility for the conflict, to smooth any ruffled feelings that may remain, and to impress upon the parties the grave consequences of repeating the offense. When a prayer of reconciliation is mandated by the court, it is performed at a later date. Often prescribed in cases of violence, the prayer is intended to create a sacred sibling bond between the parties.

Yakan courts have no formal powers of coercion with which to ensure compliance with their rulings and must therefore depend upon persuasion and compromise. Once a ruling has been given, a court will argue for compliance on its fairness and on the dangerous consequences of a refusal to abide by it. Such consequences include the possibility that God or one's ancestors will visit sickness upon an offender or upon his kin. Social consequences to the refusal to accept a court decision may be the withdrawing of support or even disowning of the offender. Judges may penalize noncompliance by threatening to retire from the case or to withdraw political support. Extreme cases may be referred to the official Philippine legal system, with its expensive procedures and severe correctional system. The possibility of these unpleasant outcomes, acting together, results in a high rate of compliance with the decisions of the Yakan community courts.

Despite the uniqueness of its procedures, the basics of the Yakan court exhibit many features found in the community courts of more highly developed societies. The absence of any professional prosecutors, defense counsel, or judges; the informal nature of the proceedings; the progressive movement of the case, beginning with presentation of the complaint and the countering statement by the defense; the submission by the presiding judge of a ruling to form the basis for resolution of the dispute; and the acceptance of the ruling as modified into final form—all are basic to the community-court approach to conflict resolution wherever found.

Papua New Guinea

"All the Western pilot projects and legal literature on dispute resolution methods, as alternatives to court processes, may be re-inventing the wheel," remarks an observer of the operation of the village courts that have always played a historic part in the resolution of conflict in Papua New Guinea.[25] Since 1974 this traditional form of settlement has been recognized by statute, and the village "big men" who were the mediators of the traditional courts have become magistrates or chief magistrates. Official recognition by statute has given added status to the village courts and "ensured that even more urbanized regions troubled by rapid social change, would have courts with a community awareness."

Village courts have jurisdiction over eighteen minor offenses; they are authorized to sentence by means of fines, compensation, or community service. Because they are not bound by the common law and do not distinguish between civil and criminal matters, many customary disputes come to them rather than to the formal courts established when New Guinea was a British colony. The traditions of the people are oral, and these have changed over the years as the natives came under the influence of the missionaries, then colonial rule, and now independence.

William Clifford, noted authority on criminal procedures in underdeveloped societies, states, "Thus Papua New Guinea is experimenting with village courts able to deal with local cases by customary law; and it may extend this experiment to the creation of special local tribunals developing their own indigenous laws and procedures for urban settlements."[26]

Mexican Zatopec Courts

Dispute settlement practices in the community courts of the native Zatopec people in the state of Oaxaca have as their goal the restoration of equilibrium among persons who know each other well because they live together and are joined by a wide variety of social bonds.[27] Three officials—the *presidente*, the *alcalde*, and the *sindico*—administer the courts. Nominated and elected by the town's citizens, they are specifically charged with "making the balance" between the accusing party and the accused.

The *presidente*, the court judge, follows a procedure much like arbitration in the disputes that come before him. He allows and encourages the conflicting parties to tell their side of the story as fully as possible, using whatever evidence they deem relevant. The *presidente* listens, tries to identify the specific nature of the dispute, and, after the issues have been clarified, speaks to both parties, seeking to alleviate any anger or outrage that has surfaced and reminding the disputants of their social obligations, such as their parental duties. The *presidente*'s decision is generally a compromise settlement, which grants some concessions to both sides. The parties generally accept the decision of the court and thereafter sign a mutual promise to abide by it.

The specific features of the Zatopec community courts are summarized by an observer as follows:

1. The procedure is seen as a way of finding out what the trouble is. Instead of the assumption that the cause of the dispute is already known and that the purpose of the proceedings is to settle it, a variety of related matters may be discussed in order to mediate the basis of the instant dispute.
2. The goal is for the parties to compromise their differences according to the "minimax" principle (give a little, get a little) rather than the zero-sum game (win or lose).
3. The decisions of the court proceed from the characteristics of the multiplex society which it serves. For regardless of who the litigants are, the wider network of relations is the basic determinant of the court decision.
4. Norms and interests are recognized.
5. There is a legal expert.
6. It is not necessary to establish past facts or to establish guilt.
7. Conclusion is an agreement.
8. Compromise prevails even if the conclusion is either/or.
9. Agreement is backed by coercive force.
10. Reasoning is prospectively oriented.
11. The principals may exchange positions as a ruling may be made on other than the original claim.[28]

An example of Zatopec court operation is provided by the case of the damaged chiles.[29] On a spring morning in the town of Ralu'a, district of Villa Alta, state of Oaxaca, there arrived at nine-thirty before this municipal authority a Sr. Ignacio Andres Zoalage, merchant, fifty-five years of age. He explained, "I am coming to make a complaint about the chauffeur of the cream-colored truck that is on the platform, in the middle of which is a bruised basket of chiles weighing forty-seven-and-a-half kilograms." The chauffeur of the cream-colored truck was called; he arrived fifteen minutes later and said that his name was Mario Valdez Herrere. The court president asked him whether it was true that he had bruised the basket of chiles, and he answered, "Actually, I bruised it, but this happened because I don't have anyone to advise me. It is also the truck owner's fault because he ought to let me have a helper. Also, I could not see because the driver's compartment is high. Besides, it is the señor's fault—they put the things they have for sale on the ground, knowing that there is truck traffic."

The president asked the complainant, "Why did you put your merchandise down, knowing that the truck would go by?" Zoalage answered that there was room for the truck to pass. The chauffeur then said this was not true because the space was at an angle. Zoalage replied, "Look, Mr. President, the truck came this way, then this way and that way." The president said that it would be most convenient in this case if the chauffeur paid for the damage he had caused and that the basket of chiles should be brought in so that an estimate could be made of how much of it had been spoiled.

The plaintiff left and the president ordered the magistrate to have the merchandise brought in. The magistrate returned with the owner, carrying a basket of chiles, which they emptied on the floor. The court magistrate observed the chiles on the floor and put aside the damaged ones. He then told the president that the quantity ruined was about one and a half kilograms. The president asked the owner of the basket how much he wanted to be paid for the damage. Zoalage answered that it was not much—three pesos. The president told the chauffeur that he had to pay three pesos for the damage, and the chauffeur agreed. Meanwhile the president reminded the plaintiff to be more careful on the next occasion and to watch where he put his booth. The case was closed and the owner walked out with his load of chile, leaving the damaged merchandise with the municipal authority.

People's Courts in India and Pakistan

In India long before the British undertook to colonize it, village councils, called *Gram Panchayat*, had been in existence.[30] These bodies administered most of the affairs of the village, including the dispensation of justice. *Gram Panchayat* means, literally, "village council." Its five members are elected by majority vote of the villagers. Generally they are elderly persons having status, respect, and influence, in whom their neighbors have faith and trust.

Until about 1870, the system of common law introduced under British rule prevailed. But at about that time, a movement for some degree of local self-government developed, and with it came the revival of the *Panchayat* village courts and their ultimate authorization by legislative acts in different provinces of India. The villages of India are where the people live, since earliest times the pivot of government administration, as the keystone of the economy.

After independence, India's new constitution left to each of the component states the working out of its own distinctive form. Generally the *Gram Panchayat*—there are said to be more than eight thousand of them in the state of Uttar Pradesh alone—is an elected body consisting of twenty-five members, divided into benches of five, each of which elects its own chairman. At least three members must participate in the hearing and disposition of disputes of all kinds, including both civil and criminal cases of a minor nature. Civil suits may be heard up to a value of 500 rupees (aproximately $65), like small-claims courts in the United States. Cases entail such matters as recovery of property, damages caused by trespassing cattle, and debts. Criminal jurisdiction of these same courts includes cases of theft, "causing hurt," creating a public nuisance, criminal trespass, and intimidation. Lawyers are not allowed to appear in behalf of clients. The *Panchayat* calls the parties concerned before it, hears the evidence, and then makes its decision, generally in the form of a compromise, compensation, and/or limited fines. After a finding of guilt, the courts may impose a fine up to a maximum of 100 rupees but not imprisonment. From this fine, compensation may be awarded by the court to the aggrieved person. Appeals from an order of the court may be taken to the regular magistrates' courts, and even up to the supreme court. It is reported that such appeals are fewer in recent years because the village court is seen to be "working satisfactorily, as the justice is quick, sure, and available at negligible cost, and given by people intimately known to both parties and who work for the welfare of the village as a whole."[31]

A murder case decided by one of these village courts was related to us by a judge in the regular criminal court of that state. The facts were simple and agreed upon by both the defendant and his victim's widow. In a sudden rage over a boundary dispute between two neighbors, the defendant had struck and instantly killed his opponent. Because the question of guilt was never at issue, consideration of the sentence to be meted out took considerable time and involved the entire community. In the end, the defendant agreed to donate two days a week to the cultivation of the land of the woman widowed by his act. In addition he consented to have dinner with her once a week in a sincere effort to reestablish at least some degree of neighborliness between them. It was testified by those who knew the two parties that the convicted man was of good and peaceful nature and that previous to the dispute the families had been friends. Some frontier regions of tribal areas in northwestern Pakistan

> have never seen the Police, the Courts or the Revenue collecting agencies since man occupied this globe. There is no Penal Code or Procedure Code, Evidence Act or any special law in the area. One drives a car without acquiring a license—can keep a gun or any explosive without permit. People are brave, very well built, frank and outspoken and live a very simple life.

Twice the government of Pakistan decided to extend the Law and Court system in this region, but the tribesmen revolted. The only liaison between them and the government is five or six political agents stationed at various places.

These people govern themselves by electing their Tribal Jirga. Members of Jirga are normally Tribal chiefs. Each and every case is decided within a week or so. The mode of justice in almost all cases is compensation to the victim. Their code is the customary Law, which has more force and effect than the secular laws.

Crime is almost nil. There are cases of clashes between one tribe or another or murder because of hot temper. Sex crimes and juvenile delinquency are not known to these people. The population is approximately two million.[32]

In certain northern parts of Pakistan there is a custom that after a murder, the villagers gather around the house of the murderer. The idea is that should the relatives of the murdered person come to take revenge, the villagers may be able to persuade them not to take law in their own hands. This custom often saves further loss of life.[33]

Community Child Welfare Boards

Although the juvenile court has spread in eighty years from Cook County, Illinois, to every part of the United States and to most of the world, some countries have never had a juvenile court. The prime example is Scandinavia where the child welfare board takes an entirely different approach to the problem of juvenile delinquency.[34] It originated in Sweden under a statute passed around 1780 for the protection of children and has since been adopted in Denmark and Norway.

The child welfare board is based on much the same concept as *parens patriae*, which views the state as the parent of all its children. The child welfare board is an entirely lay body composed of citizens in the community whose only qualification is that they be voters. A lawyer is suggested for membership on the board, which usually totals five.

Each of the one thousand communes in Sweden, including Stockholm, is empowered to create such a board "to protect children and young people from a harmful milieu . . . or to correct children who are misbehaving."[35] This legal provision views much of what is termed delinquency as mischief or misbehavior on the part of children in need of protection or correction, not of punishment. The upper age limit of board jurisdiction is twenty-one.

Measures available for disposition range from dismissal of a complaint to commitment to an institution. The child's rights are safeguarded, including that of representation by counsel. Appeal may be made to the county administration and thereafter to the district court and ultimately to the crown. The child welfare board idea, first brought to the attention of the world by the League of Nations in the mid-1930s, has not been extended beyond Scandinavia until very recently, when the effectiveness of juvenile courts has begun to be called into question and the movement began for diversion, together with a search for alternatives.

In Great Britain a government white paper issued in 1966 recommended a radical reorganization of services for delinquent children and youth. Scotland had recently all but abolished the juvenile court and established in its place a child welfare board very much like that of Scandinavia. The report recommends that special magistrates' courts be created to hear disputed issues of fact and decide treatment in matters referred to it by the family council. Such courts will also have jurisdiction over adoption and other matters affecting young people under twenty-one.

Scotland's Social Work Act took the drastic step of substituting for the juvenile court so-called children's panels with responsibility for the care and protection of children. This move has had the effect of giving to the panels a nearly exclusive jurisdiction over juvenile offenders.[36] As part of its revised Juvenile Court Act of 1971, South Australia developed juvenile aid panels as a supplement, and in some instance an alternative, to the existing juvenile courts. These panels provide a mechanism for the nonjudicial treatment of juvenile offenders. Their jurisdiction extends to age eighteen and, interestingly, sets the lower age level of jurisdiction at age ten, three years above that of most juvenile courts in the United States which follow a precedent dating from Roman times. Homicide, neglect, and guardianship matters are exempted from the panels' jurisdiction. Its objectives are:

(1) to provide an alternative to Court proceedings, and a greater degree of flexibility in dealing with young offenders and other children in trouble;

(2) to offer support to the child within his family and to preserve his links with the community;

(3) to provide the child with an opportunity for growth and development within the family and the community;

(4) to deal informally with cases of children, to avoid the stigma and procedural formality of a court appearance;

(5) to achieve consistency in the handling of children's cases without sacrificing flexibility;

(6) to reduce delinquency.[37]

The panel is composed of only two members—a senior police officer and an experienced community worker—both specially trained in techniques of interviewing. They meet to hear cases in a room in the local welfare office. "The panel makes considerable effort to learn the reason for the youth's misbehavior and does so by appealing to the youngster and to his or her parents, only rarely contacting other persons for information. This avoids some of the secondary effect of labelling often associated with juvenile court processing."[38] The importance of this procedure to avoid stigma cannot be overstressed, given the admitted deleterious effects of a court appearance on many of the children who pass through it.

Working out a course of action that is satisfactory to child and parent is the primary objective of the panel meeting. Alternatives available to it include warning to the child and parents; their signature to an agreed-upon set of conditions; counseling to the youth and/or parents; and possible referral to the juvenile court for further action. During the first five years of the operation of the plan, close to twenty-five thousand children have appeared before the panels.

Community alternatives to the juvenile court have made little progress in the United States, despite a recommendation by the President's Commission Report on Juvenile Delinquency, which, as far back as 1967, had stated:

> The formal sanctioning system and pronouncement of delinquency should be used only as a last resort. In the place of the formal system, dispositional alternatives to adjudication must be developed for dealing with juveniles, including agencies to provide and coordinate services and procedures to achieve necessary control without unnecessary stigma.[39]

This somewhat generalized reference has been made specific by the supreme court of New Jersey, which authorized the appointment of one or more juvenile conference committees for any county to "serve as an arm of the court in hearing and deciding such matters involving alleged juvenile offenders as are specially referred to it by the court. Encouraged to help forestall more serious future misconduct by the juvenile offender . . . by obtaining the voluntary cooperation of the juvenile, it is empowered to supervise and follow up its recommendations."[40] The essential characteristic of the conference committee is its voluntary nature. No person can be compelled to appear before it or to comply with its recommendation, but the sanction of referral to court may be the price of noncompliance. To date the lay juvenile conference committee has had twenty years of experience, but it has not spread from New Jersey to other jurisdictions.

The advantage of these noncourt procedures is that they decriminalize the court process for young people. Most importantly, the concept departs from the notion that the state is the ultimate parent of all children and instead says to the community, "You are the parents of the children in your neighborhood." Inherent in the idea of the community panel is the notion of decentralization of authority and the debureaucratization of official procedures for dealing with youthful misconduct. Almost everywhere government structures are overloaded with officials, bogged down by paper, confined in too many squares on organizational charts. In the process, people tend to become dossiers, lives become statistics, and human problems become cases. Just as there has been overreliance on the law for the solution of many of our social and economic problems, so has there been over-reliance on government as the ultimate arbiter for dealing with the problems of young people in trouble.

Part of the answer lies in efforts by community people to help determine the conditions under which their young people live and grow up. It is up to our communities to protest the inequities in the social and economic sphere and to take the initiative in the establishment of their own tribunals for the solution of their local problems and the resolution of their own disputes.

Epilogue

Is it so, that there is not a wise man among you? no, not one that shall be able to judge between his brethren? . . . But brother goeth to law with brother . . .

—*Paul, 1 Corinthians 6:5-6*

We have presented a number of alternatives to our current court procedures, the formal, adversary process by which guilt or innocence is established, the offender punished, the victim recompensed or ignored. We live in a time of rapidly changing values, modes of life, and governance. The provisions that any society establishes for resolving in truly just fashion the controversies between people that occur in their daily lives is a significant gauge of the level attained by that society. Our aim in offering this material has been twofold: to show the deficiencies in our present court procedures and to point the way to those who may desire to bring into the resolution of conflict a larger element of community participation than currently exists.

We are not alone in either of these respects. The Canadian Criminology and Corrections Association has written:

> If the community is to have any impact with fresh approaches in public education, prevention, restitution, diversion, prison programs and aftercare, government and the community must come together in a way they have not done up to the present. Time is running out as a great many Canadians have already lost confidence in the criminal justice system. A feeling of hopelessness in dealing with offenders seems to be taking hold. More prisons and longer sentences will not solve the problems the system faces.[1]

Criminal justice, like other integral sectors of our society, is an ever-changing dialectic, characterized by progress in some areas and regression in others. One of the unfortunate aspects of the current community-justice picture is the tendency on the part of funding agencies to support alternative projects for short demonstration periods, usually three years. Despite the proven success of some of these pilot programs, the providers of the seed money all too frequently withdraw their aid and their interest in order to invest in other projects in other places, leaving the relatively recent innovative program marooned, if not sunken. We hope that the number of new programs that are initiated each year will exceed the number of those that terminate.

Although this pattern of episodic support for worthy and proven projects is understandable, it is nonetheless disastrous for any kind of steady provision of services. The trial project has barely had a chance to prove itself when it is left to shift for itself. In some instances public support from courts or private funds is forthcoming, but in most instances the experimental demonstration project disappears. Fortunately many of these pioneering projects have inspired other groups and other communities to learn from their experiences and to adapt them to their own local conditions. In this way the movement seems to go marching on; each year a larger number of community-justice programs is in operation, proof that the movement has vitality.[2]

At the same time that we sound this optimistic and forward-looking note, we are mindful of the criticism that has been leveled against informal conflict-resolution procedures. Our desire to emphasize what we believe to be the positive aspects of these programs must take heed of those who have warned against the uncritical or too rapid spread of these schemes, lest, unwittingly, a wider net be cast to catch those who might otherwise never come before a tribunal of any kind—formal court or informal panel of neighbors. Diversion, for example, does bear within it the inherent possibility of bringing before the court persons whose cases might not be serious enough for court attention and who, except for the availability of a diversion program, might never have had their behavior adjudicated in any fashion, official or unofficial.

The same kind of warning has been sounded by legal scholar Jerold Auerbach in his comments on public law 96-190, the Dispute Resolution Act, signed by the president on February 12, 1980.[3] The purpose of this law is to encourage alternative dispute-resolution systems to handle small claims and civil cases. In the first year of its operation, $1 million would be made available to local governments, and for each of the succeeding years, $10 million. Mediation panels would be created with these funds to handle minor cases, in the hope of reducing court congestion. The chief judge of New York has advocated a similar program for that state.

Auerbach points to "the rich historical tradition of alternative dispute resolution in the United States," citing precedents that existed in seventeenth-century New England towns and among the Dutch in New York. In those days, churches of various denominations made provision for procedures that were nonsecular in auspice and conciliatory rather than adversary in nature. And immigrants from Scandinavia established here replicas of the informal community processes that they had known in the mother country. Auerbach concludes:

> Comparison of the historical pattern with current developments is suggestive. Informal dispute settlement flourished when it was indigenous to strong, tight communities (whether defined by geography, religion, ideology or occupation). It expressed a cohesive communal experience that could not tolerate conflict. Community members would not relinquish their shared values to the rules and procedures of a formal legal system. Now, however, a highly sophisticated legal culture has supplanted its

communal predecessors. Its attempt to impose informal dispute settlement
must inevitably fail without the strong community base that no longer exists.
Worse yet, it will discriminate against those who cannot afford legal services
by reducing even further their opportunity to assert their legal rights.[4]

Few basic reforms in the provision of criminal-justice services have
come about as a result of the critical efforts of bench or bar. Bernard Shaw
may have characteristically overstated the case when he declared that every
profession is a conspiracy against the public (to which one wit has added
that technical jargon is the secret code of the conspirators). Another explanation of the reluctance of the legal fraternity to make basic changes in
their professional arrangements is that under common-law tradition, they
look constantly for precedents from the past to guide present decisions. It is
difficult to press forward, it has been argued, when our eyes are turned back
to see from whence we came.

Two authorities in the field have pointed out that lawyers have little incentive "to create new legal institutions to facilitate the resolution of
disputes outside courtrooms." They suggest that three forces are likely to
discourage the new methods of dispute avoidance or resolution: economic
scarcity, the dramatic increase in the number of lawyers, and the great
preponderance of lawyers in our state legislatures (seventy-five in California). "At the same time," they continue, "the social distance between
the legal profession and the mass of middle-income Americans has increased so that most professionals are virtually uninformed about the range
and consequences of the legal problems that plague ordinary citizens."[5]

Such considerations as these make it all the more imperative that those
same ordinary citizens press for the establishment in their communities of alternatives to formal court trials, if the chronic backlog of cases is to be reduced and conflicts of a minor nature are to be dealt with before they develop
into full confrontations of a more serious, even deadly nature. Members of
our neighborhoods across the land who keenly feel this need to provide effective substitutes to traditional court dealing can draw heart not only from the
manifest needs in their own neighborhoods but from history as well.

One of the most ancient precursors of what has been referred to
throughout this work as familistic justice, an open-ended process of reconciliation that may transcend the letter of the law, is the historic Hebrew
practice of the jubilee, a year of favor from the Lord to be observed every
fifty years (after the seventh "sabbath of sabbaths").[6] Twice in a century
the prevailing practices of the law would give way to a divinely ordained
form of justice, which would initiate a process of healing and renewal. The
joy of the jubilee is manifest in the scriptural directions for its observance:

You are to count seven weeks of years—seven times seven years. . . . And
on the tenth day of the seventh month you shall sound the trumpet . . .

throughout the land. You will declare this fiftieth year sacred and proclaim the liberation of all the inhabitants of the land.[7]

Reconciliation and renewal were realized through three types of liberation: forgiveness of debts, return of lands to their original owners, and release of slaves. A natonal redistribution, in short, would even out the economic fortunes and misfortunes of the preceding five decades for all inhabitants. Those who had been forced to sell their lands or themselves into servitude would be given an opportunity to begin anew. The solidarity of the nation would thus be restored and strengthened through this expression in tangible form of God's concern for the oppressed.

As final incentive for observing the special justice of the jubilee year, there was the divine assurance that "I have broken the yoke that bound you and have made you walk with head held high."[8] The familistic justice of the jubilee with its promise of freedom and lasting peace endured from the time of Moses to the destruction of Jerusalem—more than a thousand years.

From the golden age of Greece comes a reminder that citizen involvement in the dispensation of justice is not new. Although history has deplored the sentence passed upon Socrates, nevertheless his trial was conducted in public, and the charges—refusing to recognize the official gods, introducing new divinities, and corrupting the youth—were heard and decided by a tribunal of five hundred "dicasts," citizens who functioned as both judge and jury. "The very size of their number, the fact that they were quite literally a popular court, itself had historical antecedents."[9]

It had historical sequels as well.

Medieval Lovedays

"Make Love, Not War" was a slogan popular in the 1970s, especially among young people. It was a protest against the Vietnam war, but it also expressed a certain yearning for amity and brotherhood during that period, marked by conflict, civil strife and disobedience, and urgent campaigns to reduce racial inequalities and tension. Actually the slogan itself had an honorable pacific origin: the so-called lovedays in medieval France, certain days appointed to settle by amicable arbitration the differences between parties.[10] The alternative, of course, was the adversary process, which in those days was frequently played out by force of arms and tourney.

The literary, legal, and historical records of the Middle Ages contain many references to lovedays. The first recorded instance was discovered to have been in 1194 in France, where it was cited as *dies amoris*. Whether as loveday or *dies amoris* or *jour d'amour*, it provided a means of amicable settlement of a quarrel or dispute by arbitration, or by the intervention of friends, in lieu of a legal proceeding and a legal judgment.

Toward the end of the fifteenth century, references to lovedays no longer appeared, although Chaucer's "Piers Plouman" mentions them.[11] By the time of the Reformation the term had gone out of use. Probably with the rising power of the state and the consequent concentration of authority, recourse to informal, friendly procedures gradually withered away. Only one reference to lovedays has been found in Elizabethan times: by Shakespeare in *Titus Andronicus*.[12]

From earliest Anglo-Saxon times the evidence is clear and unambiguous that the "love" of "loveday" had the common usage meaning of "reconciliation, peace and concord, amity." As early as the tenth century, the laws of King Ethelred had read in part, "The thanes have two choices, love and law, and he that chooses *lufe* is as much bound [by the agreement] as he by a court decision." Over the years the term *loveday* came to be used for all manner of peacemaking where no court was involved.

Provision was evidently made in both civil and ecclesiastical courts for settling cases out of court. Anyone, it seems, could act as the peacemaker—churchmen, priests, bishops, private friends, or public officials from the lord chief justice, to the mayor or aldermen of London. From recorded cases it appears that they were indeed frequently called upon to end quarrels and to settle disputes.

Cases in dispute involved apprentices and masters, landlords and tenants, charges of assault with a deadly weapon (a club), nonpayment of debts in amounts that seem small in today's inflated times: reaping a field of wheat owned and sown by another. In a dispute over a desk at the University of Oxford, the chancellor served as peacemaker. Cardinal Wolsey of York is recorded as having made "many agreements and concordes between gentlemen and gentlemen and between some gentlemen and their wives." In all of these disputes, the term *loveday* was used for an occasion of reconciliation and amity.

A quarrel between a saddler and a painter threatened to develop into a feud among the guilds of London in 1327, but it was resolved by the six representatives from each guild, though not without some preliminary resort to force. "Final peace and concord" were established, and the agreement was drawn in the form of a contract, with fines and penalties for non-compliance. A dispute between a judge and a group of tenants of a neighboring lord over rights of pasture required two sessions. The first broke down, but at a subsequent meeting the defendant apologized in the presence of the offended tenants, and agreed to pay five hundred marks.

"At least three different types of pacification were covered by the term loveday. It was used for private settlements out of court; less frequently for regular cases of arbitration in which the court took an active interest; and for the settlement of all kinds of private and public quarrels from the vicar's pacification of scolding women to treaty-making on the borders" with

Wales and Scotland. Disputes of a civil nature might be resolved in a religious ceremony, or the church could serve as a convenient place for secular peacemaking.

It is apparent that any kind of dispute could be settled out of court by permission or license of the court or without it. Any court could grant an adjournment of a case to allow time for a settlement to be made amicably between the disputants. Settlements by resort to lovedays are recorded in the archives of the lowest civil courts—those of the manor, the fair, borough, or village.

"Ideally, the loveday was an attempt to practice brotherly love and forgiveness among all those who professed Christianity. Practically it seems to have been used to supplement legal action, and to secure voluntary compliance where the law had too little power to enforce its decrees."

At the conclusion of the loveday settlement, it was not unusual for the disputant at fault to make an apology, to offer to make amends in money or kind, even to "kiss and make up." In the case involving rights of pasture, the apology offered by the defendant was accepted and his money offer refused, but the defendant also provided five hundred gallons of French wine, two fat oxen, and twelve fat sheep, consumed by the tenants "in a regular English jollification." There are references to other contending parties providing a feast; in the Oxford desk matter, there was also "mutual entertainment, wine and a handshake at parting."

In order to view the proceedings and their finale in perspective, it is important to recall the spirit of the times in which they took place. We are reminded that the kiss of peace was a sign of forgiveness and brotherly love, as in the neighborly exchange in the receiving of the eucharist. One wonders whether the use today of the phrase "love feast" after the resolution of contention between friends, lovers, or partners may not derive from ceremonies that celebrate the conclusion and the reconciliation of love days. Such customs as these were essentially in keeping with biblical teaching: "Whatever the abuses, the ideal of the Church to secure peace among Christians was a constant force at every level of mediaeval life."

"The word 'loveday' went out of use along with the Mass and the monks and friars, but the practice of settling cases out of court, or without recourse to the courts, by mutual agreement, or through the good offices of friends, has survived."

The medieval tradition of lovedays may indeed have provided precedent and impetus for conflict resolution outside of the courts during the earliest years of the French Revolution. After the reorganization of the French court system in 1791, all parties to litigation were required to attempt reconciliation before initiating a lawsuit. This was handled by a justice of the peace or by a "bureau of peace and conciliation," depending on the nature of the case. These bureaus, consisting of six members, two of them "men of law,'' adjudicated disputes. The procedure was evidently quite successful. In Montpelier, for example, over 40 percent of disputes were settled by the bureaus and never went to litigation.[13]

If we draw on the experience of the history of other countries and of cultures whose practices are relevant, even challenging, to our own and if we combine with that the innovative and imaginative genius of our citizenry, at the same time remaining mindful of the potential pitfalls, we may yet evolve a system of justice that has its roots in the community and can therefore serve the community more effectively. The greater the level of citizen involvement in conflict resolution, the greater the likelihood of reducing tensions at the neighborhood level. It may not be too much to hope that local communities may thus help to point out to the world at large the way to the reduction of international tensions—through arbitration, mediation, compromise, even restitution—to attain to that level of justice without which there can be no truly lasting peace.

Notes

Preface

1. Canadian Criminology and Corrections Association, *Crime: A Community Responsibility* (Ottawa: Canadian Criminology and Corrections Association, 1976), p. 7.

2. Laura Nader and Linda Singer, "Dispute Resolution," *California State Bar Journal* 51 (1976):315.

3. See David Karp, William Yoels, and Gregory Stone, *Being Urban* (Lexington, Mass.: D.C. Heath and Company, 1977), chap. 3.

4. Philip Slater, *The Pursuit of Loneliness* (Boston: Beacon Press, 1976.

5. Yitzhak Bakal, *Closing Correctional Institutions* (Lexington, Mass.: Lexington Books, D.C. Heath and Company, 1973).

Chapter 1

1. "Report of the New England Conference on Conflict between Media and the Law," duplicated (Boston, September 1974), p. 4.

2. Robert A. Nisbet, *The Sociological Tradition* (New York: Basic Books, 1966), p. 47.

3. Ibid.

4. Auguste Comte, *The System of Positive Polity* (New York: Burt Franklin, 1968), 1:278.

5. Karl Marx and Frederick Engels, "The Communist Manifesto," in Lewis S. Feuer, ed., *Marx and Engels, Basic Writings on Politics and Philosophy* (New York: Doubleday, 1959), p. 29.

6. Ferdinand Toennies, *Community and Society*, trans. and ed. Charles F. Loomis (New York: Harper and Row, 1963), p. 231.

7. Emile Durkheim, *The Division of Labor in Society*, trans. George Simpson (New York: Free Press, 1964), p. 80.

8. Robert M. MacIver, *On Community, Society, and Power*, ed. Leon Bramson (Chicago: University of Chicago Press, 1970), p. 31.

9. Pitirim A. Sorokin, *Society, Culture, and Personality* (New York: Harper and Row, 1947), pp. 116-117.

10. MacIver, *Society: Its Structure and Changes* (New York: Long and Smith, 1931), p. 5.

11. MacIver, *On Community*, p. 29.

12. Toennies, *Community and Society*, p. 57.

13. Robert and Helen Lynd, *Middletown* (New York: Harcourt Brace, 1929); Allison Davis, Burleigh Gardner, and Mary Gardner, *Deep South*

(Chicago: University of Chicago Press, 1941); W. Lloyd Warner and Paul S. Lunt, *The Social Life of a Modern Community* (New Haven: Yale University Press, 1941); J.R. Seeley, R.A. Sim, and E.W. Loosley, *Crestwood Heights* (New York: Wiley, 1963); Herbert J. Gans, *The Levittowners* (New York: Vintage Books, 1967).

14. Nels Anderson, *The Hobo* (Chicago: University of Chicago Press, 1925); Louis Wirth, *The Ghetto* (Chicago: University of Chicago Press, 1928); Harvey W. Zorbaugh, *The Gold Coast and the Slum* (Chicago: University of Chicago Press, 1929).

15. William F. Whyte, *Street Corner Society* (Chicago: University of Chicago Press, 1955); Herbert J. Gans, *The Urban Villagers* (New York: Free Press, 1962); Elliot Liebow, *Tally's Corner* (Boston: Little, Brown, 1967).

16. See Georg Simmel, *The Sociology of Georg Simmel*, trans. and ed. Kurt Wolff (New York: Free Press, 1950).

17. Louis Wirth, "Urbanism as a Way of Life," *American Journal of Sociology* 44 (1938):1-24.

18. David Karp, Gregory Stone, and William Yoels, *Being Urban: A Social Psychological View of City Life* (Lexington, Mass.: D.C. Heath and Company, 1977).

19. Carol B. Stack, *All Our Kin* (New York: Harper, 1974).

20. See, for example, the work of Harrison C. White, including *An Anatomy of Kinship* (Englewood Cliffs, N.J.: Prentice-Hall, 1963), and Chains of Opportunity (Cambridge: Harvard University Press, 1970).

21. MacIver, *Society*, pp. 9-10.

22. David Riesman, Nathan Glazer, and Raoul Denney, *The Lonely Crowd* (Garden City, N.Y.: Doubleday, 1953), p. 316.

23. Philip Slater, *The Pursuit of Loneliness* (Boston: Beacon Press, 1970), p. xiii.

24. Ibid., p. 5.

25. Maurice Stein, *The Eclipse of Community* (Princeton, N.J.: Princeton University Press, 1960), p. 45.

26. Ibid., p. 53.

27. Ibid., p. 93.

28. Karp, Yoels, and Stone, *Being Urban*, p. 79.

29. Ibid., pp. 91-92.

30. Ibid., p. 91.

31. Sorokin, *Society, Culture, and Personality*, pp. 93-118.

Chapter 2

1. John P. Frank, *American Law: The Case for Radical Reform* (New York: Macmillan, 1969), p. xxi.

2. Mauro Cappelletti and Bryant Garth, "Access to Justice: The Newest Wave in Worldwide Movement to Make Right Effective," *Buffalo Law Review* 27 (1978):185.

3. Samuel J. Brakel, *Judicare, Public Funds, Private Lawyers, and Poor People* (Chicago: American Bar Foundation, 1974), p. 124.

4. Leonard S. Janofsky, "A.B.A. Attacks Delay and the High Cost of Litigation," *American Bar Association Journal* 65 (1979):1323.

5. Such proposals range from many types of private insurance plans to the nationalization of legal services. See Laura Nader and Linda Singer, "Dispute Resolution," *California State Bar Journal* 51 (1976):281-286, 311-320.

6. Warren E. Burger, "Why Courts Are in Trouble," *U.S. News*, March 31, 1975, p. 30.

7. Ibid., p. 31.

8. Governor's Select Committee on Judicial Needs, *Report on the State of the Massachusetts Courts* (Boston: Commonwealth of Massachusetts, 1977), p. 1.

9. Thomas W. Church et al., *Pretrial Delay* (Williamsburg, Va.: National Center for State Courts, 1978), pp. 12-13.

10. Ibid., p. 45. For other statistical data on the problem of delay, see Administrative Office of the U.S. Court, *Annual Report of the Director* (Washington, D.C.: Administrative Office of the United States Courts, 1940-present).

11. Governor's Select Committee on Judicial Needs, *Report,*, p. 2.

12. Barbara Botein, "Court Reorganization in New York," *Justice System Journal* 3 (1977-78):126.

13. Joe R. Greenhill and John W. Odam, Jr., "Judicial Reform of Our Texas Courts," *Baylor Law Review* 23 (1971):205.

14. James A. Gazell, "Judicial Reorganization in Michigan," *Michigan State Bar Journal* 54 (1975):114.

15. James A. Gazell, "Lower-Court Unification in the American States," *Arizona Law Journal* (1974):653.

16. Larry C. Berkson, "The Emerging Ideal of Court Unification," *Judicature* 60 (1977):372-382. Quote is on p. 372.

17. Ernest C. Friesen, Jr., "Internal Organization and Procedures of the Courts," in National Center for State Courts, *State Courts: A Blueprint for the Future* (Williamsburg, Va.: National Center for State Courts, 1978), p. 197.

18. Earl Johnson, Jr., "Toward a Responsive Justice System," in *State Courts*, p. 115.

19. Paul C. Reardon, Foreword to *State Courts*, p. xi.

20. See National Center for State Courts, *Planning in State Courts, Trends and Developments, 1976-78* (Williamsburg, Va.: National Center for State Courts, 1978).

21. Lloyd L. Weinreb, *Denial of Justice* (New York: Free Press, 1977).

22. American Arbitration Association, *The 4-A Approach: Arbitration as an Alternative* (San Francisco: AAA, 1976), p. 1.

23. Wesley G. Skogan, "The Politics of Judicial Reform," *Justice System Journal* 1 (1975):20.

24. Robert Bergstrom, "The Struggle for Judicial Reform," *Illinois Bar Journal* 6 (1977):24.

25. Ibid., p. 25.

26. Marian Neef and Stuart Nagel, "The Adversary Nature of the American Legal System from a Historical Perspective," *New York Law Forum* 20 (1974):124.

27. Ibid., p. 161.

28. Marvin E. Frankel, "The Search for Truth: An Umpireal View," *University of Pennsylvania Law Review* 123 (1975):1033.

29. Ibid.

30. Abraham S. Blumberg, *Criminal Justice* (New York: New Viewpoints, 1974), pp. 29, 30. "In Detroit's Recorders Court . . . only three of every hundred criminal defendants is ever tried by a judge or jury." Leonard Downie, Jr, *Justice Denied* (Baltimore: Penguin Books, 1972), p. 27. See also Arthur Rosett and Donald R. Cressey, *Justice by Consent* (Philadelphia: Lipincott, 1976).

31. Mirsher v. Hayes, 434 U.S. 357 (1978).

32. Rummel v. Estelle, 63 L. Ed. 2d. (decided March 18, 1980).

33. Warren E. Burger, "Let's Stop Building Major Cases Out of Minor Disputes," *Bar Leader*, no. 2 (1977):3.

34. Lawrence E. Walsh, "How to Cut High Legal Fees," *U.S. News*, August 2, 1976, p. 39.

35. William H. Erickson, "The Pound Conference Recommendations," *Federal Rules Decisions* 76 (1978):279.

36. Roscoe Pound, "The Causes of Popular Dissatisfaction with the Administration of Justice," *Journal of the American Judicature Society* 20 (1937):408.

37. Erickson, "Pound Conference Recommendations," p. 280.

38. Ibid., pp. 280-303. "Neighborhood Justice Centers" in chap. 12 of this book, for details of the operation of the program.

39. Ibid., pp. 306-313.

40. *U.S. Code Congressional and Administrative News, 96th Congress, Second Session (March 1980)*, "Dispute Resolution Act, P.L. 96-190," pp. 3-49.

41. Ibid.

42. Richard Danzig, "Toward the Creation of a Complementary, Decentralized System of Criminal Justice," *Stanford Law Review* 26 (1973):1-54.

43. Ibid., pp. 4, 14-16.

44. Ibid., pp. 28-32.

45. Ibid., pp. 24-44.

46. Ibid., pp. 46-48.

47. Eric A. Fisher, "Community Courts: An Alternative to Conventional Adjudication," *American University Law* 24 (1975):1253-1291.

48. Ibid., p. 1287.

49. Goss v. Lopez, 95 U.S. 792 (1975).

50. The extent to which such access has become a matter of international concern and action is evidenced in the recent publication of four volumes under the overall title "Access to Justice." Sponsored by the Ford Foundation, the Italian Research Council, and the Italian Ministry of Education, the study is in four volumes totaling close to three thousand pages. The first reports the results of a world survey, the second describes "Promising Institutions," the third is on "Emerging Issues and Perspectives," and the fourth is "Anthropological Perspective Patterns of Conflict Management, Essays in the Ethnography of Law." The publisher is Sijthoff and Noordhoff, 8 Winchester Terrace, Winchester, Massachusetts 01890.

Chapter 3

1. "Any person attending a judicial proceeding which is open to the public may, as a matter of right, make written notes in an unobtrusive manner during the course of the proceedings." Franklin N. Flaschner, chief justice, District Courts of Massachusetts, Administration Regulation No. 1-75, February 7, 1975. Chief Justice Burger, in announcing the most recent Supreme Court decision on the matter, "concluded that the right of the public and press to attend criminal trials is guaranteed under the First and Fourteenth Amendments. Absent an overriding interest articulated in findings, the trial of a criminal case must be open to the public." Richmond Newspapers v. Commonwealth of Virginia (No. 79-243), *United States Law Week*, June 24, 1980, pp. 5008-5009.

Since the first juvenile court was established in Cook County, Illinois, in 1899, juvenile hearings have been closed to the public. H.H. Lou, *Juvenile Courts in the United States* (Chapel Hill: University of North Carolina Press, 1927), pp. 131-133.

2. S.R. Bing and S.R. Rosenfeld, *The Quality of Justice in the Lower Criminal Courts of Metropolitan Boston* (Boston: Lawyers' Committee for Civil Rights under Law, 1970).

3. Ibid., appendix A.

4. Ibid., p. 125.

5. Ibid., p. 51.

6. This account is abridged from Marianne Stecich, "A Survey of Court Observer Programs," *Judicature* 58 (1975):470-479.

7. "Making Sure the Courts Obey the Law," *Boston Globe*, October 15, 1973, p. 50.

8. American Friends Service Committee, *Outline of the American Friends Service Committee Activities in Monitoring Criminal Courts* (Cambridge, Mass.: AFSC Northeast Regional Office, n.d.).

9. Adapted from National Institute of Law Enforcement and Criminal Justice, *Citizen Court Working: The Consumer's Perspective* (Washington, D.C.: National Institute of Law Enforcement and Criminal Justice, 1977).

10. These recruiting methods are much the same as those used to enlist local people to volunteer in community-justice programs.

11. Step 1: Setting up the Committee; Step 2: Putting the Committee to Work; Step 3: Introducing the Project to Court Officials; Step 4: Announcing the Project to the Community; Step 5: Recruiting Volunteers; Step 6: Training the Monitors; Step 7: Scheduling Monitors; Step 8: Distributing and Collecting Forms; Step 9: Tabulating the Data; Step 10: Making Recommendations for Court Improvements; Step 11: Negotiating with Court Officials; Step 12: Reporting to your Community. *Citizen Court Working*, p. 25.

12. Ibid., pp. 31-32.

13. American Friends Service Committee, *Arbitration as an Alternative to District Courts* (Cambridge, Mass.: AFSC, n.d.).

14. This account is condensed from the voluminous files on the case at the Massachusetts Law Reform Institute (2 Park Square, Boston, Massachusetts 02116), which kindly made them available, through the courtesy of Ernest Winsor.

15. Cited from the initial grant proposal of the Justice Resource Institute, Boston, December 1974.

16. Ibid.

17. From information provided by the director of the program, 38 Linden Street, Waltham, Massachusetts 02154.

Chapter 4

1. For material on the subject of diversion at the time of arrest, and of sentencing, see Abraham Blumberg, *Criminal Justice*, 2d ed. (New York: New Viewpoints, 1979), esp. pp. 22-25, 49-51.

2. National Advisory Committee on Criminal Justice Standards and Goals, *Report on Corrections* (Washington, D.C.: Government Printing Office, 1973), p. 85.

3. The following states authorize pretrial diversion by statute: Arizona, California, Colorado, Connecticut, Florida, Illinois, Massachusetts, New York, Tennessee, and Washington. *Pretrial Reporter* 2:14.

4. National Pretrial Intervention Service Center, *Why Pretrial Intervention? A Prosecutor's Perspective* (Washington, D.C.: NPISC, 1977), p. 2.

5. Samuel J. Brakel, "Diversion from the Criminal Justice Process: Informal Discretion, Motivation, and Formalization," *Denver Law Journal* 48:213.

6. "Evaluation of Program Input and Cost Effectiveness," *Pretrial Service Annual Journal* (Washington, D.C., 1978), pp. 68-93.

7. *In re Gault*, 387 U.S. 1 (1967).

Chapter 5

1. See Stephen Schafer, *The Victim and His Criminal* (New York: Random House, 1968).

2. James L. Gibbs, Jr., "The Kpelle Moot: A Therapeutic Model for the Informal Settlement of Disputes," in John Robertson, ed., *Rough Justice* (Boston: Little, Brown, 1974), pp. 391-404.

3. See, for example, Stephen Schafer, *Theories in Criminology* (New York: Random House, 1969), chap. 4.

4. Naomi Goldstein, "Reparation by the Offender to the Victim as a Method of Rehabilitation for Both," in Israel Drapkin and Emilio Viano, eds., *Victimology, A New Focus* (Lexington, Mass.: Lexington Books, D.C. Heath and Company, 1974), 2:193-205.

5. Schafer, *Theories in Criminology*, pp. 101-102.

6. Schafer, *Compensation and Restitution to Victims of Crime*, 2d ed. (Montclair, N.J.: Patterson Smith, 1970), p. 8.

7. Richard E. Laster, "Criminal Restitution: A Survey of Its Past History," in Joe Hudson and Burt Galaway, eds., *Considering the Victim* (Springfield, Ill.: Charles C. Thomas, 1975), pp. 19-28.

8. Schafer, *Compensation and Restitution*, pp. 9-10.

9. Margery Fry, "Justice for Victims," *Journal of Public Law* 8 (1959):191-194. Reprinted in Hudson and Galaway, *Considering the Victim*, pp. 54-56.

10. See Drapkin and Viano, *Victimology*, vols. 1-4. Rivalary, or at least confusion in the international sphere of victimology is indicated in the announcement of what is termed the First World Congress of Victimology held in Washington, D.C. in the fall of 1980. Called jointly by *Victimology: An International Journal of Victimology* and by the National Institute of

Victimology, the conference, at least in its call for participants, gave no indication that three international conferences on victimology have been held previously.

11. National Office for Social Responsibility, *A Guide to Juvenile Restitution Planning* (Arlington, Va.: NOSR, 1978), pp. 4-5.

12. Kathleen Smith, "A Cure for Crime," in Hudson and Galaway, *Considering the Victim*, pp. 340-350, and "Implementing Restitution within a Penal Setting," in Joe Hudson and Burt Galaway, eds., *Restitution in Criminal Justice* (Lexington, Mass.: Lexington Books, D.C. Heath and Company, 1977).

13. Smith, "Cure for Crime," p. 340.

14. See Bruce R. Jacob, "Reparation or Restitution by the Criminal Offender to His Victim: Applicability of an Ancient Concept in the Modern Correctional Process," *Journal of Criminal Law, Criminology, and Police Science* 61 (1970):152-167.

15. "Reglamento del Centro de Adaptacion Social 'La Reforma'," San Jose, Costa Rica, Imprenta Nacional, 1977, and personal observation by the senior author.

16. Smith, "Implementing Restitution," p. 133.

17. Ibid., p. 140.

18. Ibid., p. 139.

19. Albert Eglash, "Creative Restitution: A Broader Meaning for an Old Term," in Hudson and Galaway, *Considering the Victim*, pp. 284-290, and "Beyond Restitution—Creative Restitution," in Hudson and Galaway, *Restitution in Criminal Justice*, pp. 91-99.

20. Eglash, "Beyond Restitution—Creative Restitution," pp. 91-92.

21. Ibid., pp. 94-95.

22. Stephen Schafer, "Restitution to Victims of Crime—An Old Correctional Aim Modernized," *Minnesota Law Review* 50 (1965):243-254. See esp. pp. 250-254.

23. Margery Fry, *The Arms of the Law* (London: Victor Gollancz, 1951), p. 124.

24. See, for example, Stephen Schafer, "The Proper Role of a Victim-Compensation System," *Crime and Delinquency* 21 (1975):45-49.

25. Schafer, *Compensation and Restitution*, pp. 117-129.

26. Anne L. Schneider and Peter R. Schneider, *An Overview of Restitution Program Models in the Juvenile Justice System* (Eugene, Ore.: Institute of Policy Analysis, 1979), p. 2. The Institute address is 777 High Street, Suite 227.

27. Ibid., pp. 9-13.

28. Howard F. Feinman, *Legal Issues in the Operation of Restitution Programs* (Eugene, Ore.: Institute of Policy Analysis, 1979), pp. 6-15. A further listing could be made of political issues or evaluation research

issues. See National Office for Social Responsibility, Working Paper on *Managing Juvenile Restitution Projects* (Washington, D.C.: NOSR, 1979).

29. Burt Galaway and Joe Hudson, "Issues in the Correctional Implementation of Restitution to Victims of Crime," in Hudson and Galaway, *Considering the Victim*, pp. 351-360.

30. This account is drawn from the unpublished document, "Program Description: Victim Restitution Parole Program" (Billerica, Mass.: Billerica House of Correction, 1977), and from interviews with Sheriff John J. Buckley.

31. Derived from information provided by the Victim Offender Reconciliation Project, 8 Water St. North, Kitchener, Ontario, Canada.

32. See Yitzhak Bakal, ed., *Closing Correctional Institutions* (Lexington, Mass.: Lexington Books, D.C. Heath and Company, 1973).

33. The description that follows is taken from the "Restitution Program Proposal of the Massachusetts Department of Youth Services" (January 1978, mimeographed). Interested persons are referred to the director of the program, 150 Causeway St., Boston, Massachusetts.

34. Ibid.

35. Ibid.

36. Ibid.

37. Letter to the authors from John A. Calhoun.

38. Lynn Youth Resource Bureau, "Program Description" (n.d.), pp. 1-2.

39. Ibid., pp. 4-7.

40. Lynn Youth Resource Bureau, "Job Description: Victim Advocate" (Duplicated, 1979).

41. Earn-It Program, "Alternative Work Sentencing Employment Project" (District Court of East Norfolk, Massachusetts, Duplicated).

42. Interview with Marty Thresher, Earn-It counselor.

43. *Boston Globe*, October 1, 4, 1976; *Quincy Patriot-Ledger*.

44. Station WEEI, Boston, editorial, April 20, 1977.

45. Letter to Earn-It, May 13, 1978 (author confidential).

46. *Probation Journal* 15 (September 1980):6.

47. Milton G. Rector, "The Extravagance of Imprisonment," *Crime and Delinquency*, Vol. 21 (1975), pp. 323-330.

48. Burt Galaway, "Toward the Rational Development of Restitution," in Hudson and Galaway, *Restitution in Criminal Justice*, p. 83.

Chapter 6

1. Law Commission of Canada, *Working Paper No. 3, The Principles of Sentencing* (Ottawa: Law Commission of Canada, 1974), p. 4.

2. The section that follows has been drawn from its five-year report, *Further Work in Criminal Justice Reform* (New York, Vera Institute of Justice, 1977), pp. 25-31.

3. Summarized and occasionally quoted directly from Don Helbush and David Mandel, "Aid to Victims and Witnesses," *Federal Probation* 41 (1977):3-6.

4. Summarized from materials kindly provided by the Junior League of Chicago (1447 North Astor Street, Chicago 60610), which included information from the Office of the State's Attorney of Cook County.

5. *LEAA Newsletter* 8 (October 1979):14.

6. Ibid., p. 7.

7. Wayne A. Kerstetter, *Pretrial Settlement Conference: An Evaluation* (Washington, D.C.: Government Printing Office, 1979).

8. Herbert S. Miller, James A. Cramer, and William F. McDonald, *Plea Bargaining in the United States: Phase I Report* (Washington, D.C.: Government Printing Office, 1978), p. 19.

9. Criminal Justice Research Center, *Compensating Victims of Violent Crimes* (Washington, D.C.: Government Printing Office, 1978), pp. 34, 37.

10. Cesare Beccaria, *On Crimes and Punishment* (New York: Bobbs-Merrill, 1963).

11. *Time*, September 11, 1978, p. 41.

12. Ibid.

Chapter 7

1. Israel Drapkin and Emilio Viano, *Victimology: A New Focus, Society's Reaction to Victimization*, (Lexington, Mass.: Lexington Books, D.C. Heath and Company, 1974), p. 139.

2. Exodus 21:18-19.

3. M. Wolfgang, "Victim Compensation of Crimes of Personal Violence," *Minnesota Law Review* 50 (1965):223-224.

4. Clarence R. Jeffrey, "The Development of Crime in Early English Society," *Journal of Criminal Law, Criminology and Police Science* 47 (1956):655.

5. It is important to note the difference between compensation and restitution. As defined by Stephen Schafer in *The Victim and His Criminal* (New York: Random House, 1968), p. 112, "Compensation calls for action by the victim in the form of an application and *payment by society*; restitution calls for a decision by a criminal court and *payment by the offender* (emphasis added)."

6. Drapkin and Viano, *Victimology*, p. 85.

7. "Note, The New Jersey Criminal Injuries Compensation Act," *Rutgers Law Review* 27:727-729.

8. McAdam, Michael R., "Emerging Issues, An Analysis of Victim Compensation in America, *Urban Lawyer* 8:346-350.

9. Comment, "Compensations to Victims of Violent Crimes," *Northwestern University Law Review* 61 (1966):72-85.

10. *Congressional Record*, June 1, 1955.

11. McAdam, "Emerging Issues," p. 350.

12. LeRoy L. Lamborn, "The Methods of Governmental Compensations of Victims of Crimes," *University of Illinois Law Review* (1971):655, 657.

13. Drapkin and Viano, *Victimology*, p. 131.

14. H.R. 4257 (1979).

15. As of the end of 1979, Alaska, California, Connecticut, Delaware, Florida, Hawaii, Illinois, Kentucky, Maryland, Massachusetts, Michigan, Minnesota, Montana, Nevada, New Jersey, New York, North Dakota, Ohio, Oregon, Pennsylvania, Tennessee, Virginia, Washington, and Wisconsin had enacted victim-compensation schemes.

16. A showing of financial need is required in California, Florida, Kentucky, Maryland, Michigan, New Jersey, Virginia, and Wisconsin.

17. *Correctional Forum* (June-July 1980):4.

18. *New Zealand Parliamentary Debates* 336 (1963):1865.

19. Drapkin and Viano, *Victimology*, p. 107.

20. Ibid., p. 111.

21. Only Prince Edward Island and Nova Scotia have failed to do so.

22. Minister of Supply and Services, *Community Participation in Sentencing* (Ottawa: Minister of Supply and Services, 1976), p. 23.

23. Ibid.

24. Ibid., p. 26.

25. New South Wales, Queensland, Western Australia, Victoria, and South Australia. Tasmania has yet to follow.

26. New South Wales Act, sec. 3.

27. Ibid., sec. 5(1).

28. Criminal Code Amendment of 1968, sec. 663D(1), (5).

29. Council of Europe, *Compensation for Victims of Crime* (Strasbourg: Council of Europe 1975), p. 22.

30. Ibid., p. 54.

31. Ibid., p. 45.

32. Ibid., p. 40.

33. Ibid., p. 50.

34. Ibid., p. 73.

35. Ibid., p. 35.

36. Ibid., p. 29.

Chapter 8

1. John C. Cratsley, "Community Courts: Offering Alternative Dispute Resolution within the Judicial System," *Vermont Law Review* 3 (1978):6.

2. Geraldine Mund, "The Need for Community Arbitration," *Arbitration Journal* 31 (1976):115.

3. Eric A. Fisher, "Community Courts: An Alternative to Conventional Adjudication," *American University Law Review* 24 (1975):1263.

4. George Nicolau and Gerald Cormick, "Community Disputes and the Resolution of Conflict: Another View," *Arbitration Journal* 27 (1972):98-112.

5. Ibid., pp. 108-109.

6. This account is freely adapted from Joseph Stulberg, " A Civil Alternative to Criminal Prosecution," *Albany Law Review* 39 (1975):359-376; Center for Dispute Settlement, "Annual Report, 1979" (duplicated); interview with Michael Weaver, tribunal administrator, the Center for Dispute Settlement.

7. Stulberg, "Civil Alternative," pp. 363-364.

8. Ibid., p. 362.

9. Ibid., p. 366.

10. Ibid., p. 370.

11. Ibid., p. 368.

12. District Attorney of Los Angeles County, Annual Statistical Reports.

13. Mary Gardner Jones, "Wanted: A New System for Solving Consumer Disputes," *Arbitration Journal* 25 (1970):235.

14. Aryeh Friedman, "The Effectiveness of Arbitration for the Resolution of Consumer Disputes," *New York University Review of Law and Social Change* 6 (1977):176-177.

15. Thomas Eovaldi and Joan Gestrin, "Justice for Consumers: The Mechanisms of Redress," *Northwestern University Law Review* 66 (1971):283.

16. Friedman, "Effectiveness of Arbitration," p. 182.

17. Eovaldi and Gestrin, "Justice for Consumers," p. 297.

18. Ibid., p. 299.

19. Ibid., p. 300.

20. Ibid.

21. The bureau has introduced minor changes in these rules to suit its own purposes.

22. Friedman, "Effectiveness of Arbitration," pp. 195-196.

23. Ibid., pp. 196-199.

24. Jones, "Wanted," pp. 245-246.

25. Robert Wexler, "Court-Ordered Consumer Arbitration," *Arbitration Journal* 28 (1973):180.

26. John J. McGonagle, Jr., "Arbitration of Consumer Disputes," *Arbitration Journal* 27 (1972):77.

27. Ibid.

28. 15 U.S.C., 1975 Supp., 2301-2312.

29. Friedman, "Effectiveness of Arbitration," pp. 200-201.

30. Ibid., p. 202.

31. See Douglas Rossi, "Incentives for Warrantor Formation of Informal Dispute Settlement Mechanisms," *Southern California Law Review* 52 (1978):235.

32. For a review of recent developments, see Barbara Berger Opotowsky, "The Arbitration of Consumer Disputes," *A.L.I.-A.B.A. Course Materials Journal* 4 (1979):115-122.

33. Carol Holliday Blew and Robert Rosenblum, *An Exemplary Project, The Community Arbitration Project, Anne Arundel County, Maryland* (Washington, D.C.: Government Printing Office, 1979).

34. Ibid., p. 6. See also "Community Arbitration Project, Anne Arundel County, Maryland," pp. 16-17, in newsletter of the National Institute of Law Enforcement and Criminal Justice (Fall 1979). For an evaluation of the project, see M.A. Morash, *Some Preliminary Results of An Impact Assessment of the Community Arbitration Project, Anne Arundel County, Maryland* (Washington, D.C.: National Criminal Justice Reference Service, 1977).

35. Leonard Orland, *Prisons: Houses of Darkness* (New York: Free Press, 1975), p. 7.

36. John R. Hepburn and John H. Laue, "The Resolution of Inmate Grievances as an Alternative to the Courts," *Arbitration Journal* 35 (1980):12.

37. J. Michael Keating, Jr., "Arbitration of Inmate Grievances," *Arbitration Journal* 30 (1975):177-190.

38. John F. Lillard III, "Arbitration of Medical Malpractice Claims," *Arbitration Journal* 26 (1971):199-200.

39. See Duane H. Heintz, "Medical Malpractice Arbitration: A Successful Hospital-Based Application," *Insurance Law Journal* (September 1979):515-523. Also see Medical Bar Association, *Medical Malpractice Arbitration Bibliography* (Washington, D.C.: MBA, 1976).

40. Marilyn M. Glynn, "Arbitration of Landlord-Tenant Disputes," *American University Law Review* 27 (1977-78):417-418.

41. Daniel McGillis, "Neighborhood Justice Centers and the Mediation of Housing-Related Disputes," *Urban Law Journal* 17 (1979):245-269. Statistics are taken from pp. 259-265.

42. Janet Maleson Spencer and Joseph P. Zamnit, "Reflections on

Arbitration under the Family Dispute Services,'' *Arbitration Journal* 32 (1977):111-112.

43. Margaret S. Herrman, Patrick C. McKenry, and Ruth Weber, "Mediation and Arbitration Applied to Family Conflict Resolution: The Divorce Settlement," *Arbitration Journal* 34 (1979):19.

44. Spencer and Zamnit, "Reflections," p. 117. See also Raymond Pauley, "Mandatory Arbitration of Support Matters in the Family Courts," *New York State Bar Journal* 47 (January 1975):27-29, 58-62.

45. Stulberg, "Civil Alternative," p. 376.

Chapter 9

1. The account that follows is drawn from the following: Department of Justice, *Citizen Dispute Settlement, The Night Prosecutor Program of Columbus, Ohio* (Washington, D.C.: Government Printing Office, 1974); John W. Palmer, "Pre-Arrest Diversion: The Night Prosecutor's Program in Columbus, Ohio," *Crime and Delinquency* 21 (1975):100-108.

2. Department of Justice, *Citizen Dispute Settlement*, p. 29.

3. Ibid., pp. 3-6.

4. Ibid., p. 17.

5. Paul Wahrhaftig and Michael J. Lowy, "Mediation at the Police Station: A Dialogue on the Night Prosecutor Program, Columbus, Ohio," in Paul Wahrhaftig, ed., *The Citizen Dispute Resolution Organizer's Handbook* (Pittsburgh, Pa.: Grassroots, 1979), p. 28.

6. This account is drawn from Luis Salas and Ronald Schneider, "Evaluating the Dade County Citizen Dispute Program," *Judicature* 63 (1979):174-183.

7. Ibid., pp. 180-182.

8. Wahrhaftig, ed., *Handbook*, pp. 47-48.

9. The discussion is developed from the following sources: Justice Resource Institute, "The Urban Court Program," duplicated (Boston: JRI, 1975); Frederick E. Snyder, "Crime and Community Mediation, The Boston Experience: A Preliminary Report on the Dorchester Urban Court Program," *Wisconsin Law Review* (1978):737-790; and interviews with and statistical data provided by program staff.

10. Community Boards, "Community Board Program," duplicated (San Francisco, 1977). The program's address is 149 Ninth St., San Francisco.

11. *San Francisco Examiner*, October 17, 1977, p. 4.

12. Ibid., January 3, 1978.

13. Laura Nader and Linda R. Singer, "Dispute Resolution and Law in the Future: What Are the Choices?" *California State Bar Journal* 51 (1976):285.

14. Issued by the center, 9 Caldwell Place, Elizabeth, New Jersey 07201.

15. Information derived from "Proposal to Establish the Boston Municipal Court Mediation Program" (May 1980). The foundation is at 31 St. James Avenue, Suite 348, Boston, Massachusetts 02116.

16. Crime and Justice Foundation, "Mediation Programs," duplicated (Boston: Crime and Justice Foundation, 1980).

17. The Center is a project of the Criminal Justice Institute, with offices at 60 East 42nd Street, Suite 956, New York City, 10017.

18. "Mediation in Prison Disputes: a New Way to Settle Bitter Conflicts," 1980, p. 5.

Chapter 10

1. Law Commission of Canada, *The Principles of Sentencing*, Working Paper No. 3 (Ottawa: Law Commission of Canada, 1976), p. 6.

2. Emile Durkheim, *The Division of Labor in Society* (New York: Free Press, 1969), esp. chap. 2.

3. Instances that come to mind in this regard are Judge Thayer who presided at the trial of Sacco and Vanzetti in the 1920s, Judge Kaufman in the Rosenberg trial in the 1950s, and Judge Hoffman in the trial of the Chicago Seven in the 1970s, all of them highly political trials.

4. Justice Resource Institute, "The Urban Court Program" (Boston, 1975, duplicated).

5. The responsibility of the victim aide or advocate is to represent the victim, to obtain documentation of the losses he has sustained, and to verify them. The aide is expected to be present throughout the hearing in order to provide the panel and the defendant with the victim's version of the incident and to ensure that his interests are protected at all stages of the proceedings.

6. Memorandum, March 25, 1977, pp. 2, 3.

7. Justice Resource Institute, "The Urban Court Program," p. 21.

8. John Newton, "Some Criminological Issues in Finland," *Quarterly Newsletter of the Australian Institute of Criminology* 4:14.

9. Ibid., p. 6.

10. From *American Bar Association Journal* 65 (1979):1165; *Time*, October 15, 1979; director of the program (West Side Court Building, 924 West Colfax St., Denver, Colorado 80204) to the senior author, November 16, 1979.

11. *McLean's Magazine*, November 15, 1979, p. 48.

Chapter 11

1. President's Commission on Law Enforcement and the Administration of Justice, *The Challenge of Crime in a Free Society* (Washington, D.C.: Government Printing Office, 1967), p. 14.

2. Joe Hudson and Burt Galaway, eds., *Considering the Victim* (Springfield, Ill.: C.C. Thomas, 1975), p. 106.

3. Milton Rector, "The Extravangance of Imprisonment," *Crime and Delinquency* 21 (1975):328-329.

4. John Robson, "Crime and Penal Policy in New Zealand," *New Zealand Journal of Public Administration* (March 1971):36. See also Research Section, Justice Department, "Periodic Detention in New Zealand" (Wellington, New Zealand, 1973).

5. David M. Margolick, "Penalties That Pay Dividends," *National Law Journal* 1 (March 1979):1, 16.

6. Letter to the authors from John A. Calhoun.

7. Interview with Judge Albert Kramer, *Boston Globe*, January 31, 1980.

8. Much of this text is drawn from the testimony of Judge Kramer before U.S. House, Committee on Education and Labor, Subcommittee on Human Resources, March 20, 1979.

9. From information received from the office of the district attorney of Bronx County. Further details may be obtained from that office in the Criminal Court Building, Room M29, 125 161st Street, Bronx, New York, or from the Bronx Frontier Development Corp., 1180 Leggett Avenue, Bronx, New York.

10. Penal law, sec. 65.10(f.1), as amended July 24, 1978.

11. Summarized from Bailey Brown "Community Service as a Condition of Probation," *Federal Probation* 41 (1977):7-9.

12. For a comprehensive account of the origins and operation of the British scheme, see Hudson and Galway, *Considering the Victim*, chap. 8. Advisory Council on the Penal System, *Non-Custodial and Semi-Custodial Treatment of Offenders* (London: HMSO, 1970).

13. British Home Office, *Research Studies No. 29, Community Service Orders* (London: HMSO, 1975).

14. Ibid.

15. G. Kaufman, "Community Service Volunteers: A British Approach to Delinquency Prevention," *Federal Probation* 37 (1973):36-40.

16. M.H. Hogan, probation inspector, Home Office, London, to the authors.

17. Jenny West, "Community Service Orders—How Different," *Probation Journal* (London) 24:113.

18. M. Kay Harris, *Community Service by Offenders* (Washington, D.C.: American Bar Association, 1979), p. 20.

19. Quoted, with permission, from "Community Service: Promise or Peril," *Jericho*, no. 19 (Winter 1979-1980):10. The study from which these extracts have been taken is available from the National Council on Crime and Delinquency, 1706 R Street, N.W., Washington, D.C. 20036.

20. WNAC-TV, Boston. In addition, 110,000 teachers are assaulted by students or intruders and 280,000 students are injured violently. "One in every 10 schools has serious violence . . . A climate of fear is paralyzing the learning process." WCBS-TV, August 31, 1980.

21. *Boston Globe*, November 1, 1979, p. 1.

22. *Washington Post*, December 12, 1979, pp. D1, 8.

23. Ibid., February 8, 1980.

24. Directors of Criminological Institute, *Report* (Strasbourg, 1972).

25. William C. Nagel, *Prisonia—America's Growing Megalopolis* (Philadelphia: American Foundation, 1979).

26. Director of the Institute (Sachar International Building, Brandeis University, Waltham, Massachusetts 02154) to the authors, July 27, 1980.

27. Quoted in *Jericho* 4, 1, p. 12.

Chapter 12

1. Drawn from E. Adamson Hoebel, "Keresan Pueblo Law," in Laura Nader, ed., *Law in Culture and Society* (Chicago: Aldine, 1969), pp. 92-116. See also Samuel J. Brakel, "American Indian Courts: Separate? 'Yes' Equal? 'Probably Not.' " *American Bar Association Journal* 62 (1976):1002-1006.

For alternative court procedures in countries not described in this chapter, see Laura Nader and Harry F. Todd, eds, *The Disputing Process—Law in Ten Societies* (New York: Columbia University Press, 1978); Mauro Cappelletti and Bryant Garth, "Access to Justice: The Newest Wave in the Worldwide Movement to Make Rights Effective," *Buffalo Law Review* 27 (1978):181-292.

2. Hoebel, "Keresan Pueblo Law," pp. 97-98.

3. Ibid., p. 108.

4. Ibid., p. 109.

5. For a more extended account of American Indian justice, see Samuel J. Brakel, *American Indian Tribal Courts, The Costs of Separate Justice* (Chicago: American Bar Foundation, 1978).

6. The discussion that follows is based on Robert Beresford and Jill Cooper, "A Neighborhood Court for Neighborhood Suits," *Judicature* 61 (1977):185-190.

7. Ibid., p. 189.

8. Ibid., p. 190.

9. The source for this description is Leigh-Wai Doo, "Dispute Settlement in Chinese-American Communities," *American Journal of Comparative Law* 21 (1973):627-663.

10. Ibid., p. 643.

11. Ibid., p. 648.

12. The account below is abridged from James Yafe, *So Sue Me! The Story of a Community Court* (New York: Saturday Review Press, 1972), pp. 47-50.

13. Ibid., p. 7.

14. Ibid., p. 13.

15. Ibid., p. 40.

16. Ibid., pp. 47-50.

17. The discussion that follows is drawn from the following sources: Daniel McGillis, *Neighborhood Justice Centers, An Analysis of Potential Models* (Washington, D.C.: Government Printing Office, 1977); Daniel McGillis, "The Quiet (R) Evolution in American Dispute Settlement," *Harvard Law School Bulletin* (Spring 1980):20-25; Jack Etheridge, "The Atlanta Neighborhood Justice Center," *Harvard Law School Bulletin* (Spring 1980):26-29; Daniel McGillis, "Policy Brief: Neighborhood Justice Centers" (Washington, D.C.: National Institute of Justice, 1980); Roger F. Cook, Janice A. Roehl, and David I. Sheppard, *Neighborhood Justice Centers Field Test, Executive Summary, Final Evaluation Report* (Washington, D.C.: Law Enforcement Assistance Administration, 1979).

18. Public Law 96-190. Reprinted in McGillis, "Policy Brief," pp. 13-15.

19. American Bar Association, *Report of the Pound Conference Follow-up Task Force* (Washington, D.C.: ABA, 1976).

20. Frank E.A. Sander, "Varieties of Dispute Processing," *Federal Rules Decisions* 70 (1976):111-134.

21. McGillis, *Neighborhood Justice Centers*, pp. 25-28.

22. U.S. Department of Justice, news release, November 23, 1977.

23. Office for Improvements in the Administration of Justice, *Neighborhood Justice Center Program* (Washington, D.C.: Department of Justice, July 11, 1977), p. 1.

24. Ibid.

25. Law Enforcement Assistance Administration, *Newsletter* 8 (No. 3):1, 5.

26. Cook, Roehl, and Sheppard, *Neighborhood Justice Centers Field Test*, p. iii.

27. *Dispute Resolution*, newsletter of the American Bar Association, Special Committee on Resolution of Minor Disputes (Winter 1980):5.

Chapter 13

1. The following account is based on Bernard A. Ramundo, "The Comrades' Court: Molder and Keeper of Socialist Morality," *George*

Washington Law Review 33 (1964-1965):692-727; and Gordon Smith, "Popular Participation in the Administration of Justice in the Soviet Union: Comrades' Courts and the Brezhnev Regime," *Indiana Law Journal* 49 (1973-74):238-252.

2. L.B. Smirnov (chairman of the Russian Soviet Socialist Republic Supreme Court), "Comradeship Courts and Related Innovations in the Soviet Union" (address presented at the Third United Nations Crime Congress, Stockholm, 1965).

3. Ramundo, "Comrades' Courts," pp. 704-706.

4. Smith, "Popular Participation," p. 246.

5. Ramundo, "Comrades' Courts," p. 711. "Hooliganism" is a distinctively Soviet term, which encompasses delinquency, vandalism, malicious mischief, and general disrespect for authority.

6. For a fuller account of the procedures of the comrades' courts, see ibid., pp. 715-725.

7. For further discussion of the Soviet comrades' courts, see James L. Hildebrand, "The Sociology of Soviet Law: The Heuristic and Parental Functions," *Case Western Reserve Law Review* 22 (1971):157-229, and Harold J. Berman, "The Educational Role of the Soviet Court," *International and Comparative Law Quarterly* 2 (1972):81-94.

8. This presentation is drawn from Edith Brown Weiss, "The East German Social Courts: Development and Comparison with China," *American Journal of Comparative Law* 20 (1972):266-289.

9. Weiss interprets the emphasis on formalism, law, and guilt as part of the heritage of German culture, which distinguishes the social courts of that nation from its counterparts in other socialist countries. See ibid., pp. 288-289.

10. The sources for this discussion are Jesse Berman "The Cuban Popular Tribunals," *Columbia Law Review* 69 (1969):1217-1354; Karen Wald, *Children of Che* (Palo Alto, Calif.: Ramparts Press, 1978), and personal observation of the popular tribunals, by Benedict Alper.

11. Wald, *Children of Che*, p. 288.

12. Ibid., pp. 288-291.

13. Berman, "Cuban Popular Tribunals," pp. 1321-1323.

14. Ibid., p. 1328.

15. Ibid., pp. 1334-1338.

16. Jack Spence, *Search for Justice: Neighborhood Courts in Allende's Chile* (Boulder, Colo.: Westview Press, 1979), p. 159. See also Spence, "Institutionalizing Neighborhood Courts: Two Chilean Experiences," *Law and Society Review* 13 (1978):139ff.

17. This account of Chinese communty courts is drawn from the following sources: Stanley Lubman, "Mao and Mediation: Politics and Dispute Resolution in Communist China," *Indiana Law Review* 55 (1967):

1289-1359, and "On Understanding Chinese Law and Legal Institutions," *American Bar Association Journal* 62 (1976):597-600; Jerome A. Cohen, "The Criminal Process in the People's Republic of China: An Introduction," *Harvard Law Review* 79 (1966):469-533, and "Reflections on the Criminal Process in China," *Journal of Criminal Law and Criminology* 68 (1977):323-355; Daniel J. Hoffheimer, "Law and Modernization in China: The Juridical Behavior of the Chinese Communists," *Georgia Journal of International and Comparative Law* 7 (1977):515-550; and Victor H. Li, *Law without Lawyers* (Stanford Calif.: Stanford Alumni Association, 1977). (See also Bao Ruo-wang and Rudolph Chelminski, *Prisoner of Mao*.)

18. Lubman, "Mao and Mediation," pp. 1291-1300.

19. Ibid., p. 1313. For a fuller discussion of the organizational structure of the mediation committees, see esp. pp. 1330-1337.

20. Li, "Law without Lawyers," pp. 9-10.

21. J. Anthony Kline, "Law Reform and the Courts: More Power to the People or to the Profession," *California State Bar Journal* (January-February 1979):16.

Chapter 14

1. Allen Ashman and David L. Lee, "Non-Lawyer Judges: The Long Road North," *Chicago-Kent Law Review* 53 (1977):566.

2. Ibid., p. 569.

3. Ibid., p. 572.

4. Comment, "The Justice of the Peace in Virginia: A Neglected Aspect of the Judiciary," *Virginia Law Review* 52 (1966):158.

5. See Roland Johnson, Matthew Chapman, Jay Clifton, and James Waggoner, "Justice Courts in Oregon," *Oregon Law Review* 53:411-441.

6. See Mary T. Hennessy, "The Qualification of California Judges," *Pacific Law Journal* 3 (1972):439-474.

7. Irving F. Reichert, "The Magistrates' Courts: Lay Cornerstone of English Justice," *Judicature* 57 (1973):138-143.

8. Interview with Joseph E. Diniger, JP, of London, February 18, 1980.

9. Ibid.

10. Reichert, "Magistrates' Courts," pp. 140-142.

11. Gerhard Casper and Hans Zeisel, "Lay Judges in the German Criminal Courts," *Journal of Legal Studies* 1 (1972):135.

12. Ibid.

13. Ibid., p. 137.

14. Eric A. Fisher, "Community Courts: An Alternative to Conventional Adjudication," *American University Law Review* 24 (1975):1283n.

15. Stanislaw Pomorski, "Lay Judges in the Polish Criminal Courts: A Legal and Empirical Description," *Case Western Reserve Journal of International Law* 7 (1975):198-209.

16. Ibid, pp. 202-203.

17. Ibid., p. 206.

18. Stephen J. Adler, "The Israel Labor Courts," *Labor Law Journal* 28 (1977):13-19.

19. Ibid., p. 15.

20. Harry Kalven, Jr., and Hans Zeisel, *The American Jury* (Chicago: University of Chicago Press, 1971), p. 3.

21. Adapted from Casper and Zeisel, "Lay Judges," p. 142.

22. The following is drawn from Charles O. Frake, "Struck by Speech: The Yakan Concept of Litigation," in Laura Nader, ed., *Law in Culture and Society* (Chicago: Aldine, 1969), pp 147-167.

23. Ibid., pp. 153-158.

24. Ibid., pp. 164-165.

25. David Cruickshank, "Dispute Resolution—Melanesian Style," *Harvard Law School Bulletin* (Spring 1980):30-35. See also N.D. Dram, "Grass Roots Justice: Village Courts in Papua New Guinea," in William Clifford, ed., *Innovations in Criminal Justice in Asia and the Pacific* (Canberra: Australian Institute of Criminology, 1979).

26. "Crime Prevention in Papua New Guinea," in David Biles, ed., *Crime in Papua New Guinea* (Canberra: Australian Institute of Criminology, 1976), p. 84.

27. Laura Nader, "Styles of Court Procedure: To Make the Balance," in Nader, ed., *Law in Culture and Society*, pp. 69-91.

28. Ibid., pp. 87-88.

29. Ibid., p. 74-75.

30. United Nations Asia and Far East Intitute on Prevention of Crime and Treatment of Offenders, *Report of 1970* (Fuchu, Japan: UNAFEI, 1971), p. 156.

31. Udai Saroji Sah, "Gram Panchayats and Nyaya Panchayats," unpublished paper (Durgakund, India, 1973).

32. This account is drawn from Benedict S. Alper, *Prisons Inside-Out, Alternatives in Correctional Reform* (Cambridge, Mass.: Ballinger, 1974), pp. 191-193.

33. Interview with Habib-Ur-Rahman Khan, participant from Pakistan at the 33rd Course at UNAFEI, April 1973.

34. Benedict S. Alper, "The Children's Court at Three Score and Ten: Will it Survive Gault?" *Albany Law Review* 34 (1969):62-63.

35. Swedish Ministry of Justice, *The Child Welfare Act of Sweden* (Stockholm: Ministry of Justice, 1965).

36. *Social Work Act* (Scotland), chap. 49 (London: HMSO, 1968).

37. Office of the Attorney General, *Revised Juvenile Code* (Canberra, Australia, 1971).

38. Ibid.

39. President's Commission on Law Enforcement and Administration of Justice, Task Force on Juvenile Delinquency, *Task Force Report: Juvenile Delinquency and Youth Crime* (Washington, D.C.: Government Printing Office, 1967), p. 2.

40. Soney and Sage, *Rules Governing the New Jersey Courts*, pt. VI, "Rules Governing the Juvenile and Domestic Relations Court," pp. 537-538 (State of New Jersey, 1968).

Epilogue

1. Canadian Criminological Corrections Association, *Crime: A Community Responsibility* (Ottawa: Canadian Criminology and Corrections Association, 1976), pp. 6, 7.

2. This vitality was evidenced in the calling of the Fourth National Symposium on Restitution and Community Sentencing, Minneapolis September 24-26, 1980.

3. Jerold S. Auerbach, "The Two-Track Justice System," *Nation*, April 5, 1980, pp. 399-400.

4. Ibid.

5. Laura Nader and Linda R. Singer, "Dispute Resolution and Law in the Future: What Are the Choices?" *California State Bar Journal* 51 (1976):314-315.

6. This account is drawn from Robert Bryan Sloan, Jr., *The Favorable Year of the Lord* (Austin, Tex.: Schola Press, 1977), chap. 1. See also R. North, *The Sociology of the Biblical Jubilee* (Rome: Pontifical Institute, 1954).

7. Leviticus 24:8-10, Jerusalem Bible.

8. Ibid., 26:11-13.

9. We are grateful for the reminder to Dr. John L. Robson's *Values and Criminal Justice*, Occasional Papers in Criminology, No. 3 (Wellington, New Zealand: Victoria University, Institute of Criminology), p. 1.

10. We are indebted to Susan Sperling in whose *Poplollies and Bellibones* (Harmondsworth: Penguin, 1979) we first came on a reference to lovedays, which she had discovered in William Toone's *Glossary and Etymological Dictionary* (London: William Pickering, 1832), p. 318. Thereafter Professor Samuel Thorne of Harvard Law School kindly directed us to Josephine W. Bennett, "The Mediaeval Loveday," *Speculum* 33 (July 1968):351-370. We have culled and quoted briefly from her and recommend the entire article for its scholarship and fascinating detail.

11. Cf. John W. Spargo, "Chaucer's Love-Days," *Speculum* 15 (1940):36-55.

12. Act 1, Sc. 1.

13. Jacques Godechet, *Les institutions de la France sous la revolution et l'empire* (Paris, 1968), p. 148, and Albert Grivel, *La justice civile dans le district de Montpelier 1790-91* (Montpelier, 1928), pp. 67-68. We are indebted to Michael F. Fitzsimmons, doctoral candidate in the Department of History, University of North Carolina, Chapel Hill, for the references.

Bibliography

An extensive bibliography on alternative methods of dispute resolution is available at $2.50 per copy from the American Bar Association Special Committee on Minor Disputes, 1800 M Street, NW, Washington, D.C. 20036.

General Sources

Brantley, James R., and Kravitz, Marjorie. *Alternatives to Institutionalization, A Definitive Bibliography*. Washington, D.C.: National Criminal Justice Reference Service, 1979.

Cain, A.A., and Kravitz, M., eds. *Victim/Witness Assistance—A Selected Bibliography*. Washington, D.C.: Law Enforcement Assistance Administration, 1978.

Church, Thomas W., Jr.; Lee, Jo-Lynne Q.; Tan, Teresa; Carlson, Alan; and McConnell, Virginia. *Pretrial Delay, A Review and Bibliography*. Williamsburg, Va.: National Center for State Courts, 1978.

Levin, Edward, and DeSantis, Daniel V. *Mediation, An Annotated Bibliography*. Ithaca, N.Y.: Cornell School of Industrial Relations, 1978.

Medical Bar Association. *Medical Malpractice Arbitration Bibliography*. Washington, D.C.: Medical Bar Association, 1976.

National Criminal Justice Reference Service. *Annotated Bibliography: Alternative Dispute Resolution*. Washington, D.C.: Law Enforcement Assistance Administration, 1980.

Sander, Frank E.A., and Snyder, Frederick E. *Alternative Methods of Dispute Settlement—A Selected Bibliography*. Washington, D.C.: American Bar Association, 1979.

Yngvesson, B., and Hennessey, P. "Small Claims, Complex Disputes: A Review of the Small Claims Literature." *Law and Society Review* 9 (1975):219.

Other Sources

Abel, Richard L. "A Comparative Theory of Dispute Institutions in Society." *Law and Society Review* 8 (1973):217-347.

Adler, Stephen J. "The Israel Labor Courts." *Labor Law Journal* 28 (1977): 13-19.

Administrative Office of the United States Courts. *Annual Report of the Director*. Washington, D.C.: Administrative Office of the United States Courts, 1940-present.

Alaska Judicial Council. *Anchorage (AK) Citizen Dispute Center—A Needs Assessment and Feasibility Report*. Washington, D.C.: Department of Justice, 1977.

American Bar Association. *Report of the Pound Conference Follow-Up Task Force*. Washington, D.C. ABA, 1976.

Ashman, Allan, and Lee, David L. "Non-Lawyer Judges: The Long Road North." *Chicago-Kent Law Review* 53 (1977):565-580.

Bakal, Yitzhak. *Closing Correctional Institutions*. Lexington, Mass.: Lexington Books, D.C. Heath and Company, 1973.

Barnett, Randy E., and Hagel, John, eds. *Restitution—A New Paradigm of Criminal Justice*. Cambridge, Mass.: Ballinger, 1977.

Baxi, U. "Panchayat Justice: An Indian Experiment in Legal Access." In Cappelletti and Garth, eds. *Access to Justice, Vol. 3*.

Bazelon, David L. "Institutionalization, Deinstitutionalization and the Adversary Process." *Columbia Law Review* 75 (1975):897-912.

Beck, M.A. *Alternative Approaches to Dispute Resolution*. Washington, D.C.: National Criminal Justice Reference Service, 1977.

Beha, J.; Carlson, K.; and Rosenblum, R.H. *Sentencing to Community Service*. Cambridge, Mass.: ABT Associates, 1977.

Bell, Griffin B. "Responses of the Justice Department." *American Bar Association Journal* 64 (1978):53-59.

————. *Statement before the Senate Subcommittee on Improvements in Judicial Machinery, April 14, 1978*. Washington, D.C.: Department of Justice, 1978.

Bennett, Josephine W. "The Mediaeval Loveday." *Speculum* 33 (1958): 351-370.

Beresford, Robert, and Cooper, Jill. "A Neighborhood Court for Neighborhood Suits." *Judicature* 61 (1977):185-190.

Berger, Peter L., and Neuhaus, Richard J. *To Empower People*. Washington, D.C.: American Enterprise Institute for Public Policy Research, 1977.

Bergman, Howard Standish. "Community Service in England: An Alternative to Custodial Sentencing." *Federal Probation* 39 (1975):43-46.

Bergstrom, Robert. "The Struggle for Judicial Reform." *Illinois Bar Journal* 66 (1977):22-37.

Berkson, Larry C. "The Emerging Ideal of Court Unification," *Judicature* 60 (1977):372-382.

Berman, Harold J. "The Educational Role of the Soviet Court." *International and Comparative Law Quarterly* 21 (1972):81-94.

Berman, Jesse. "The Cuban Popular Tribunals." *Columbia Law Review* 69 (1969):1317-1354.

Billerica House of Corrections. "Program Description." Unpublished, 1977.

Bing, S.R., and Rosenfeld, S.R. *The Quality of Justice in the Lower Criminal Courts of Metropolitan Boston.* Boston: Lawyers' Committee for Civil Rights under Law, 1970.

Blew, Carol Holliday. *Community Arbitration Project—Anne Arundel County, Maryland.* Cambridge, Mass.: ABT Associates, 1979.

Blew, Carol Holliday, and Rosenblum, Robert. *An Exemplary Project, The Community Arbitration Project, Anne Arundel County, Maryland.* Washington, D.C.: Government Printing Office, 1979.

Blomberg, T. "Diversion and Accelerated Social Control." *Journal of Criminal Law and Criminology* 68 (1977):274-282.

Board of Directors. National Council on Crime and Delinquency. "The Nondangerous Offender Should Not Be Imprisoned." *Crime and Delinquency* 21 (1975):315-321.

Boetin, Barbara. "Court Reorganization in New York: The Role of Bernard Botein, 1958-73." *Justice System Journal* 3 (1977-1978):126-142.

Brakel, Samuel J. *American Indian Tribal Courts: The Costs of Separate Justice.* Chicago: American Bar Foundation, 1978.

_____ . "American Indian Tribal Courts: Separate? 'Yes,' Equal? 'Probably Not.'" *American Bar Association Journal* 62 (1976):1002-1006.

_____ . "Diversion from the Criminal Justice Process: Informal Discretion, Motivation and Formalization." *Denver Law Journal* 48 (1971-1972):211-238.

_____ . *Judicare, Public Funds, Private Lawyers, and Poor People.* Chicago: American Bar Foundation, 1974.

Bridenbeck, M.L., and Planchard, J.B. "Citizen Dispute Settlement: The Florida Experience." *American Bar Association Journal* 65 (1979): 570-573.

Burger, Warren E. "Agenda for 2000 A.D.—A Need for Systematic Anticipation." *Federal Rules Decisions* 70 (1976):83-95.

_____ . "Let's Stop Building Major Cases out of Minor Disputes." *Bar Leader*, no. 2 (1977):2-3.

_____ . "Why Courts Are in Trouble." *U.S. News*, March 31, 1975, pp. 28-32.

Cahn, Edgar S., and Cahn, Jean C. "What Price Justice: The Civilian Perspective Revisited." *Notre Dame Lawyer* 41 (1966):927-960.

Canadian Ministry of Justice. *Community Participation in Sentencing.* Ottawa; Printing and Publishing Supply, 1976.

Cappelletti, Mauro, and Garth, Bryant. "Access to Justice: The Newest Wave in the Worldwide Movement to Make Rights Effective." *Buffalo Law Review* 27 (1978):181-292.

Casper, Gerhard, and Zeisel, Hans. "Lay Judges in the German Criminal Courts." *Legal Studies* 15 (1972):135-191.

Cavoukian, A. "Examination of the Diversion Concept." *Canadian Criminology Forum* 1 (1979):25-31.

Chesney, S.L. *Assessment of Restitution in the Minnesota Probation Services—Summary Report.* St. Paul: Minnesota Department of Corrections, 1976.

Cohen, Jerome A. "Chinese Mediation on the Eve of Modernization." *California Law Review* 54 (1966):1201.

_____ . "The Criminal Process in the People's Republic of China: An Introduction." *Harvard Law Review* 79 (1966):469-533.

_____ . "Reflections on the Criminal Process in China." *Journal of Criminal Law and Criminology* 68 (1977):323-355.

Colson, C.W. and Benson, D.H. "Restitution as an Alternative to Imprisonment." *Detroit College Law Review* 1980:523-598.

Comment. "Non-Traditional Remedies for the Settlement of Consumer Disputes." *Temple University Law Quarterly* 49 (1976):385-427.

Conn, Stephen, and Hippler, Arthur E. "Conciliation and Arbitration in the Native Village and the Urban Ghetto." *Judicature* 58 (1974): 228-235.

Conner, R.F., and Surette, R. *Alternatives to Court, An Evaluation of the Orange County (Fla.) Bar Association's Citizen Dispute Settlement Program.* Washington, D.C.: American Bar Association, 1977.

Connolly, Paul K. "The Possibility of a Prison Sentence Is a Necessity." *Crime and Delinquency* 21 (1975):356-359.

Coons, J.E. "Compromise as Precise Justice." *California Law Review* 68 (1980):250-262.

Cotchett, Joseph, W. "Community Courts: A Viable Concept." *Trial* 14 (1978):45-47.

Cratsley, John C. "Community Courts: Offering Alternative Dispute Resolution within the Judicial System." *Vermont Law Review* 3 (1978): 1-69.

Curran, Barbara A. *The Legal Needs of the Public: The Final Report of a National Survey.* Washington, D.C.: American Bar Foundation, 1977.

Danzig, Richard. "Toward the Creation of a Complementary, Decentralized System of Criminal Justice." *Stanford Law Review* 26 (1973): 1-54.

Danzig, Richard, and Lowy, Michael J. "Everyday Disputes and Mediation in the United States: A Reply to Professor Felstiner." *Law and Society Review* 9 (1975):675-694.

Divito, Sal, and McLaughlin, Frank. *Consumer Complaints: Public Policy Alternatives.* Washington, D.C.: Acropolis Books, 1975.

Doo, Leigh-Wai. "Disputes Settlement in Chinese-American Communities." *American Journal of Comparative Law* 21 (1973):627-663.

Drapkin, Israel, and Viano, Emilio, eds. *Victimology: A New Focus.* 5 vols. Lexington, Mass.: Lexington Books, D.C. Heath and Company, 1974-1975.

Earn-It Program. "Alternative Work Sentencing Employment Project." District Court of East Norfolk, Massachusetts, 1976, duplicated.

Ebel, D.M. "Landlord-Tenant Mediation Project in Colorado." *Urban Law Annual* 17 (1979):279-286.

Edelhertz, H. *Public Compensation to Victims of Crime.* New York: Practicing Law Institute, 1974.

Edmonton Family Court Conciliation Service. *The Edmonton (Canada) Family Court Marriage Conciliation Service, Five-Year Summary of Operations.* Edmonton, Alberta: Edmonton Family Court, 1978.

Eglash, Albert. "Beyond Restitution—Creative Restitution." In Joe Hudson and Burt Galaway, eds., *Restitution in Criminal Justice.* Lexington, Mass.: Lexington Books, D.C. Heath and Company, 1977.

_____. "Creative Restitution: A Broader Meaning for an Old Term." In Joe Hudson and Burt Galaway, eds., *Considering the Victim.* Springfield, Ill.: C.C Thomas, 1975.

Ehrhardt, C.W. "One Thousand Seven Hundred Days: A History of Medical Malpractice Panels in Florida." *Florida State University Law Review* 8 (1980):165-208.

Eisenstein, M. "The Swedish Public Complaints Board: Its Vital Role in A System of Consumer Protection." In Mauro Cappelletti and J. Weisner, eds., *Access to Justice*, vol. 2. Netherlands: Sijthoff and Noordhoff, 1978.

Eovaldi, Thomas, and Gestrin, Joan. "Justice for Consumers: The Mechanisms of Redress." *Northwestern University Law Review* 66 (1971):281-325.

Erickson, William H. "New Directions in the Administration of Justice: Responses to the Pound Conference." *American Bar Association Journal* 64 (1978):48-61.

_____. "The Pound Conference Recommendations: A Blueprint for Justice in the Twenty-First Century." *Federal Rules Decisions* 76 (1978): 277-319.

Fahey, Richard P. "Native American Justice: The Courts of the Navajo Nation." *Judicature* 59 (1975):10-17.

Feeley, Malcolm M. "Two Models of the Criminal Justice System: An Organizational Perspective." *Law and Society Review* 7 (1973):407-425.

Feinman, Howard F. *Legal Issues in the Operation of Restitution Programs.* Eugene, Ore.: Institute of Policy Analysis, 1979.

Felstiner, William. "Avoidance as Dispute Processing: An Elaboration." *Law and Society Review* 9 (1975):695-706.

_____. "Influences of Social Organization on Dispute Processing." *Law and Society Review* 9 (1974):63-94.

_____. "Mediation as an Alternative to Criminal Prosecution—Ideology and Limitations." *Law and Human Behavior* 2 (1978):223-244.

Felstiner, William, and Drew, Ann Barthelmes. *European Alternatives to Criminal Trials and Their Applicability in the United States*. Washington, D.C.: Government Printing Office, 1978.

———— . "European Alternatives to Criminal Trials: What We Can Learn." *Judges Journal* 17 (1978):18-24, 50-53.

Fetter, Theodore J. "The History of the Lay Judge." *State Court Journal* 2 (1978):9-12.

Fisher, Eric A. "Community Courts: An Alternative to Conventional Adjudication." *American University Law Review* 24 (1975):1253-1291.

Florida Office of the State Courts Administrator. *The Citizen Dispute Settlement Process in Florida: A Study of Five Programs*. Tallahassee, Fla.: Office of the State Courts Administrator, 1979.

Forbes, F.S. "Arbitration of Small Business Disputes: The Potential for Nebraska." *Arbitration Journal* 35 (1980):17-24.

Ford Foundation. *New Approaches to Conflict Resolution*. New York: Ford Foundation, 1978.

Frake, Charles O. "Struck by Speech: The Yakan Concept of Litigation." In Laura Nader, ed., *Law in Culture and Society*. Chicago: Aldine, 1969.

Frankel, Marvin E. "From Private Fights toward Public Justice." *New York University Law Review* 51 (1976):516-537.

———— . "The Search for Truth: An Umpireal View." *University of Pennsylvania Law Review* 123 (1975):1021-1059.

Freedman, Monroe H. "Judge Frankel's Search for Truth." *University of Pennsylvania Law Review* 123 (1975):1060-1066.

Friedman, Aryeh. "The Effectiveness of Arbitration for the Resolution of Consumer Disputes." *New York Review of Law and Social Change* 6 (1977):175-215.

Friesen, Ernest C., Jr. "Internal Organization and Procedures of the Courts." In *State Courts: A Blueprint for the Future*. Williamsburg, Va.: National Center for State Courts, 1978.

Fry, Margery. *The Arms of the Law*. London: Victor Gollancz, 1951.

———— . "Justice for Victims." In Joe Hudson and Burt Galaway, eds., *Considering the Victim*. Springfield, Ill.: C.C Thomas, 1975.

Fuller, Lon L. "The Forms and Limits of Adjudication." *Harvard Law Review* 92 (1978):353-409.

———— . "Mediation: Its Forms and Functions." *Southern California Law Review* 44 (1971):305-339.

Galaway, Burt. "Is Restitution Practical?" *Federal Probation* 41 (1977): 3-8.

———— . "The Use of Restitution." *Crime and Delinquency* 23 (1977): 57-67.

Gazell, James. "Judicial Reorganization in Michigan." *Michigan State Bar Journal* 54 (1975):113-121.

_____. "Lower-Court Unification in the American States." *Arizona Law Journal* (1974):653-678.

Gibbs, James. "The Kpelle Moot: A Therapeutic Model for the Informal Settlement of Disputes." In John A. Robertson, ed., *Rough Justice*. Boston: Litle, Brown, 1974.

Glazer, Nathan. "The Judiciary and Social Policy." In Leonard J. Theberge, ed., *The Judiciary in a Democratic Society*. Lexington, Mass.: Lexington Books, D.C. Heath and Company, 1979.

Glick, Henry R. "The Promise and Performance of the Missouri Plan." *University of Miami Law Review* 32 (1978):509-541.

Glynn, Marilyn M. "Arbitration of Landlord-Tenant Disputes." *American University Law Review* 27 (1977-1978):405-432.

Goldbeck, Willis B. "Mediation: An Instrument of Citizen Involvement." *Arbitration Journal* 30 (1975):241-252.

Goldstein, Naomi. "Reparation by the Offender to the Victim as a Method of Rehabilitation for Both." In Israel Drapkin and Emilio Viano, eds., *Victimology: A New Focus*, vol. 2. Lexington, Mass.: Lexington Books, D.C. Heath and Company, 1974.

Governor's Select Committee on Judicial Needs. *Report of the Committee on Judicial Needs*. Boston: Massachusetts State Legislature, 1977.

Greenhill, Joe R., and Odam, John W., Jr. "Judicial Reform of Our Texas Courts." *Baylor Law Review* 23 (1971):204-226.

Griffiths, John. "Ideology in Criminal Procedure or a Third 'Model' of the Criminal Process." In John A. Robertson, ed., *Rough Justice*. Boston: Little, Brown, 1974.

Gulliver, P.H. "Negotiation as a Mode of Dispute Settlement: Towards a General Model." *Law and Society Review* 7 (1973):667-691.

Hannah, Susan B. "Competition in Michigan's Judicial Elections: Democratic Ideals vs. Judicial Realities." *Wayne Law Review* 24 (1978): 1267-1306.

Hawes, Douglas W. "Medical Malpractice Arbitration: A Comparative Analysis." *Virginia Law Review* 62 (1976):1285-1310.

Hays, Stephen W. *Court Reform: Ideal or Illusion*. Lexington, Mass.: Lexington Books, D.C. Heath and Company, 1978.

Heintz, Duane H. "Medical Malpractice Arbitration: A Successful Hospital-Based Application." *Insurance Law Journal* (September 1979): 515-523.

Hepburn, John R., and Laue, James H. "The Resolution of Inmate Grievances as an Alternative to the Courts." *Arbitration Journal* 35 (1980): 11-16.

Herrman, Margaret S.; McKenry, Patrick C.; and Weber, Ruth E. "Mediation and Arbitration Applied to Family Conflict Resolution: The Divorce Settlement." *Arbitration Journal* 34 (1979):17-21.

Hildebrand, James L. "The Sociology of Soviet Law: The Heuristic and 'Parental' Functions." *Case Western Reserve Law Review* 22 (1971): 157-229.

Hoebel, E. Adamson. "Keresan Pueblo Law." In Laura Nader, ed., *Law in Culture and Society*. Chicago: Aldine, 1969.

Hoelzel, E. "Survey of Twenty-Seven Victim Compensation Programs." *Judicature* 63 (1980):485-496.

Hoffheimer, Daniel J. "Law and Modernization in China: The Juridical Behavior of the Chinese Communists." *Georgia Journal of International and Comparative Law* 7 (1977):515-550.

Hofrichter, R. "Justice Centers Raise Basic Questions." *New Directions* 2 (1977):168-172.

Holmstrom, Lynda Lytle, and Burgess, Ann Wolbert. "Rape Victimology: Past, Present, and Future Research." in Edith E. Flynn and John Conrad, eds., *The New and Old Criminology*. New York: Praeger, 1978.

―――― . *The Victim of Rape, Institutional Reactions*. New York: Wiley, 1978.

Horowitz, Donald. *The Courts and Social Policy*. Washington, D.C.: Brookings Institution, 1977.

Hubbard, F. Patrick. "Taking Persons Seriously: A Jurisprudential Perspective on Social Disputes in a Changing Neighborhood." *Cincinnati Law Review* 48 (1979):15-41.

Hudson, Joe, and Galaway, Burt. "Restitution and Rehabilitation: Some Central Issues." *Crime and Delinquency* 18 (1972):403-410.

―――― . eds. *Considering the Victim*. Springfield, Ill.: C.C. Thomas, 1975.

―――― . *Offender Restitution in Theory and Action*. Lexington, Mass.: Lexington Books, D.C. Heath and Company, 1978.

―――― . *Restitution in Criminal Justice*. Lexington, Mass.: Lexington Books, D.C. Heath and Company, 1977.

Hudson, Joe; Challeen, D.A.; and McLagan, J. "Self-Sentencing Restitution Program." *Law Journal of the American Criminal Justice Association* 41 (1978):23-28.

Hufstedler, S. and Nejelski, P. "ABA Action Commission Challenges Litigation Cost and Delay." *American Bar Association Journal* 66 (1980):965-969.

Jacob, Bruce R. "Reparation or Restitution by the Criminal Offender to His Victim: Applicability of an Ancient Concept in the Modern Correctional Process." *Journal of Criminal Law, Criminology, and Police Science* 61 (1970):152-167.

Janofsky, Leonard S. "A.B.A. Attacks Delay and the High Cost of Litigation." *American Bar Association Journal* 65 (1979):1323-1324.

Johnson, Earl, Jr. *Assessment of Alternative Policy Options in Dispute Resolution: A Proposal.* Washington, D.C.: Law Enforcement Assistance Administration, 1976.

_____ . "Let the Tribunal Fit the Case—Establishing Criteria for Channeling Matters into Dispute Resolution Mechanisms." *Federal Rules Decisions* 80 (1979):167-180.

_____ . "Thinking about Access—A Preliminary Typology of Possible Strategies." In Mauro Cappelletti and Bryant Garth, eds., *Access to Justice*, vol. 3. Netherlands: Sijthoff and Noordhoff, 1979.

_____ . "Toward a Responsive Justice System." In *State Courts: A Blueprint for the Future.* Williamsburg, Va.: National Center for State Courts, 1978.

Jones, Mary Gardner. "Wanted: A New System for Solving Consumer Disputes." *Arbitration Journal* 25 (1970):234-247.

Justice Resource Institute. "The Urban Court Program." Boston, 1975, duplicated.

Karp, David; Yoels, William; and Stone, Gregory. *Being Urban.* Lexington, Mass.: Lexington Books, D.C. Heath and Company, 1977.

Keating, J. Michael, Jr. "Arbitration of Inmate Grievances." *Arbitration Journal* 30 (1975):177-190.

_____ et al., *Grievance Mechanisms in Correctional Institutions.* Washington, D.C.: National Institute of Criminal Justice and Law Enforcement, 1975.

Kennedy, Edward M. "Equal Justice and the Problems of Access." *Loyola of Los Angeles Law Review* 11 (1978):485-491.

Kirkaldy, A.D. *Community Service Order Program, The British Columbia Experience.* Victoria, B.C.: Department of the Attorney General, 1977.

Klein, J.H.; Ratcliffe, J.; Griseta, J.; and Risk, C. *Neighborhood Justice in Chicago, City of Neighborhoods.* Chicago: Chicago Bar Association, 1978.

Laster, Richard E. "Criminal Restitution: A Survey of Its Past History." In Joe Hudson and Burt Galaway, eds., *Considering the Victim.* Springfield, Ill.: C.C. Thomas, 1975.

Laszlo, A.T. "Court Diversion, An Alternative for Spousal Abuse Cases." In U.S. Commission on Civil Rights, *Battered Women, Issues of Public Policy.* Washington, D.C.: U.S. Commission on Civil Rights, 1978.

LaTour, Stephen, et al. "Some Determinants of Preference for Modes of Conflict Resolution." *Journal of Conflict Resolution* 20 (1976):319-356.

Law Enforcement Assistance Administration. *Citizen Dispute Settlement: An Exemplary Project.* Washington, D.C.: LEAA, 1974.

Law Enforcement Assistance Administration, *Deinstitutionalization of Status Offenders, Program Announcement*. Washington, D.C.: LEAA, 1975.

Lawyers' Committee for Civil Rights under Law. *The Quality of Justice*. Boston: LCFCRUL, 1970.

Leng, S.C. "The Role of Law in the People's Republic of China as Reflecting Mao Tse-tung's Influence." *Journal of Criminal Law and Criminology* 68 (1977):356-373.

Li, Victor. *Law without Lawyers*. Stanford, Calif.: Stanford Alumni Association, 1977.

Lesnick, Howard. "Grievance Procedures in Federal Prisons." *University of Pennsylvania Law Review* 123 (1974):1-44.

Lillard, John F. III. "Arbitration of Medical Malpractice Claims." *Arbitration Journal* 26 (1971):193-218.

Loyola of Los Angeles Law Review. "Streamlining the Justice System: Proposal and Alternatives. *Loyola of Los Angeles Law Review* 11 (June 1978).

Lubman, Stanley. "Mao and Mediation: Politics and Dispute Resolution in Communist China." *California Law Review* 55 (1967):1284-1359.

———. "On Understanding Chinese Law and Legal Institutions." *American Bar Association Journal* 62 (1976):597-600.

Lynn Youth Resource Bureau. "Program Description." Lynn, Mass., duplicated.

MacArthur, Virginia. "Inmate Grievance Mechanisms: A Survey of 209 Prisons." *Federal Probation* 38 (1974):41-47.

McDonald, W.F. *Criminal Justice and the Victim*. Beverly Hills, Calif.: Sage Publications, 1976.

McGillis, Daniel. *Neighborhood Justice Centers: An Analysis of Potential Models*. Washington, D.C.: Government Printing Office, 1977.

———. "Neighborhood Justice Centers and the Mediation of Housing-Related Disputes." *Urban Law Journal* 17 (1979):246-269.

———. "The Quiet (R) Evolution in American Dispute Settlement." *Harvard Law School Bulletin* (Spring 1980):20-25.

McGonagle, John J., Jr. "Arbitration of Consumer Disputes." *Arbitration Journal* 27 (1972):65-84.

Massachusetts Department of Youth Services. "Restitution Program Proposal." Boston, 1978, duplicated.

Medical Bar Association. *Medical Malpractice Arbitration Bibliography* Medical Bar Association, 1976.

Merry, S.E. "Going to Court: Strategies of Dispute Management in an American Urban Neighborhood." *Law and Society Review* 13 (1979): 891-925.

Metropolitan Human Relations Commission. *Portland (Oregon) Neigh-borhood Mediation Pilot Project*. Portland, Ore.: Metropolitan Human Rights Commission, 1979.

Miller, Sheldon L. "Mediation in Michigan." *Judicature* 56 (1973):290-294.

Minneapolis City Attorney's Office. *Citizens Dispute Settlement Project: Evaluation*. Washington, D.C.: National Criminal Justice Reference Service, 1977.

Morash, M.A. *Annapolis (Maryland): The Impact of the Community Ar-bitration Program on the Police*. Washington, D.C.: National Criminal Justice Reference Service, 1976.

_____ . *Some Preliminary Results of An Impact Assessment of the Com-munity Arbitration Project, Anne Arundel County, Maryland*. Wash-ington, D.C.: National Criminal Justice Reference Service, 1977.

Nader, Laura. "Disputing without the Force of Law." *Yale Law Journal* 88 (1979):998-1021.

_____ . "Forums for Justice: A Cross-Cultural Perspective." *Journal of Social Sciences* 31 (1975):151.

_____ . ed. *Law in Culture and Society*. Chicago: Aldine, 1969.

Nader, Laura, and Singer, Linda. "Dispute Resolution and Law in the Future: What Are the Choices?" *California State Bar Journal* 51 (1976): 281-286, 311-320.

Nader, Laura, and Todd, Harry F., eds. *The Disputing Process: Law in Ten Societies*. New York: Columbia University Press, 1978.

National Advisory Committee on Criminal Justice Standards and Goals. *Report on Corrections*. Washington, D.C.: Government Printing Of-fice, 1973.

National Center for State Courts. *Planning in State Courts, Trends and Developments, 1976-78*. Williamsburg, Va.: National Center for State Courts, 1978.

_____ . *Small Claims Courts, A National Examination*. Williamsburg, Va.: National Center for State Courts, 1978.

_____ . *State Courts: A Blueprint for the Future*. Williamsburg, Va.: National Center for State Courts, 1978.

National Conference on the Judiciary. *Addresses and Papers of the Na-tional Conference on the Judiciary, Consensus Statement*. Williams-burg, Va.: National Center for State Courts, 1978.

National Institute of Law Enforcement and Community Justice. *The Com-munity Arbitration Project*. Washington, D.C.: NILECJ, 1979.

National Office for Social Responsibility. *A Guide to Juvenile Restitu-tion Planning*. Arlington, Va.: NOSR, 1978.

_____ . *Working Paper: Managing Juvenile Restitution Projects*. Ar-lington, Va.: NOSR, 1979.

National Pretrial Intervention Service Center. *Why Pretrial Intervention? A Prosecutor's Perspective*. Washington, D.C.: NPISC, 1977.

Neef, Marian, and Nagel, Stuart. "The Adversary Nature of the American Legal System from a Historical Perspective." *New York Law Forum* 20 (1974):123-164.

Nejelski, Paul. "Court Annexed Arbitration." *Forum* 14 (1978):215-221.

_____. "The 1980 Dispute Resolution Act." *Judges Journal* 19 (1980): 33-35, 44-45.

_____. "Diversion: The Promise and the Danger." *Crime and Delinquency* 22 (1976):393-410.

_____. *Neighborhood Justice Centers: Traditional Questions and New Issues*. Washington, D.C.: Department of Justice, 1978.

Newton, A. "Aid to the Victim, Part I: Compensation and Restitution." *Crime and Delinquency Literature* 8 (1976):368-390.

Nicolau, George, and Cormick, Gerald. "Community Disputes and the Resolution of Conflict: Another View." *Arbitration Journal* 27 (1972): 92-112.

Nimmer, R.T. *Diversion: The Search for Alternative Forms of Prosecution*. Washington, D.C.: Law Enforcement Assistance Administration, 1974.

Ontario. Ministry of the Attorney General. *Background Paper on Community Service Orders*. Ottawa, Ont.: Ontario Ministry of Correctional Services, 1977.

Opotowsky, Barbara Berger. "The Arbitration of Consumer Disputes." *A.L.I.—A.B.A. Course Materials Journal* 4 (1979):115-122.

Orland, Leonard. *Prisons: Houses of Darkness*. New York: Free Press, 1975.

Palmer, John W. "The Night Prosecutor: Columbus Finds Extrajudicial Solutions to Interpersonal Disputes." *Judicature* 59 (1975):22-27.

_____. "Pre-Arrest Diversion: The Night Prosecutor's Program in Columbus, Ohio." *Crime and Delinquency* 21 (1975):100-108.

Pauley, Raymond. "Mandatory Arbitration of Support Matters in the Family Courts." *New York State Bar Journal* 47 (1975):27-29, 58-62.

Pierce, Julian T. "Due Process and Lay Judges." *North Carolina Central Law Journal* 6 (1975):339-349.

Pines, B. "Noncriminal Solutions for Minor Misdemeanor Complaints." *American Bar Association Journal* 63 (1977):1208-1211.

Pomorski, Stanislaw. "Lay Judges in the Polish Criminal Courts: A Legal and Empirical Description." *Case Western Reserve Journal of International Law* 7 (1975):198-209.

Pound Conference on the Causes of Popular Dissatisfaction with the Administration of Justice. *Federal Rules Decisions* 70 (1976):79-246.

Pound, Roscoe. "The Causes of Popular Dissatisfaction with the Administration of Justice." *Journal of the American Judicature Society* 20 (1937):178-187.

Ramundo, Bernard A. "The Comrades' Court: Molder and Keeper of Socialist Morality." *George Washington Law Review* 33 (1964-1976): 692-727.

Rector, Milton G. "The Extravagance of Imprisonment." *Crime and Delinquency* 21 (1975):323-330.

Reichert, Irving F. "The Magistrates' Courts: Lay Cornerstone of English Justice." *Judicature* 57 (1973):138-143.

Reveley, P.M. *Deinstitutionalization: Problems and Opportunities.* Washington, D.C.: National Technical Information Service, 1976.

Robertson, John A. *Rough Justice.* Boston: Little, Brown 1974.

Rogers, J.D. "Alternative to a Housing Court." *Urban Law Journal* 17 (1979):177-185.

Ross, H. Laurence, and Littlefield, Neil O. "Complaint as a Problem-Solving Mechanism." *Law and Society Review* 12 (1978):199-216.

Rossi, Douglas. "Incentives for Warrantor Formation of Informal Dispute Settlement." *Southern California Law Review* 52 (1978):235ff.

Rubenstein, Leonard S. "Procedural Due Process and the Limits of the Adversary System." *Harvard Civil Rights-Civil Liberties Law Review* 11 (1978):48-96.

Ruhnka, J.C., and Martin, J.A. *Small Claims Courts, A National Examination.* Williamsburg, Va.: National Center for State Courts, 1978.

Russ, Kenneth. "The People's Courts in China." *Chicago Bar Record* 58 (1976):96-100.

Rutherford, A. "Decarceration of Young Offenders in Massachusetts." In Norman Tutt, ed., *Alternative Strategies for Coping with Crime.* Oxford, Eng.: Blackwell, 1978.

Salas, Luis, and Schnedier, Ronald. "Evaluating the Dade County Citizen Dispute Program." *Judicature* 63 (1979):174-183.

Sander, Frank E.A. *Report of the National Conference on Minor Dispute Resolution.* Washington, D.C.: American Bar Association, 1978.

_____ . "Varieties of Dispute Processing." *Federal Rules Decisions* 70 (1976):111-134.

Schaeffer, Ivan M. "Justice, Justice Shalt Thou Follow." *Case and Comment* 79 (1974):37-41.

Schafer, Stephen. *Compensation and Restitution to Victims of Crime.* 2d ed. Montclair, N.J.: Patterson Smith, 1970.

_____ . *Introduction to Criminology.* Reston, Va.: Reston Publishing Co., 1976.

_____ . "The Proper Role of a Victim-Compensation System." *Crime and Delinquency* 21 (1975):45-49.

_____ . "Restitution to Victims of Crime—An Old Correctional Aim Modernized." *Minnesota Law Review* 50 (1965):243-254.

_____ . *The Victim and His Criminal.* New York: Random House, 1968.

Schneider, Anne L., and Schneider, Peter R. *An Overview of Restitution*

Program Models in the Juvenile Justice System. Eugene, Ore.: Institute of Policy Analysis, 1979.

Scull, Andrew T. *Decarceration, Community Treatment and the Deviant, A Radical View.* Englewood Cliffs, N.J.: Prentice-Hall, 1977.

Sheppard, David I.; Roehl, Janice A.; and Cook, Roger. *Neighborhood Justice Centers Field Test: Interim Evaluation Report.* Washington, D.C.: Law Enforcement Assistance Administration, 1979.

Siegel, L. "Court-Ordered Victim-Restitution: An Overview of Theory and Action." *New England Journal of Prison Law* 5 (1979):135-150.

Silberman, Charles E. *Criminal Violence, Criminal Justice.* New York: Random House, 1978.

Silberman, Linda J. *Non-Attorney Justice in the United States: An Empirical Study.* Washington, D.C.: Institute of Judicial Administration, 1978.

Singer, Linda. "Nonjudicial Dispute Resolution Mechanisms: The Effect on Justice for the Poor." *Clearinghouse Review* 13 (1979):569-583.

Skogan, Wesley G. "The Politics of Judicial Reform: Cook County, Illinois." *Justice System Journal* 1 (1975):11-23.

Smith, Gordon. "Popular Participation in the Administration of Justice in the Soviet Union: Comrades' Courts and the Brezhnev Regime." *Indiana Law Review* 49 (1973-1974):238-252.

Smith, Kathleen. "A Cure for Crime." In Joe Hudson and Burt Galaway, eds., *Considering the Victim.* Springfield, Ill.: C.C. Thomas, 1975.

————. "Implementing Restitution within a Penal Setting." In Joe Hudson and Burt Galaway, eds., *Restitution in Criminal Justice.* Lexington, Mass.: Lexington Books, D.C. Heath and Company, 1977.

Snyder, Frederick. "Crime and Community Mediation—The Boston Experience: A Preliminary Report on the Dorchester Urban Court." *Wisconsin Law Review* (1978):737-790.

Sorokin, P.A. *Society, Culture, and Personality.* New York: Harper and Row, 1947.

Spence, Jack. "Institutionalizing Neighborhood Courts: Two Chilean Experiences." *Law and Society Review* 13 (1978):139-182.

Spencer, Janet Maleson, and Zamnit, Joseph P. "Reflections on Arbitration under the Family Dispute Services." *Arbitration Journal* 32 (1977):111-122.

Stanley, Justin A. "The Resolution of Minor Disputes and the Seventh Amendment." *Marquette Law Review* 60 (1977):963-972.

Statsky, W.P. "Community Courts—Decentralizing Juvenile Jurisprudence." *Capital University Law Review* 3 (1974):1-31.

Steich, Marianne. "A Survey of Court Observer Programs." *Judicature* 58 (1975):470-479.

Steggerda, R.O., and Dolphin, S.P. *Victim Restitution, An Assessment of the Restitution in Probation Experiment Operated by the Fifth Judicial District Department of Court Services, Polk County, Iowa.* Washington, D.C.: Law Enforcement Assistance Administration, 1975.

Stevenson, Adlai E. "Reform and Judicial Selection." *American Bar Association Journal* 64 (1978):1283-1285.

Stulberg, Joseph. "A Civil Alternative to Criminal Prosecution." *Albany Law Review* 39 (1975):359-376.

_____ . *Training Impartial Intervenors to Resolve Community Disputes.* New York: American Arbitration Association, 1977.

Tomlanovich, S. "Michigan's Medical Malpractice Legislation—Prognosis: Curable Defects." *University of Detroit Journal of Urban Law* 55 (1978):309-344.

U.S. Congress. House. Committee on the Judiciary. *Dispute Resolution Act: Hearings before the House Subcommittee on Courts, Civil Liberties, and the Administration of Justice.* 95th Cong., 2d. sess., July 27, August 2, 1978.

U.S. Congress. Victims of Crime Act of 1977.

U.S. Department of Justice. *Citizen Dispute Settlement, The Night Prosecutor Program of Columbus, Ohio.* Washington, D.C.: Government Printing Office, 1974.

_____ . *Community Relations Service (C.R.S.), A National Review.* Washington, D.C.: Government Printing Office, 1978.

Uviller, H. Richard, "The Advocate, the Truth, and Judicial Hackles: A Reaction to Judge Frankel's Idea." *University of Pennsylvania Law Review* 123 (1975):1067-1081.

von Hentig, Hans. *The Criminal and His Victim.* New Haven: Yale University Press, 1948.

Wahrhaftig, Paul. "Citizen Dispute Resolution—An Answer to the Liberal's Dilemma." In Rodger O. Darnell et al., eds. *Alternatives to Prisons: Issues and Options.* Iowa City: University of Iowa School of Social Work, 1979.

_____ . ed. *Citizen Dispute Resolution Organizer's Handbook.* Rev. ed. Pittsburgh: Grassroots, 1979.

_____ . ed. *Community Mediation of Interpersonal Disputes, Readings.* Pittsburgh: American Friends Service Committee, 1974.

_____ . ed. *The Mooter.* Pittsburgh: American Friends Service Committee, 1980.

Walsh, Lawrence E. "How to Cut High Legal Fees." *U.S. News,* August 2, 1976, pp. 39-42.

Warman, J.V. "Mountain View Rental Housing Mediation—A Grass Roots Program." *Urban Law Annual* 17 (1979):271-278.

Weber, J.R. *Georgia's Residential Restitution Center.* Lexington, Ky.: Council of State Governments, 1978.

Weisbrod, Ann. *The Institute for Mediation and Conflict Resolution, Final Report*. Washington, D.C.: Law Enforcement Assistance Administration, 1976.

Weiss, Edith Brown. "The East German Social Courts: Development and Comparison with China." *American Journal of Comparative Law* 20 (1972):266-289.

Wexler, Robert. "Court-Ordered Consumer Arbitration." *Arbitration Journal* 28 (1973):175-184.

Winter, Ralph K. "The Growth of Judicial Power." In Leonard J. Theberge, ed., *The Judiciary in a Democratic Society*. Lexington, Mass.: Lexington Books, D.C. Heath and Company, 1979.

Willis, J. "Sentencing Alternatives Involving Community Service—First Report of the Sentencing Alternatives Committee." *Law Institute Journal* 53(1979):570-574.

Wolff, L.B.; Herbert, B.S.; and Reichers, M. "'HOW' Settles Consumer Disputes." *Urban Law Annual* 17 (1979):333-341.

Yaffe, James. *So Sue Me!* New York: Saturday Review Press, 1972.

Zimring, F.E. *The Court Employment Project*. New York: Court Employment Project, 1973.

National Directory of Conflict-Resolution Programs

Arizona

Pima County Attorney's Mediation
  Service
111 West Congress
Tucson   85701

The Problem Solvers
2619 West Bethany Home Road
Suite 5
Phoenix   85017

Pima County Attorney's Diversion
  Program
600 Administration Building
131 West Congress Street
Tucson   85701

Arkansas

Small Claims Program
Little Rock Municipal Court
102 Pulaski County Courthouse
Little Rock   72201

California

Housing Alliance of Contra Costa
  County
2480 Pacheco Street
Concord

California State Mediation/
  Conciliation Service
107 South Broadway Room 7039
Los Angeles   90012

Conciliation Court
County of Los Angeles
111 North Hill Street, 241
Los Angeles   90012

Los Angeles City Attorney Program
200 North Main Street

1700 City Hall East
Los Angeles   90012

Neighborhood Justice Center
Los Angeles County Bar Association
606 Olive Street
Los Angeles   90014

Mountain View Rental Housing
  Mediation Group
City Hall—540 Castro
Mountain View

Rental Housing Mediation Task Force
250 Hamilton Avenue
Palo Alto   94301

Resolve: Center for Environmental
  Conflict Resolution
360 Bryant Street
Palo Alto   94301

Dispute Resolution
Suite 2, Essex Center
412 Red Hill Avenue
San Anselmo   94960

Executive Director
Center for Collaborative Problem
  Solving
149 Ninth Street
San Francisco   94103

Community Boards Program
149 Ninth Street
San Francisco   94103

Community Dispute Services
American Arbitration Association
445 Bush Street, 5th Floor
San Francisco   94108

Mediation Institute of California
P.O. Box 26490
San Jose   95159

California *(cont.)*

Neighborhood Mediation and
Conciliation Services
70 West Hedding Street, 5th Floor
San Jose   95110

Neighborhood Small Claims
Night Court
200 West Hedding Street
San Jose   95110

Division of Mediation Services
Room 423
Civic Center
San Rafael   94903

Family Mediation Center of
Marin County
610 D Street
San Rafael   94901

Mediation Services
Civic Center, Room 423
San Rafael   94903

Mediation/Arbitration Program
for Consumer
701 Ocean Street, Room 240
Santa Cruz   95060

Rental Information and Mediation
Service
Laurel Community Center
301 Center Street
Santa Cruz   95060

Colorado

Center for Dispute Resolution
310 East Cedar Avenue
Denver   80209

Center for Environmental Problem
Solving
5500 Central Avenue, Suite A
Boulder   80301

Denver Custody Mediation
Department of Sociology
University of Denver
Denver   80210

Landlord/Tenant Mediation Program
1445 Cleveland Place, Room 307
Denver   80202

Neighborhood Justice Program
11 East Vermijo Street
Colorado Springs

Connecticut

Connecticut Pre-Trial Commission
75 Elm Street
Hartford   06106

Delaware

Citizens' Dispute Center
City County Building
800 French Street
Wilmington   19801

Family Court of Delaware
Mediation/Arbitration Units
P.O. Box 2359
Wilmington   19899

District of Columbia

Citizens' Complaint Center
Superior Court Building B
5th & F Street, N.W.   20001

Community Mediation Center
1470 Irving Street, N.W.   20010

14th Street Inter-Agency
Community Services Center
3031 14th Street, N.W.   20010

Florida

Citizen Dispute Settlement Program
Hall of Justice
Bartow   33830

Citizens' Dispute Settlement Program
2115 Second Street
P.O. Box 398
Fort Meyers   33902

Community Arbitration Program
State Attorney's Office
125 East Orange Avenue
Daytona Beach   32074

Citizen Dispute Program
Broward County
305 South Andrews Avenue
Fort Lauderdale   33301

Citizen Dispute Settlement Program
305 South Andrews Avenue
Suite 218
Fort Lauderdale   33301

Citizen Dispute Settlement Program
Eighth Judicial Circuit
State Attorney's Office
P.O. Box 1437
Gainesville   32601

Citizen Dispute Settlement Program
State Attorney's Office
Duval County Courthouse
330 East Bay Street
Jacksonville   32202

Citizen Dispute Settlement Program
Metropolitan Justice Building
1351 Northwest 12th Street
Miami   33125

Citizen Dispute Settlement Program
1351 N.W. 12th Street
5th Floor
Miami   33199

Citizens' Dispute Settlement Program
Room 81, Building A
Collier County Courthouse
Naples   33942

Citizen Disposition Settlement
55 E. Washington Street
Orlando   32804

Citizen Dispute Settlement Program
14 East Washington Street
Suite 402
Orlando   32801

Citizen Dispute Settlement Program
150 Fifth Street, North
St. Petersburg   33701

Citizen Dispute Settlement Program
Hillsborough County Courthouse
Tampa   33602

Citizens' Dispute Settlement Program
County Courthouse
Titusville   32780

Citizen Dispute Settlement
West Palm Beach Courthouse
West Palm Beach   33401

Georgia

Neighborhood Justice Center
   of Atlanta
1118 Euclid Avenue, N.E.
Atlanta   30307

Hawaii

Community Mediation Service
2424 Maile Way
Honolulu   96822

Neighborhood Justice Center
   of Honolulu, Inc.
1538 Makiki Street
Honolulu   96822

Illinois

Neighborhood Justice of Chicago
Suite 1122
4753 North Broadway
Chicago   60640

Indiana

Elkhart County Pact, Inc.
115 West Cleveland Avenue
Elkhart   46515

Night Prosecutor's Program
Prosecutor's Office—6th Floor
County-City Building
South Bend   46601

Kentucky

Pretrial Services
Administrative Office of the Courts
403 Wapping Street
Frankfort   40601

Citizen Dispute Hearing Project
Fayette District Court
140 Walnut Street
Lexington   40507

Dispute Mediation
Pretrial Services
200 S. 7th Street, Room 203
Louisville   40202

Pretrial Services Agency
300 Legal Arts Building
Louisville   40202

Maine

Court Mediation Service
Ninth District Court
142 Federal Street
Portland   04101

Maryland

Community Arbitration
Juvenile Services Administration
102 Cathedral Street
Annapolis   20401

Arbitration Service Committee
Montgomery County Bar Association
17 Jefferson Street
Rockville   20850

Montgomery County Office
   of Consumer Affairs
611 Rockville Pike, Room 201
Rockville   20852

Massachusetts

Municipal Court Mediation Program
Crime and Justice Foundation
31 South James Avenue
Boston   02116

Cambridge Dispute Settlement Center
99 Bishop Allen Drive
Cambridge   02139

Urban Court Mediation Component
560A Washington Street
Dorchester   02124

Neighborhood Mediation Project
Youth Services Bureau
One Market Street
Lynn   01001

Bristol County Probate and Family
   Court Mediation Service
441 County Street
New Bedford   02740

Salem Mediation Program
65 Washington Street
Salem

Court Mediation Services
4 Court Street
Suite 23-24
Taunton   02780

Center for Collaborative Planning
   and Community Service
12 Cottage Street
Watertown   02172

Minnesota

Citizens' Dispute Settlement Program
A-1700 Hennepin Co. Government Center
Minneapolis   55487

Family Dispute Services
515 South 7th Street
Minneapolis   55414

New Hampshire

Mediation Program
88 North Main Street
Concord   03310

New Jersey

Family Counseling Unit
East Orange Municipal Court
221 Freeway Drive East
East Orange   07018

Neighborhood Dispute Center
355 Main Street
Hackensack   07601

Neighborhood and Family Dispute
   Settlement Project
595 Neward Avenue, Room 404
Jersey City   07306

Millville Neighborhood Dispute
   Panel
18 South High Street
Millville

Informal Hearing Program of
   Mercer County
870 South Broad Street
Trenton   08611

New York

Albany Dispute Mediation Program
727 Madison Avenue
Albany   12208

Youth Advocacy Project
55 Columbia Street
Albany   12207

Community Mediation Center
356 Middle Country Road
Coram   11727

Neighborhood Justice Project
   Dispute Mediation
300 Lake Street
Elmira

Volunteer Mediation Center
151 South Main Street
New City   10956

Dispute Resolution Center
425 West 144th Street
New York   10031

Community Mediation Center
Box 112
Port Jefferson   11777

Center for Dispute Settlement
36 West Main Street
Rochester   14614

Community Dispute Settlement
   Program
35 State Street
Troy   12180

North Carolina

Dispute Settlement Center
105 N. Columbia Street
P.O. Box 464
Chapel Hill   27514

Dispute Settlement Center
Box 762
Chapel Hill   27514

Neighborhood Justice Program
316 Princess Street
New Hanover County Courthouse
Wilmington   28401

Family Service Mediation
310 West Fourth Street
First Union Building, Suite 735
Winston-Salem   27101

Ohio

Community Dispute Settlement
   Program
177 South Broadway Street
Akron   44308

Cincinnati Institute of Justice
222 East Central Parkway
Cincinnati   45202

Private Complaint Program
222 East Central Parkway
Cincinnati   45202

Community Dispute Settlement
   Program
215 Euclid Avenue, Room 930
Cleveland   44114

City Prosecutor's Office
Municipal Court Building
375 South High Street
Columbus   43215

Ohio (*cont.*)

Court Watching Project
35 Midland Avenue
Columbus   43223

Municipal Court Pretrial Unit
375 South High Street, 8th Floor
Columbus   43215

Night Prosecutor's Program
Municipal Court Building
375 South High Street
Columbus   43215

Night Prosecutor's Program
65 South Front Street
Columbus   43215

Night Prosecutor's Program
16 East Broad Street
Columbus   43215

Night Prosecutor's Program
145 East Rich Street
Columbus   43215

Night Prosecutor's Program
Capital University
2199 East Main Street
Columbus   43215

Night Prosecutor's Program
90 West Broad Street
City Hall
Columbus   43215

Small Claims Division
Franklin County Municipal Court
375 South High Street
Columbus   43215

Night Prosecutor's Program
335 West 3rd Street
Safety Building, Room 338
Dayton   45402

Community Dispute Settlement
   Program
Elyria City Hall
Elyria   44035

Night Prosecutor's Program
30 North Fourth Street
Newark   43055

Night Prosecutor's Program
14 West Locust Street
Newark   43055

Citizens Dispute Settlement Program
Toledo Municipal Court
555 North Erie Street
Toledo   43624

Oklahoma

Citizens' Dispute Settlement Program
700 Couch Street
Oklahoma City   73102

Dispute Services
Oklahoma State University
Stillwater   74074

Oregon

Family Mediation Center
3434 SW Kelly Street
Portland   97201

Neighborhood Center Project
Room 312
430 SW Morrison
Portland

Neighborhood Mediation Center
4815 NE 7th, Room 20
Portland   97211

Pennsylvania

Philadelphia Municipal Court
   Arbitration Division
City Hall Annex, Room 1224
Philadelphia   19107

Dispute Resolution Program
601 City Hall Annex
Philadelphia   19107

Mediation Program
4721 Stanton Avenue
Pittsburgh   15201

Westchester Dispute Settlement
123 North Church Street
Westchester   19380

Tennessee

Baptist Center Dispute Program
1230 West Scott Street
Knoxville   37921

Citizens' Dispute Program
128 Adams Street, Room 120
Memphis   38103

Citizens' Dispute Program
110 Public Square
Nashville   37201

Texas

Neighborhood Justice
1300 Texas Commerce Building
707 Travis Street
Houston   77002

Virginia

Family Mediation Service
935 Swinke Mill Road
McLean   22101

Neighborhood Justice Project
409 East High Street
Charlottesville   29901

Washington

Citizens' Dispute Settlement Program
315 Lowman Building
107 Cherry Street
Seattle   98104

Municipal Court of Seattle
Citizen Dispute Pilot Project
612 Smith Tower
Seattle   98104

Northwest Mediation Service
P.O. Box 2385
Seattle   98104

Wisconsin

Public Mediation Center
1605 Monroe Street
Madison   53711

Wisconsin Dispute Settlement Council
135 W. Wells Street—509
Milwaukee   53203

Canada

Community Mediation Service
27 Roy Street
Kitchener, Ontario   N2H4B4

Index

About the Authors

Benedict S. Alper, visiting professor of criminology since 1966 at Boston College, has also taught at the Law Faculty of Victoria University, Wellington, New Zealand; the Australian Institute of Criminology, Canberra; the United Nations Crime Institute, Tokyo; the Rutgers Law School, Newark; and the New School for Social Research, New York. His initial apprenticeship as a juvenile probation officer was followed by posts at the state, national, and international level. He administered five prisons in Trieste after World War II and thereafter served as the first chief of the Section on Crime and Criminal Justice at the United Nations. He has participated in United Nations Crime Congresses in Stockholm, Geneva, Kyoto, and San José, Costa Rica. Professor Alper has published many articles and books, the most recent of which is *Prisons Inside-Out*.

Lawrence T. Nichols, a Ph.D. candidate in the Department of Sociology at Boston College, received the A.B. and M.A. from St. Louis University. He has taught at Boston College, Suffolk University, and University of Massachusetts at Boston. His interests include delinquency and criminology, sociological theory and social change, problems of aging, and corporate social responsibility.